THE MOST FAMOUS IRISH PEOPLE

YOU'VE NEVER HEARD OF

COLIN MURPHY was the Creative Director of one of
Ireland's leading advertising agencies for twelve years,
during which time he was involved in a huge number of
national and international award-winning advertising
campaigns. He has a great interest in all aspects of history
and has written a light-hearted look at Ireland's past, *The
Feckin' Book of Irish History*. With Donal O'Dea he is the
author of the best-selling 'Feckin'' series, published by
The O'Brien Press. When not writing, he can usually be
found wandering the mountains of Wicklow, Kerry or
Connemara. He was born in Dublin where he still lives
with his wife, Grainne, and their two children Emmet
and Ciara.

THE
MOST
FAMOUS
IRISH
PEOPLE
YOU'VE NEVER
HEARD OF

Colin Murphy

THE O'BRIEN PRESS
DUBLIN

First published 2009 by The O'Brien Press Ltd.
12 Terenure Road East, Rathgar, Dublin 6, Ireland.
Tel: +353 1 4923333; Fax: +353 1 4922777
E-mail: books@obrien.ie
Website: www.obrien.ie

ISBN: 978-1-84717-163-4

A catalogue record for this title is available from The British Library

1 2 3 4 5 6 7 8
09 10 11 12 13

Printed and bound in the UK by J F Print Ltd, Sparkford, Somerset.

For my mother and father,
Eileen & John Murphy.

Acknowledgements

Many years ago, while on a holiday visiting my sister Pauline in Western Australia, she first introduced me to the genius that was C.Y. O'Connor; his was a story that first aroused my interest in Irish people who achieved greatness abroad, but remain largely unknown in Ireland. Subsequent research revealed countless Irish men and women of a similar nature. This book attempts to bring the achievements of a mere handful of those people to light. A thousand other stories remain untold.

This book would not have been possible without the help and support of a great number of people. First among them is my aforementioned big sister, Pauline, in Perth, for my initial insight into C.Y. O'Connor, but also for her suggestion of Paddy Hannan's inclusion and for her photographs of the prospector's statue. I would also like to thank Pauline's friends, Kerry Doust, Laraine Cook and Leith Murphy who went to a great deal of trouble to send me images of the other Hannan statue in Kalgoorlie.

Extreme gratitude to Sean O'Sullivan of the Ballingeary and Inchigeela Local History Society for his invaluable work in helping to track down Mary Harris' (Mother Jones) lineage.

My gratitude also to Gary McCue for granting me access to his extensive work on John Philip Holland and also to Bruce Ballistrieri, Curator of The Paterson Museum, New Jersey, for his permission to reproduce the images of Holland. Also to Maureen Comber of the Clare County Library for granting me permission to reference their files on both John Holland and Paddy Hannan.

My thanks to Bruce Seymour, author of *Lola Montez : A Life*, who kindly granted me access to his original research material.

Special mention to Brian Fleming, author of *The Vatican Pimpernel*, to the staff at Collins Press and especially to Deirdre Waldron of the Hugh O'Flaherty Memorial Society for their assistance in providing images of Monsignor O'Flaherty. Also to Barry O'Sullivan at Fuzion Communications, Cork.

For my research on Albert Cashier I would like to thank Mike Stoecklin, former Mayor of Saunemin, Illinois and also Tony and Marylin Thorsen & Ruth Morehart of Dwight Historical Society, Illinois for supplying me with an image of Albert.

My gratitude to Anne O'Neill at the Philatelic Advisory Committee of An Post for permission to reproduce the James Hoban commemorative stamp.

My thanks to Helen O'Carroll, curator of Kerry County Museum for her invaluable help with research material and images of William Melville and also to Peter Staunton who first introduced me to Melville's character while climbing a mountain in Kerry! Also to John V. Sullivan and Dan Downing of the *Sneem Parish News*.

I am also eternally grateful to the following people who gave me permission to use their photographs in the book. Unfortunately due to space restrictions, not all the images could be used, but my thanks nonetheless to: Facundo A. Fernández, Tony Jones, Brian O'Donovan, Andrei Roman, Harry Hunt, Nancy Spraker, Dermot Hurley and Bob Mendelsohn.

For various inputs, assistance and suggestions, my thanks to Donal O'Dea, Brendan O'Reilly, Bridget Costello and my long-suffering family, Grainne, Emmet and Ciara.

Most importantly I would like to express my heartfelt thanks to Michael O'Brien of The O'Brien Press for supporting this book from the word go and also to Helen Carr, my editor. Also my thanks to Emma Byrne for her first-class design and layout and Erika McGann for her work in production.

Lastly, I'd like to thank all the Irish men and women who did their country proud the world over.

CONTENTS

Contents

Introduction

In virtually every corner of the world you'll find Irish people have left their mark – and still continue to do so. But some more than others made an enduring impression on their adopted homeland. Occasionally on our travels as tourists, we stumble across clues to their endeavours – streets with Irish names in remote South American villages, plaques on walls in Australian towns, imposing statues of Irish men or women in some European or North American square, many of them born long ago in impoverished Irish villages yet still today proudly staring down at us from the past. In foreign fields far and wide they became famous, or occasionally, infamous. But in the land of their birth, most of them remain virtually unknown. This book attempts to set that record straight for at least some of these remarkable individuals. And if we only learn one thing from throwing a light on their accomplishments, it is probably that Ireland was so much poorer for their loss.

Paddy Hannan and Charles Yelverton-O'Connor

Paddy Hannan
Prospector who discovered the Kalgoorlie goldfields and set in
motion the largest goldrush in history

Charles Yelverton-O'Connor
Legendary Australian civil engineer

RICH MAN, POOR MAN

They were two very different men from utterly diverse backgrounds, yet the roads they took in their lives, their fates, seemed to be intimately coiled around each other like a double helix. To our knowledge, these two roads never actually crossed, yet between them, they would lay the foundations for developing what is the largest state in the world, Western Australia.

They were both born in Ireland in the early 1840s, Paddy Hannan making his debut in the world on 24 April

1840 in the village of Quin, Co. Clare to proud parents John Hannan and Bridget Lynch. Less than three years later, Charles Yelverton O'Connor would be born in quite different circumstances a hundred miles to the east in Gravelmount, Co. Meath, about six miles north-east of the historic town of Kells.

The 1845 *Parliamentary Gazetteer of Ireland* describes Paddy Hannan's birthplace as *'a wreched collection of poor cabins'*, the population of the broader townland comprised over three thousand Catholics and forty Protestants and, although the *Gazetteer* doesn't mention it, 95 per cent of the wealth was in the hands of that tiny minority. The poor were poor indeed and though it would have seemed impossible to them at the time, things were about to get a lot worse.

One of those thousands of impoverished Catholics was Paddy Hannan who was just six years old when the Great Famine struck. By the time its dark cloud had passed over the land, fifty thousand Clare natives would have died, almost a fifth of the county's population. The same number would have fled aboard tall, creaky ships to unfamiliar far-off lands that at least offered the prospect of a life with dignity.

Not much is known about Paddy Hannan's early life except that he was one of a family of seven children and he was educated in the village's National School, although he was eight before he first set his bare foot inside its door. This was to be the sum total of his education, at basic primary level, although he was a bright youngster who friends would later recall, *'wrote with a remarkably good hand and a habit of precise thought'*.

It's not known if Paddy Hannan lost any of his family in the famine, though if they survived unscathed they truly were an exception. One way or another, by the time he was a young man he would have a wealth of experience of two things: poverty and death. Yet the career he would eventually choose for himself may have found it roots in another experience from his childhood home. Just two miles from Quin in the parish of Doora was a lead and silver mine, which had been accidentally discovered in 1833 by a farmer cutting a drain though his bog. The deposits were found to be high grade and an extensive mining operation was put into place. It is highly likely Paddy Hannan like many of the local men, bereft of wealth after the ravages of famine, obtained employment in this mine.

His uncle, as well as many of his brothers, had already emigrated by the time the 1860s arrived and Paddy would soon down tools himself and board a ship for a land as far removed from Clare as is possible on this earth, in every sense. It would be six months before the golden sands of Australia appeared over his horizon and he would walk down the gangplank in Melbourne and place his foot on the soil that would bring him fame and fortune.

The farms in Paddy Hannan's home county were, like most in Ireland at that time, in the hands of a wealthy Protestant ascendancy who leased tiny plots to hundreds of tenant farmers, who in turn endured a subsistence living in which 90 per cent of their diet consisted of potatoes. When the blight destroyed the entire crop, the people starved and many landlords did little or nothing to help. Rents were still demanded and, with their livelihoods wiped out, it was impossible for people to pay, so they were frequently evicted. The shocking lack of human compassion of these wealthy individuals would become the wellspring that would ultimately feed a surge in growth of Irish nationalism and lead to armed rebellion.

But not every landlord in Ireland could be tarred with the same brush. A number of them did everything they could to help their tenants, some walking themselves to the edge of bankruptcy. One such was John O'Connor in Co. Meath. An 1837 topographical dictionary of Ireland describes his property as follows: *'Gravelmount ... in the occupation of J. O'Connor, Esq., is a spacious and handsome house; the demesne comprises about 160 statute acres, and the grounds are tastefully laid out. A manufacture of tiles, garden pots, and all kinds of coarse pottery is carried on at this place.'*

While part of the relatively small estate's business may have been devoted to making pottery, the majority of it was allotted to tenant farmers. While the more arable soil of Co. Meath allowed for a greater diversity of crops, most of the farmers still allocated a large proportion of land to potatoes as they in turn supplied a large proportion of the body's nutritional needs.

When John O'Connor's young wife Mary Elizabeth

announced to him in the spring of 1842 that he was to be a father, he must have been overjoyed. They had their health, a fine late-Georgian style country home, they had a considerable income, contented tenants and now the prospect of a family. In just a few short years that future would have been erased.

Charles Yelverton-O'Connor was born on 11 January 1843, the 'Yelverton' an inheritance from a famed family connection on his mother's side. When he was three the famine struck and, luckily for his tenants, John O'Connor proved himself quite the exception to the landed gentry of the time. Many of his kind were absentee landlords residing in England who delegated the responsibility of rent collection to land agents, so could comfortably turn a blind eye to the horror of what was happening in Ireland. John O'Connor, on the other hand, witnessed the effects of the famine first hand. He was of a compassionate nature and over the course of the tragedy he first sold his estate piece by piece, and finally sold his home to provide food and shelter to his tenants. By the time the famine had passed in 1850 he was almost penniless. One of the few things he had left to bequeath to his son was his conscientious character.

Left with no choice, John O'Connor went in search of work and secured an appointment as the secretary of the The Dublin, Wicklow and Wexford Railway Company, a move that would play a major part in the direction of his son's life. While his father worked to rebuild his life,

Charles was sent to live with his aunt who provided him with his basic education until his father's work brought the family to Waterford. Here Charles resumed his studies at Waterford Endowed School, also known as Bishop Foy's School; their choice of school is a pointer to the fact that they were still struggling financially, as Bishop Foy had specifically set up his schools to provide a free education to the poorer class of Protestant boys.

At the age of sixteen, Charles was apprenticed to one of Ireland's leading civil engineers, Mr J. Chaloner Smith, his father's connections with the railway company no doubt a factor in his choice of career. Chaloner Smith was a much-admired man who among other things was responsible for the Loopline Bridge across Dublin's River Liffey. Smith would come to like and admire his new apprentice and instructed him brilliantly, not only in railway construction and surveying, but also in mathematical and accounting skills, a necessity when working on major public infrastructural projects. Despite his youth, Charles also displayed a talent for organising and instructing the men who worked for him Besides surveying lines for railways, one of the major projects he was assigned was the construction of a number of weirs on the River Bann in the north of Ireland, his first experience of construction in an aquatic environment. Many of the weirs are still in existence today.

In 1863, the year that Paddy Hannan emigrated to Australia, Charles suffered a double tragedy when first his father and then his mother fell ill; they died within months of each other. This event must have had a profound influence on him for within a year he had decided to leave his homeland behind, and perhaps also the terrible childhood memories of the famine and the sudden loss of both parents. With the successful conclusion of his apprenticeship in 1864, Charles purchased a ticket on the ship *Pegasus* and followed in Paddy Hannan's wake towards the burgeoning colonies of Australasia.

NEW BEGINNINGS

Paddy Hannan didn't see a great deal of Australia's famed sunshine during his first years in his new home. Upon arrival in Melbourne he'd headed about sixty miles north to the town of Ballarat, the site of Australia's first real gold rush and the home of his mother's brother, William Lynch. There he quickly secured a job as a miner, working underground for up to twelve hours a day. The town was well established in 1863, having enjoyed a frenzied influx of treasure seekers a decade earlier when gold had been discovered.

Gold rush fever brought mixed fortunes to those infected with the desire to become wealthy overnight. Instantaneous wealth was possible, but rare. Some Australian goldfields literally consisted of large beds of nuggets lying scattered around on or near the surface and 'mining'

THE EUREKA STOCKADE – THE BIRTH OF AUSTRALIAN DEMOCRACY?

In 1854, the Victorian town of Ballarat was the centre of a vast mining operation involving as many as twenty-five thousand miners, or 'diggers' as they were known, the majority of whom were Irish. Unrest had long been brewing at the enforced payment of a miners' licence, irrespective of whether one found any gold or not. On top of that, the digggers had no vote and the police were also widely believed to be corrupt. The seething discontent exploded into armed rebellion and violence when a small group of miners hoisted the Southern Cross flag above a hastily-assembled stockade of carts and timbers. Their appointed leader was one Peter Lalor from Co. Laois. The password at the so-called Eureka Stockade was 'Vinegar Hill' – scene of the battle in the 1798 rebellion in Ireland. The authorities refused to bow to any demands and sent in a large force of troops. The 'battle' was little more than a slaughter, lasting ten minutes. Reports indicate that the soldiers killed indiscriminately, even after some diggers had surrendered. Twenty-two diggers died along with five soldiers. Yet when word of the rebellion and the killings leaked out, there was outrage and the government found it had a public relations disaster on its hands. Ultimately they backed down and virtually all the diggers' demands were conceded, including revoking the licences and the right of men to vote (this excluded Aborigines). Peter Lalor, who had an arm amputated as a result of the battle, would go on to have a noteworthy career as a politician and in later life be elected Speaker of the Legislative Assembly of Victoria. Some historians view the Eureka Stockade incident as a labour rebellion against powerful business interests, others a revolt in the name of freedom against a monarchy and others as the birthplace of true democracy in Australia. On a visit to the Victorian goldfields in 1895, Mark Twain said of Eureka – '... It is another instance of a victory won by a lost battle. It adds an honorable page to history; the people know it and are proud of it. They keep green the memory of the men who fell at the Eureka Stockade, and Peter Lalor has his monument.'

involved sticking a shovel into the ground and shaking off the excess dirt leaving the heavier metal behind, often in pieces the size of a walnut. But like the angler describing the size of the fish he'd caught, tales of beds of glistening gold were usually exaggerated and early prospectors had discovered quickly that the quest for gold often brought severe hardship under a merciless sun and worst of all, a terrible isolation for months on end.

Instead of nuggets, the gold was often in the form of pieces not much bigger than grains of sand and because water was so scarce, no sluice systems could be used to separate the two. Early Australian miners used a hand-shaker, a series of sieves mounted one above the other. This was backbreaking work carried out in boiling heat with little or no shade. Countless would-be millionaires, unused to the harshness of the Australian outback, died poor and alone in the wilderness before they'd even seen their first glint of gold.

When a rich goldfield was discovered however, the rewards were potentially great, especially for the first to stake a claim. After a number of years' work on a site, the surface gold would be exhausted and the only way to mine it would be with larger, commercially-orientated, steam-driven machinery. Miners would often sell their claim to a company and move on, leaving the giant mechanical diggers and drills to open up an underground world of wealth. And it was in one of these that Paddy Hannan found himself still toiling in 1868, digging gold to put into someone else's hand. It was time, he decided, to go in search of his own glittering prize and, thanks to another Irishman, he knew just where to go.

BREAKING NEW GROUND

Charles Yelverton O'Connor had spent a great deal of his voyage around the globe studying the use of a sextant, a parting gift from his employer John Chaloner Smith. Bypassing Australia, where his future lay, he instead navigated his way to the north island of New Zealand.

After a brief stay on the North Island he was offered the position of assistant engineer for the Westland Province, an impressive appointment for a man so young. Among his first tasks was to survey the construction of a road and rail link over the Southern Alps to facilitate the rush to the new found goldfields at Hokitika. The problems he faced were literally mountainous. The terrain was rugged and steep, constantly subject to heavy rains and bitter cold even in the summer months. His superiors noted his skills in handling his men and his ability to overcome obstacles with unique solutions and his work moved along on schedule and in budget. In effect he opened up the region to the thousands waiting to exploit its golden harvest; among them was Paddy Hannan, freshly arrived in 1868 from Australia.

C.Y. O'Connor was still moving up, meanwhile, not over mountains, but back down to sea level where, as Senior Engineer to Westland Province, he was given the task of developing the ports on the west coast, valuable marine experience that would stand to him in later life. In 1872 he secured the prominent appointment of District Engineer for Canterbury Province and as a result he was responsible for a great deal of the infrastructure around Christchurch, much of it still visible today.

But he'd also been busy building a relationship, and on 5 March 1874 at the age of thirty-one, he married Susan Laetitia Ness, a girl of twenty-five from Durham in the north of England. Susan would bear him eight children, all but one of whom would survive.

Over the next decade he gained extensive experience

on a broad range of infrastructural projects, including hugely expanding the island's rail network, building ports, roads and bridges. By 1883 his works had so impressed that he was appointed Under-Secretary for Public Works for New Zealand. He continued to lay the foundations for the country's development over the next seven years, winning the praises of public, press and politicians. And yet in 1890, after almost a quarter of a century's work, he was bitterly disappointed not to be offered the position of department head. He immediately began to survey the horizon for another job.

Then in the early spring of 1891, a letter fell through his letterbox that had begun its journey in the office of the Premier of Western Australia, Mr John Forrest.

John Forrest was himself a skilled surveyor and also a successful explorer, having led expeditions into the burning heart of Australia and along its southern coastline. He'd eventually be appointed to the prestigious job of Surveyor General and in 1890 been made the first Premier of the State of Western Australia.

Forrest knew the daunting task facing him. Perth was one of the most isolated cities on the planet, the vastness of the Indian Ocean to the west, the Southern Ocean to the south and in every other direction for a thousand miles lay a wilderness of mostly desert. If the colony were to survive and thrive it would need to overcome infrastructural problems that were in many ways unique. As Premier he could not undertake the task himself. He was quickly made aware of C.Y. O'Connor's work in New Zealand and as a surveyor himself he could appreciate the achievements the Irishman had made in demanding environments. Charles was just the man he was looking for and he wrote to him personally with an offer of a salary of £1,000, an impressive amount for its time. Charles turned him down, despite the fact that the job in New Zealand only paid £750! But Forrest was determined to get his man and having batted it back and forth a little, Charles finally accepted the post for the sum of £1,200, plus the costs of relocating his family. New Zealand's loss was Australia's gain and in May 1891 the O'Connor family moved into their new home in Fremantle, the then tiny port which provided one of the state's few connections with the rest of the world. That was about to change.

HEART OF GOLD

After many years and modest success in New Zealand, Paddy Hannan had returned to Australia some time in the 1870s and resumed his new-found passion of prospecting for gold. He was a tough man, well used to enduring the hardships demanded of the prospector. But he was never rash and always set out well prepared, usually in company and with horses. He also learned to source water before trying to source gold, because in the wilds each was as valuable as the other.

THE IRISH WOMAN WHO WENT WALKABOUT

Among the most unusual and fascinating Irish people to gain fame in Australia was Daisy Bates, born in Tipperary in 1859. At the age of twenty-three, she emigrated to Australia (after rumours of a sexual scandal in the house in which she was governess) and embarked on a life that was in many ways pioneering and in others highly controversial. She was married at least twice, the second time reputedly bigamous, and eventually, through her interaction with the Aboriginal people (both her husbands were drovers and bushmen) became a champion of the natives' human rights. She would ultimately spend most of her life living among them, making major anthropological studies of them and writing almost three hundred articles and books, most controversially about Aboriginal cannibalism. She wore a pistol to protect 'her natives' and fought to protect Aboriginal women against sexual exploitation by whites and against the incursion of European culture, technology and disease. Yet she cut a strange figure in the outback – insisting on wearing traditional Victorian dress. Her work prompted governments to introduce laws to give the Aboriginal people some measure of protection and she was awarded the CBE in 1934. She lived to the grand old age of ninety-two.

As the century progressed the earlier finds to the east of the country were beginning to play out, at least for individual exploitation. Most of the goldfields in Victoria and New South Wales enjoyed a reasonable sprinkling of rain, moderate temperatures and closer proximity to civilisation. But the discovery of gold in the west demanded a new genus of prospector, altogether tougher and more resilient, patient and level-headed. If C.Y. O'Connor's qualities made him the ideal candidate for the job of Surveyor General, Paddy Hannan's character and skills likewise made him the perfect man for the job of disappearing into the desert for months on end, eyes on the ground and nose to the grindstone.

Just as Paddy had preceded Charles in his departure from Ireland by one year, again he preceded his arrival in Western Australia by a single year, getting his first glimpse of the immense dry plains of the state interior in early 1890.

The Western Australian goldrush wouldn't begin in earnest until 1893, when it would become the largest gold migration in history. But the whole thing was really kick-started on a much smaller scale by another Irishman, Mick Toomey, and his fellow prospector Thomas Risely when they found gold at the town of Southern Cross in 1888. Actually it wasn't a town at all then, but a bit of outback in the shire of Yilgarn – in the middle of nowhere, 370 km from Perth, but they named the spot for the constellation that had guided them there. The same stars soon guided thousands more, including Paddy Hannan, but the glittering light they sought came not from above their heads, but from below their feet.

By the time Paddy had caught up with the thousand other prospectors around Southern Cross, pickings were slim, yet he persisted for a couple of years in his efforts to locate a commercially viable field. He'd been almost three years in Western Australia when, on 17 September 1892, an Australian called Arthur Bayley hit the jackpot at a place called Fly Flat, the east of Southern Cross. This was a larger find than the first and the snowball that had begun rolling a few years earlier now gathered momentum as it hurtled further east into the desert, picking up thousands more fortune seekers as it rolled. The town of Coolgardie was born around Bayley's find; today it has a population of eight hundred, then it had about twenty thousand. Paddy Hannan was happy to number himself among them as this time he'd gotten in early.

Violence and theft were a common feature of the various gold rushes, for the thief it could be all too easy to simply kill someone in the middle of nowhere and walk away with a fortune in his saddle bags and with only the lizards as witnesses. This was one of the reasons Paddy Hannan rarely travelled alone, that and the innate human requirement for company. As a general rule of thumb, people aligned themselves with others of their own nationality, the largest groups of prospectors being Irish, British, Australian and Chinese. Paddy Hannan formed a friendship with two other Irishmen, Thomas Flanagan and Dan O'Shea, both of whom had arrived in Australia about ten years after him and both of whom had previous experience of prospecting in the eastern rush.

But Hannan had been in the Yilgarn the longest and was the most experienced at coping with the particular demand of the terrain and climate and the Irish lads were keen to accept his guidance. Their efforts around Coolgardie were reasonably successful, but really sufficient only to keep the ball rolling by financing continued prospecting into 1893.

Like Charles O'Connor, Paddy Hannan had been in search of a substantial success for over a quarter of a century. In O'Connor's case, when a letter had dropped into his hallway he had no idea that within its folds lay his destiny. Similarly, on 10 June 1893, Paddy Hannan had no idea that the footprints he would leave in the sand that day would soon be obliterated by a stampede.

'RAILWAYS, HARBOURS, EVERYTHING...'

When C.Y. O'Connor had at one point written to John Forrest to enquire the precise nature of what he was expected to oversee, the Premier had immediately cabled him back '*Railways, harbours, everything.*'

Indeed, when he arrived he quickly realised the task he was facing would require a Herculean effort. But mountains had failed to stop him before, deserts, oceans and isolation from the rest of the civilised world were simply other obstacles to be surmounted.

In his early years in Western Australia, or WA as it was known, O'Connor undertook two mammoth projects, the development of the railway system and the expansion of Fremantle Harbour. With the discovery of gold at Southern Cross, the demand for a rail line became deafening. The trains were needed to transport not just gold-hunters to the region, but more importantly, water.

In the summer months the demand for water became so great that any enterprising individual who managed to transport a large container of water the three hundred or so kilometres into the Yilgarn could have literally sold it at the same price as whiskey and made a small fortune. One of the more unusual modes of transport to appear on the scene were camels, which could carry up to three hundred kilograms of water and food each. A team of Afghan Muslim cameleers had arrived in the southern port of Albany with a hundred camels when word of the problems in the west of the continent reached their ears. They were soon operating a thriving business and would develop into what was then the largest Muslim community in Australia.

At that time the railway 'network' in the region was woefully inadequate, consisting of about 190 miles of track. To put this in context, the Yilgarn region alone was just under half the size of southern Ireland. The 'network' was poorly designed with over-steep gradients, excessively heavy rolling stock and under-powered engines. The maintenance depot was situated at Fremantle, which was a totally unsuitable location for hub.

O'Connor immediately surveyed and re-built the existing lines, turning its annual loss of £40,000 into an operating profit. But his efforts to shift the central depot to Midland Junction (about sixteen kilometres from what is now Perth) were met with political fudging and manoeuvring. The government did vote to build a line to the Yilgarn, but didn't provide the necessary money. He was having some early lessons in the political wrangling and bureaucracy that would ultimately be his downfall.

A couple of frustrating years dragged by, but eventually the funding was approved to properly complete the rail line to Southern Cross in 1893. But of course building a train track into the middle of a desert isn't as simple as it seems. The engines ran on steam and as the prospectors could have told you for nothing, water was in pretty short supply. So besides the hundreds of workers surveying land and laying track, many others had to be engaged in building reservoirs at key points along the way, many of these are still in existence today. It was a huge logistical undertaking.

After four years in the job the rail network around Fremantle had been transformed. Although O'Connor's demand for a new depot wouldn't be realised for another six years, he had yet succeeded in providing new lines to Yilgarn (now extending beyond Coolgardie) as well as lines to the south-west and the north, each with important branch lines. The network was slowly spreading like a spider's web across the entire region.

In a reflection of his father's character, it was noted that C.Y. O'Connor was always concerned for the well-being of the rail workers. He reported that they were underpaid, overworked and poorly trained. He insisted on improved conditions, believing that a more contented workforce is a more efficient workforce. His recommendations were taken on board and new recruits had the education and training necessary. Within a few years the entire operation was turning a profit.

SEA CHANGES

C.Y. O'Connor was an incredibly disciplined man with a logical mind, capable of thinking his way around almost any obstacle. One might imagine such a character to be clinical and distracted by the cogs and wheels constantly turning in his mind. And yet he seems to have been quite the opposite. He was completely devoted to his family and though he travelled a great deal on his various surveying expeditions, he desperately tried to make up for it when he was back in their Fremantle home in Quarry Street, overlooking the Swan River. Visitors to their home without exception commented on the warmth of the welcome they received, his Irish hospitality having accompanied him to Australia.

He was an accomplished horseman and often rode out in the mornings accompanied by one of his daughters, usually the eldest, Aileen, sometimes bringing her on casual 'inspections' of his ongoing works in which she had developed a keen interest. (His horse, Moonlight, would win the first Hunt Club Cup run in Western Australia in 1901, bearing his emblem of Irish harps against a shamrock green background).

One of the projects he frequented on his early morning rides was what he regarded as his finest personal achievement – the complete reconstruction of Fremantle Harbour, a colossal undertaking even by today's standards.

At the time, trade with Perth had to be serviced through the natural harbour at Albany, which was about four hundred kilometres away to the south. Goods would then be transported on a privately-owned sub-standard rail line, which was very costly and extremely slow. Fremantle couldn't offer the natural shelter afforded by Albany – it was shallow and exposed to winds and, worst of all, it faced directly into the powerful currents created by the Indian Ocean. The Swan River, which emptied into the bay, had a shallow, rocky bar that was actually exposed at low tide. Yet Premier Forrest wanted a harbour that could accommodate some of the largest ships afloat at the time, huge trans-oceanic steamers carrying goods and mail from all over the globe. An earlier report had indicated that there were serious problems with extensive sand travel and that any attempts at deepening the harbour would fail as it would soon silt up again.

O'Connor set about months of investigation, surveying the minutiae of every aspect of the harbour and its environs. He consulted local fishermen and visited ships' captains, building up an extensive knowledge of the area's winds and currents. His earlier harbour development in New Zealand stood to him. He worked up detailed budgets and after seven months' planning, he presented them to Premier Forrest.

Initially sceptical, Forrest was nonetheless loyal and accepted O'Connor's assurances that the project was viable. There was fierce opposition from other engineers sceptical about O'Connor's claims. The costs would be astronomical, it couldn't be achieved in any reasonable time frame, it would silt up and prove to be the greatest white elephant in Australian history: opponents threw everything they had at O'Connor. But Forrest held firm and ultimately forced the plan through, though the bickering did delay the work for a couple of years.

At a ceremony in 1892 to mark the commencement of the project, John Forrest gave a speech that gives us a fair indication of the nature of C.Y. O'Connor:

'Last year I was not in favour of C.Y. O'Connor's plan because I thought then it would cost too much money and there was too much risk connected with it. But the Engineer in Chief has stuck to his scheme, he urged it with all his power, and Parliament decided we should have the works as he planned them. In this

action of the engineer you see the character of the man; he was not afraid to take responsibility of this great work. I believe that in him we have an able and energetic, a brave and a self reliant man, and I only hope in this great work he has undertaken that he will be successful.'

The entire plan would take eight years to complete and would cost £800,000, an enormous outlay at the time. Besides the deepening and widening of the Swan it also envisaged the construction of two harbour moles – massive stone walls constructed in the sea as a breakwater to protect ships at anchor from the destructive power of the ocean. The larger of these would stretch a kilometre out into the ocean.

Five years on and the bed of the Swan had been lowered so far that it now offered depths of thirty feet at low tide and its mouth had also been widened to two hundred feet. Within a couple of years the harbour was welcoming ships of 10,000 tons, something unthinkable a few years earlier. There was now almost two kilometres of wharfage, a rail bridge spanned the river, the moles were completed, huge cargo terminals rose all around the harbour, and everything had been completed on schedule and on budget. Some years after C.Y. O'Connor died, the HMS *Hood* berthed in Fremantle. She was then, at 42,000 tons, the largest ship afloat on the world's oceans.

In 1900, Fremantle became the official port serving Perth. The project had been a huge triumph for O'Connor and Forrest. Cynics were silenced – at least for the time being. Over a century after C. Y. O'Connor completed his harbour, which critics claimed would silt up within a few years, it remains, despite constant use by heavy shipping, as deep, as calm and as sound as ever.

But his work was not done. As Paddy Hannan had, in the meantime, presented Premier Forrest with a serious logistical problem, one that could only be solved through the largest civil engineering project Australia

MAKING IT BIG

Born in Castlebar in 1852, Louis Brennan would become one of the best-known inventors of his day. Excelling at all things mechanical as a child, when his parents moved to Australia, Louis received an education in a Melbourne Technical College and aged twenty-two, his first successful invention was the steerable torpedo for which the British government paid the extraordinary sum of £100,000 for the patent. (It was trialled in Crosshaven in Cork in 1877). He was responsible for countless inventions including a futuristic monorail train kept upright by a gyroscope, an early helicopter, a miniature recording machine and mechanical starting devices for internal combustion engines. Sadly a car powered by such an engine struck him while on holiday in Switzerland in 1932 and he died as a result of his injuries, aged eighty.

had ever undertaken.

SITTING ON A GOLD MINE

There are slightly conflicting accounts of what exactly happened under the warm outback sun on 10 June 1893, about fifty kilometres east of Coolgardie.

Rumours were abroad all over Coolgardie of a substantial find further to the east at a place called Mount Youle. Just about everyone, the Irishmen included, decided to set off to the area in search of a claim of their own. This so-called find turned out to be fruitless and hundreds of men were left to make the sad, dejected journey back to town as poor as when they'd left.

According to some accounts the three Irishmen, Hannan, Flanagan and O'Shea, were together. Other versions, including Hannan's, say that O'Shea had gone on ahead alone while the other two sought to buy horses. The legend is that they actually found gold while looking for a stray horse, but again Hannan's version doesn't mention this. What is more likely is that the horse went astray earlier, delaying their departure from Coolgardie which led to their being separated from the hordes who had already left. With just the two men alone, they were free to wander the outback without the prying eyes of hundreds of other gold-hungry prospectors.

Three days out of Coolgardie they arrived at a slight rise

known as Mount Charlotte. They then began a thorough search of the area, inch by inch as far as a point called Maritana Hill. To his great excitement he and Flanagan spotted gold simply lying on the surface. Hannan himself said that Flanagan actually picked up the first nugget, but as he was the one to volunteer to go and register the claim, his name would forever be associated with the largest gold rush in history. It is interesting to note that the two locations of Mount Charlotte and Maritana Hill are now virtually in the centre of Kalgoorlie, the town that sprang up around the claim. Paddy Hannan stated in his account that as Dan O'Shea was their mate from previous outings, they went in search of him so that he could share in their find, though O'Shea refuted this when he was an old man, claiming he found the first piece of gold! As he was unable to give accurate accounts of where and when he had precisely made his find, Hannan's version was generally believed.

Whatever happened, it was decided that Paddy Hannan, being the youngest of the three men, should ride back to Coolgardie as quickly as possible to officially register the claim. But they still had one major problem – they were perilously short of water, with only four pints left between them. It is very possible they might have perished where they sat and their dust ended up mingling with the very gold dust they craved. But as though the gods had smiled upon them, that very day the heavens opened. He recounts:

'The water difficulty, which was usually great, was solved. Rain began to fall when I was on my way into Coolgardie, and continued for some time. The fall was fairly heavy, and, of course, exceedingly welcome. The downpour left plenty of water in the lake, and the supply lasted till the following November.'

When he arrived in Coolgardie, he immediately went to the 'office' – a tent with a sign outside – to register his claim. He was carrying a package of gold as evidence of the find and as it was not made common knowledge how much or of what quality the gold was, naturally wild rumours began to circulate. When his claim was posted, in keeping with the law, there was a virtual stampede out of town. It is estimated that within two days there were seven hundred men scouring the area and that Coolgardie had been reduced to a virtual ghost town in a matter of hours.

In their excitement, many left unprepared, without proper equipment, maps or water. Some were lost in the outback and some only made it after days of wandering. But for the majority, their nose for the rich scent of gold led them straight to the area. By the time Paddy Hannan returned a couple of days later, Flanagan and Shea had collected over a hundred ounces of gold, a huge return in such a short time. To put this in context, at today's prices that would be worth approximately 50,000 euro – not a bad return for two days' work.

Within a fortnight, over a thousand prospectors were furiously digging into the arid earth around Mount

Charlotte, praying with each thrust of the shovel to feel the solid clumps of once molten gold clink against the metal of their spades. What had just weeks before been a small area of infertile outback, indistinguishable from the vast open countryside that surrounded it, was suddenly a tented city. It gives an indication of the continued influx of new arrivals that before Christmas, two hotels had been built and a solid town was beginning to spring from the desert. This was the birth of Kalgoorlie, the town called after the Aboriginal name for an indigenous scrub, 'galgurlie'.

Paddy Hannan remained to mine his fortune early into the following year until he decided he'd earned sufficient funds to leave himself comfortable for the rest of his days. He was fifty-four years old and wasn't feeling in the best of health on top of which he '*hadn't seen the sea in five years*'. He decided to go on an extended holiday and sold his original claim. He was by no means a rich man, not actually realising the extent of the goldmine he'd discovered. But Hannan, Flanagan and Shea's find did make many a millionaire. Within a year the alluvial gold had pretty much yielded up its riches and it was left to the mining companies to dig deep into the rich reefs of gold that lay hidden far beneath the surface. In 1895 literally hundreds of companies speculating on the yields were floated on the London stock exchange and by the end of the decade Australia had become the world's largest exporter of gold. It is estimated that the Kalgoorlie field contributed

£100,000,000 to the Australian economy.

To Premier John Forrest, news of the extent of the find was greeted with elation; it was just the economic boost the fledgling territory demanded. But of course it immediately threw up new challenges. Thousands were now flocking to the area, all in need of transport and more importantly, water. Carrying it by train simply wasn't practicable, it was logistically impossible to supply that much water; even if the trains ran day and night they couldn't hope to cope with the demands. He had to find another solution. And he knew just the man to help him.

PIPE DREAMS

By the spring of 1895 it was reported that the miners in Kalgoorlie had been reduced to surviving on four pints of water a day, a trifling amount in the arid, sun-baked landscape. The demand for a solution became a clamour and C.Y. O'Connor was handed the task of somehow satiating the ever-growing thirst for a commodity that seemed to be in shorter supply than gold.

He turned his attention to the east of Perth towards a low escarpment rising to about six hundred metres called the Darling Ranges, which were cut by a series of deep ravines. After an extensive study of over thirty potential sites, he settled on a ravine in the Mundaring area cut through by the Helena River.

His proposal was considered by some foolhardy and by others simply outlandish. He proposed to build a dam across the ravine trapping a vast reservoir of water which would first have to be pumped over three hundred metres upwards over the escarpment and then through a pipeline stretching another 530 kilometres across the plains to a second reservoir at Coolgardie, delivering 5,000,000 gallons of water every day. To meet the needs of the towns and farms, which were springing up along its path, water would be reticulated at key points.

Greeted with intense scepticism, O'Connor was yet convinced his design was practical and could be constructed within three years and within his budget of £2,500,000.

In 1897, C.Y. O'Connor finally received official recognition for his earlier works, particularly Fremantle Harbour and was invited to London to be invested with the Order of the Companion of St Michael and St George by the Prince of Wales, an honour granted for making an outstanding contribution to the development of the Commonwealth. And while undoubtedly delighted to be so praised, ever the pragmatist, while there he also took the time to consult with Britain's leading civil engineers on his proposed pipeline. While expressing the view that the design would be the largest civil engineering project of its kind ever undertaken, they also endorsed it as highly achievable.

Despite political and media opposition, parliament

approved the plan and work commenced on the Mundaring Weir, an immense project in itself. The Helena River had to be diverted, a rail line built to supply the work, a towering retaining wall constructed some three hundred metres across the valley and to a height of forty metres enclosing a reservoir with a surface area of almost seven square kilometres. To ensure it would contain the huge volume of water, the foundations had to be dug by hand thirty metres straight down into bedrock. Such was the brilliance of O'Connor's design that when the weir height was raised by another ten metres half a century later, no further reinforcement of the foundation was deemed necessary.

Alongside this, a pumping station was constructed and the first of the pipes began to snake their way up and over the escarpment and out into the wilds. But this was no ordinary water pipe. It requires 60,000 sections, each nine metres long and weighing one ton, connected together with a newly-developed interlocking system. Much of the pipeline would have to run underground depending on the terrain, which involved a huge digging and tunnelling operation; to maintain the pressure a whole series of pumping stations at intervals along the pipe's length would be necessary.

The logistics were simply incredible and yet somehow O'Connor managed to keep the entire project on course and on time and that despite the biggest obstacle the pipeline was facing – not a mountain or impermeable rock or a cliff face, but the bitter wrath of the press.

TRIUMPH AND TRAGEDY

By 1902 the pipeline was nearing completion. But Sir John Forrest had by now moved on and the engineer's support in Parliament was waning. Competing political factions were using the cost of the project as a political football and O'Connor was being unjustly berated by much of the press. The *Australian Sunday Times*, in particular, was vitriolic in its attacks, labelling O'Connor a '*palm greaser*' and accusing him of having made a personal fortune from the project. This would prove to be completely without foundation.

He fought back, rebutting all of the accusations made against him and continuing to fight for his vision, just as he had during the construction of Fremantle Harbour. He was forced to attend commissions of inquiry while continuing to oversee the work, which put him under mental and physical strain.

Early in 1902 he traveled to Adelaide at the request of the senior railways engineer to bring his advice and expertise to another huge infrastructural undertaking, the building of a transcontinental railway line. While away, the scurrilous attacks of the press intensified, claiming his trip was a means of avoiding the responsibility for a scheme that could not possibly work and would drain the state of vast sums of taxpayers' money. One particularly sensationalist and uninformed article claimed that engineers feared the Mundaring Dam would burst under the pressure, flooding all of Perth and drowning thousands. There were no such fears in reality and in any case the predicted catastrophe was actually impossible as the reservoir was more than forty kilometres from the city and the water would have simply dispersed in the countless arid gullies and valleys that separated Perth from the Darling Ranges.

One *Sunday Times* article in February is known to have deeply upset Charles O'Connor and so burdened him he could barely function.

'*... And apart from any distinct charge of corruption this man has exhibited such gross blundering or something worse, in his management of great public works it is no exaggeration to say that he has robbed the taxpayer of this state of many millions of money ... in all the great undertakings in which he has misguided this state there are now nothing but gigantic monuments to confront him with reckless audacity, incompetence, and that unmentionable quality which has ever kept his eye on the main chance ... we need a Court of Justice in which to investigate O'Connor's relationship to his contractors.*'

Yet through all of this he continued to strive to complete the pipeline. On 8 March, he ran a test over a ten-kilometre length of the most difficult part of the pipeline. Inspection revealed just one minor leak, which was quickly repaired, but other than that, the water flowed precisely as he had predicted.

The following weekend he sat down and wrote a note:

'*The position has become impossible. Anxious important work to do and three commissions of enquiry to attend to. We may not have done as well as possible in the past but we will necessarily be too hampered to do well in the future. I feel that my brain is suffering and I am in great fear of what effect all this worry may have upon me – I have lost control of my thoughts. The Coolgardie Scheme is alright and I could finish it if I got a chance and protection from misrepresentation, but there is no hope of that now and it is better that it should be given to some entirely new man to do who will be untrammeled by prior responsibility'.*

Ever the professional he added a further line at the base:

'Put the wing walls to Helena Weir at once.'

At 7 a.m. on 10 March he rose as usual to go for his morning ride. His youngest daughter, Bridget, usually accompanied him, much as her sister Aileen had in earlier years, but she wasn't feeling very well so he set off alone. He rode down to Fremantle Harbour and looked proudly out over the now bustling waters, busy with ships, fishing boats and pleasure craft. He then continued south until he came to South Beach where he rode his horse into the shallows, placed a gun in his mouth and shot himself.

In January 1903, the steam pumps were turned on at Mundaring and a short time later millions of gallons of clean, fresh water began to gush from the pipe in Coolgardie. There was great jubilation and fanfare, but one man was missing from the celebrations. Everything had worked precisely as Charles O'Connor had predicted it would.

C.Y. LIVES ON

A huge congregation attended the funeral of C.Y. O'Connor on 12 March 1902. He was interred in the newly-opened cemetery at Palmyra overlooking the harbour that he considered his finest work. A great Celtic cross marks his final resting place.

In the weeks and months that followed, a government commission of enquiry determined that there had been no grounds whatsoever for the malicious accusations that had been laid at his feet. When his will was read, it was discovered his assets amounted to £200, hardly the estate of a man who'd had his 'palm greased' by contractors for years.

The *Sunday Times* didn't apologise or acknowledge the part they'd played in his death. Instead they printed an article lamenting his passing and begrudgingly acknowledging his contribution to Western Australia, but justifying their stance on the basis of the management of large public works.

The pipeline would continue to supply water to the goldfields and farms along its path until the mid-1960s, when the steam pumps would need to be replaced with electric centrifugal pumps. It is the longest freshwater pipeline in the world and incredibly, it is still fully functional today, over a century later. It truly was a work of engineering genius.

In 1912 an imposing statue of Charles Yelverton O'Connor by renowned Italian sculptor Pietro Porcelli was erected overlooking Fremantle Harbour. The beach where Charles ended his life was renamed 'C.Y. O'Connor Beach' and in the shallows stands a haunting bronze sculpture by Tony Jones depicting a half-submerged man on a horse.

A number of institutions and electoral districts are also named after him, as well as the O'Connor Centre, which was the site of his office when the harbour was being built. The huge reservoir trapped behind the giant edifice of Mundaring Dam has also been named 'C.Y. O'Connor Lake'.

Charles' wife Susan would outlive him by almost four decades. She died in November 1941 at the ripe old age of ninety-two.

Charles O'Connor was a rarity, a true visionary who was prepared to stand behind his visions come hell or high water, refusing to pander to any self-serving interest group or any shallow political machinations, and at great personal expense, in the end paying the ultimate price. How Ireland, Australia, or any country for that matter, could use a man of his genius today.

GOLDEN YEARS

Paddy Hannan would also outlive C.Y. O'Connor by many years. In 1897, having enjoyed the fruits of his labour on his holiday he returned to Kalgoorlie, where he was immediately recognised and feted as a hero, being driven around in a coach drawn by five horses, which was an improvement on his transportation when he'd last been there. He was escorted to the spot where he'd first found gold and he ceremonially planted a pepper tree on the spot. A reporter for *The Kalgoorlie Miner* described Paddy as '*very pleasant and genial, as his nationality could not well prevent him from being, while in appearance a ruddy complexion betokens a healthy and vigorous outdoor life. Concerning himself he is not disposed to be very communicative.*'

Indeed the description of Paddy Hannan tallies very much with other accounts of his character. He was an extremely temperate man, rarely taking more than one or two drinks, which was anathema to his fellow miners. He was also quietly spoken, unassuming and of a kindly disposition. He was a modest man and never made any great claims about the gold find of the century; in fact he was always quick to point out that the glory for the strike should have been shared with O'Shea and especially with Flanagan.

In later years, most of his money spent, he tried his hand at prospecting once again, but with little success on this occasion and in 1904 the government granted him a pension of £100 in recognition of his contribution to the state. It was a reasonable amount in those days, but considering how much his find had contributed to state coffers, one would have to say the government got the better deal.

Paddy Hannan never married, which is hardly

surprising given the amount of time he'd spent in the wilderness or in towns populated almost exclusively by men. The relative isolation in which he'd lived wouldn't exactly have tutored him greatly in the social or 'courting' arts. He spent the remaining years of his life with his sister in Melbourne. He died peacefully in 1925 at the age of eighty-five leaving an estate of £1,400 – hardly a goldmine.

In 1929 a bronze statue of Paddy Hannan was erected in Kalgoorlie's Hannan Street portraying a weatherworn, bearded Paddy with a pickaxe and a water bag, which also doubles as a fountain. Another bronze statue was later erected in Burswood Park, Perth depicting him pushing a barrow, and in recent years his hometown of Quin in Co. Clare unveiled a plaque in his honour opposite Quin Abbey.

It is not known if Paddy Hannan and Charles O'Connor ever met, but their destinies were in many ways entwined. Charles' work paved the way for Paddy to set out on his first prospecting adventure in New Zealand, and later the development of the railway system in Western Australia facilitated the opening up of the goldfields to Paddy and thousands of others. In return, Paddy's find at Kalgoorlie launched the greatest gold rush in history, which initiated Charles O'Connor's monumental Goldfields Pipeline project for which he is best remembered and admired.

In a final twist of irony, *The Sunday Times*, which had so vilified one Irishman, C.Y. O'Connor, published an obituary on the occasion of Paddy Hannan's death, which celebrated his achievements. They may have been profoundly in error on the first occasion, but their words were a fitting homage to a poor boy from Co. Clare who, through hard work and dedication, literally went from rags to riches.

'The annals of our goldfields history will ever remember at the pinnacle of the roll of honour the name of Patrick Hannan, the discoverer of the richest goldfield in the world, to which fluctuated in an incredibly short time the most cosmopolitan crowd that riches ever beckoned from the far corners of the earth ... The State owes today to Hannan and the kind of men who were contemporaneous with him in the discovery and all the hardship that it meant, a debt which it can never pay'.

Alejandro O'Reilly

Spanish Count, Field Marshal in the Spanish Army, Governor of Madrid, Cadiz and Louisiana, 'Father of the Puerto Rican Military', respected military reformer.
(1722 – 1794)

WHAT'S IN A NAME?

Just off the Avenue de Paula San Pedro which skirts the waterfront of old Havana, you happen upon a street bearing a name that would be more at home in Co. Meath or Cavan than in the Spanish influenced Caribbean island of Cuba – Calle O'Reilly. Although it's been a part of this beautiful but crumbling maze of narrow streets for centuries, the 'O'Reilly' street sign still seems a little out of place among the 'San Ignacios', the 'Tejadillos' and the 'Obispas', a little like a tourist who's wandered into a remote tavern in a far-flung corner of the earth, only to bring stares and mutterings from the locals.

As you wander along Calle O'Reilly under the near constant sweltering sun, an old projecting sign offers you blessed relief – advertising the aptly-named Café O'Reilly. With its old, intimate, wooden interiors, overhead fans and Latin, white-shirted waiter it is so like a scene from an old movie, the temptation is irresistible and within seconds you are sitting at a table sipping a mojito or a cold beer and possibly puffing on a genuine Cuban at a cost of a couple of 'convertible' pesos.

Sitting there in Café O'Reilly watching Havana as it goes about its business, it's difficult not to be intrigued as to who exactly Senor O'Reilly was that he would merit a street named in his honour among so many local heroes, leaders and saints from Cuba's fascinating history.

Of course, the voices in the bustling, narrow streets of this part of Havana echo back long before Cuba's relatively recent history of communist rule, American blockades and conflict with the west. The foundations for the city were clearly laid by Spain and find their origins back when Spain was, like the US today, one of the world's most powerful and influential countries, possessed of an army and seafaring prowess to match the finest in the world. And in the midst of this continuing military struggle can be found an Irishman from Co. Meath, one Alejandro O'Reilly, regarded in his day in the mid-eighteenth century as one of Spain's greatest generals and a brilliant military strategist.

It's not too surprising that Alejandro would develop a

reputation for himself in matters military considering his lineage. Back in 1690, his grandfather, John, had raised a regiment of dragoons for the Catholic King James and fought in the Jacobite army against William of Orange at the Battle of the Boyne. So from the moment of his birth in Baltrasna, Co. Meath in 1722, Alexander, as he was christened, already had the army gene in his blood. His parents were Thomas O'Reilly, a Catholic nobleman and master of Baltrasna estate, and Rose McDowell.

INTO BATTLE

The political climate of the day was particularly oppressive for Catholics and, like so many thousands of so-called 'Wild Geese' before them, Thomas and Rose decided to uproot their family from the dark, damp earth of Meath and sow the seeds of their future in the much more hospitable climes of Spain. Alexander, who was by then a boy of about twelve, must have gawped in wonder at the alien landscape, the dark-skinned faces, the mysterious language and the peculiar and exotic meals and fruits of his new home in Zaragoza. But he was a bright boy and capable of quickly adapting to new circumstances. He easily picked up the language and performed well in his studies, somewhere along the way adopting the Spanish version of his name – 'Alejandro'. Yet he had not forgotten his Irish roots, as when still a teenager, he opted to enlist as a cadet in the

Hibernia Regiment of the Spanish army, which was one of six complete Irish infantry regiments serving in the Spanish Empire at that time.

In his twenty-first year Alejandro would receive an unfortunate memento from an Austrian soldier at the Battle of Camposanto – a gunshot wound to his leg – which would give him a pronounced limp for the rest of his days. Yet despite this impediment, he persevered with his military career and continued to see active service, rising to the rank of Sergeant Major by the time he was twenty-five.

After the 1748 Treaty of Aix-la-Chappelle brought a temporary peace to much of western Europe, Alejandro was afforded the opportunity to serve in the Austrian army and further enhance his knowledge and understanding of military strategy. While serving in France during these years he reputedly impressed Louis XV so much that he earned himself a personal recommendation and was duly promoted to the rank of colonel.

By 1762 Alejandro O'Reilly had returned to the dusty soil of his adopted homeland and to the ranks of the Spanish army who were about to invade their neighbours, Portugal. His strategic nous in this campaign won the admiration of his commanders who rewarded him with a promotion to Brigadier General at the age of forty.

A year later, Cuba and the Americas were to make their first appearance on Alejandro's horizon. The Irishman was assigned to accompany the Spanish Governor, the Count of Ricla, to Havana as his second-in-command. The city had fallen to the British in the Seven Years' War and under the terms of the Treaty of Paris was now to be handed back to Spain. O'Reilly landed on the spot which would later become the street that would bear his name, and from this point watched as the last of the British ships disappeared around the curve of the harbour. He then turned his eye on the city itself and within weeks had analysed its defences, which he considered had crumbled all too easily to the British guns. He recommended sweeping changes to the fortifications, troop practises and training; such was the reputation he'd garnered for himself that he was virtually given *carte blanche* by the Spanish crown to set his plans in motion. Much of this work is still visible to visitors today, particularly the Fortaleza de San Carlos de la Cabaña, more simply known to the locals as La Cabaña, an impressive fort located on the eastern side of the harbour entrance. La Cabaña incidentally, would later play an interesting role in another chapter of Havana's history when in 1959 it would be captured by Che Guevara and used as a HQ from which to direct the revolution.

TAKING ON THE PUERTO RICAN ARMY

It proved an eventful year in Alejandro's life as he also fell in love with and married Dona Rosa de Las Casas, who was the Governor of Cuba's sister. Dona Rosa would bear five children thereby ensuring that not only Alejandro's works, but also his bloodline would be permanent fixtures in the history of Cuba and Spain.

His labours in Cuba winning much admiration, King Carlos III decided to employ Alejandro's leadership and organisational skills to greater effect within the sphere of Spain's Caribbean colonies. In 1765 the now Field Marshall O'Reilly was sent to Puerto Rico where again he would make an indelible mark on the island and ultimately be

HOTEL PALACIO O'FARRILL

Another of the Wild Geese who made his name in Cuba was the exotically-titled Don Ricardo O'Farrill and O'Daly who in 1715 arrived in Havana from Monserrat, which is often nicknamed 'The Emerald Isle of the Caribbean' due to its many Irish connections. The Irish in Monserrat had been heavily involved in the slave trade and Don Ricardo used his experience of this to set up a thriving slave business in Cuba, as well as a sugar trading business. He was soon one of the wealthiest men in Cuba, became a Spanish citizen and married the daughter of an influential politician, establishing a dynasty that would endure for centuries. The palace he built for himself in Havana is now the recently-restored, elaborately ornate Hotel Palacio O'Farrill, one of the best-known hotels in the capital where, in a nod to its former owner's Irish roots, green predominates on everything from the walls to the stained-glass windows.

remembered as 'The father of the Puerto Rican military'. Having taken a thorough census of the island he then began a series of sweeping reforms of the army. This was something of a mixed blessing for the soldiers as one of his reforms ensured they were paid regularly and directly and not via their immediate superiors, who would often subtract a large 'fee' for themselves. On the other hand, the rigid discipline he instilled shocked both officers and regulars from their complacent and casual approach to their duties. Ultimately they would thank him, as over the following three years he would completely transform the military from a slack, rag-tag organisation to a highly trained, well-oiled machine. As in Havana, O'Reilly also initiated a mammoth program to strengthen the island's fortifications and one of those, the magnificent and imposing Castle of Old San Juan, was developed considerably under his recommendation and is now a World Heritage site.

O'Reilly's influence would resound long after he'd left. When thirty years later the English attacked with a massive force of 14,000 men, the Puerto Ricans routed them over two weeks of disciplined battle. This event is still celebrated on the island today and much credit for the famous victory is reserved for the training and strategies instilled by O'Reilly. It must have indeed heartened him that his influence had helped defeat the English – not only the enemy of his adopted homeland, Spain, but also the enemy of the country of his birth and from which his parents had been forced to flee.

FIT FOR A KING

Winston Churchill's favourite quote was said to be 'Know you are in the right place at the right time in your journey.' A year later O'Reilly was back in Madrid and it seemed almost instinctively that he had chosen the right place at

POETIC VICTORY

Alejandro O'Reilly would earn a mention in Lord Byron's famous epic poem 'Don Juan', not for any of his successes, but for his abortive attack in Algiers. Ironically, the character of Donna Julia in the poem mistakenly attributes him with a victory rather than defeat.

'Was it for this that no Cortejo e'er
I yet have chosen from out the youth of Seville?
Is it for this I scarce went anywhere,
Except to bull-fights, mass, play, rout, and revel?
Is it for this, whate'er my suitors were,
I favor'd none—nay, was almost uncivil?
Is it for this that General Count O'Reilly,
Who took Algiers, declares I used him vilely?

Byron would later remark that 'General Count O'Reilly did not take Algiers, Algiers took him'.

the right time. In an episode that quirkily became known as 'the Hat & Cloak riots', a despised minister decided to outlaw the wearing of a traditional cloak and hat! Motivated by this and by a shortage of bread, the people rioted and attacked several government buildings eventually turning their attentions to the palace where Carlos III was resident. With reports of killings reaching the palace, Field Marshall O'Reilly quickly mobilised and organised his forces and despite being vastly outnumbered by the hordes that had by now broken through the gates, he held sway and prevented the mob from reaching the King. Ultimately the riot would abate and become a footnote in Spain's history, but O'Reilly's actions in saving the King's life would be remembered for a long time by Carlos, who took a personal shine to the courageous and affable Irishman and rewarded him by making him Commander-in-Chief of a major expeditionary force headed for what is now the American state of Louisiana.

History has a way of remembering individuals as either famous or infamous, depending on which side you happen to be on. And it was his next appointment in 1769 as the Governor and Captain General of Louisiana that would see him loved and loathed in equal proportion by the opposing forces.

Originally a long-held colony of France (Louisiana is named after King Louis XIV), Spain gained possession of the territory as a result of a treaty six years earlier. With generations of French blood in their veins, many of the locals saw this as a betrayal and refused to accept Spanish rule. King Carlos handed O'Reilly the task of quelling the ensuing revolt, and by making him governor, also handed him real political power for the first time.

The Commander-in-Chief embarked for Havana where he mustered two thousand of the troops he'd earlier helped to train and sailed for New Orleans with twenty-four warships, dropping anchor in the sweltering humidity of an August day in 1769. He first took formal possession of the colony and then decided to hold a reception in the governor's palace, inviting many of New Orleans' most influential citizens among whom he had already identified the main rebel leaders. The French Creole guests were said to have been taken aback at O'Reilly's geniality towards them, given the rebellious state of affairs and his appointed task of punishing the insult to the Spanish crown.

They were even more taken aback when, with their bellies full and the wine having dulled their senses, O'Reilly suddenly ordered the six chief rebel leaders seized and arrested. The following day he made all the colonists swear an oath to the Spanish Crown and as an act of benevolence towards a now fearful population, he announced that only the ringleaders would face retribution. After a series of trials over the coming months, he sentenced six men to death and many more to long prison sentences. One of the six died in prison and on 25 October, the remaining five were executed by firing squad. This act would earn him the epithet 'Bloody O'Reilly' and a place of infamy in Louisiana's history.

If this episode demonstrated the ruthless side of O'Reilly's nature, many of the laws passed under his reign would display his humanist tendencies. When he'd arrived a few months earlier, many of the locals were amazed that a great proportion of his force, including officers, were black Cuban men. In a territory where slavery was an accepted part of the colonists' life, men and women stood and gawped as the troops marched past. Their jaws would drop even further when the governor strictly banned the enslavement of Indians in the state and introduced laws that would make it easier for existing slaves to buy their freedom. While the French Creoles regarded him a brutal dictator, the 'coloureds', as they were known, saw him as an enlightened humanitarian. Many of his other reforms would meet with general approval – the regulation of the medical profession, the regularisation of weights and measures in the trading community, another large programme of public works including levee and bridge improvements, as well as a host of other laws regulating the sale of alcohol and improving education for the colonists' children.

His work done, he handed the governorship over to another and the following year returned to Spain and to have first, the title 'Conde de O'Reilly' (Count O'Reilly) bestowed on him by the King and then to be handed the governorship of the city at the heart of the Spanish

Empire, Madrid.

Despite his new political appointment, the Spanish were anxious not to let Alejandro's tremendous organisational and motivational skills go to waste. With the threat of war between Spain and its old enemy Britain ever-present and one of its potential flashpoints being his familiar stomping ground of the Caribbean, he was now handed the task of organising six new regiments to be trained near Cadiz, a task he took to with his usual gusto, again impressing his superiors with the quality of fighting men he seemed to manufacture as easily as the dusty Spanish soil produced olives.

DOWN BUT NOT OUT

But in 1775 aged fifty-three and at the height of his career, Alejandro O'Reilly would have to face the only major setback of his career. The Spanish-Moroccan stronghold of Melilla had come under a combined attack from Algerian and Moroccan forces. The Conde de O'Reilly was now put in command of a large force of 18,000 men to re-assert Spain's authority in the region. They arrived in the Bay of Algiers in early July 1775 and prepared to besiege the city. Unfortunately, most of the men, while highly trained, had little or no experience of battle and combined with delays imposed on O'Reilly, the Algerians routed the Spanish force. One of the few saving graces for the Conde was his order to his former Hibernia regiment to take the lead in the battle, the more experienced unit reputedly holding off the north African force long enough for the rest to make their escape and prevent a wholesale massacre.

This defeat did little to blemish his reputation as his old admirer King Carlos and his ministers decreed that the entire expedition was ill-conceived from the start. The man who had ordered the attack was blamed and removed from power and O'Reilly was promptly made Captain-General of Andalucia, the highest possible military rank in the region!

FINAL PORT OF CALL

The Conde de O'Reilly would continue to serve in his military capacity in Andalucia for the next decade, during which he also found the time to accept a new political appointment, this time as the Governor of Cadiz.

The southern city had recently attained a new level of prosperity, replacing Seville as Spain's most important port. He may have been selected for this role specifically because of his Irish roots as at that time Irish merchants were enjoying tremendous success in the city and exercising a disproportionately large influence in the wealthier circles, highly regarded as patrons of the arts and general cultural life of the city. Now in his sixties, his military career was drawing to a close, but his energy and sense of purpose remained undimmed. The Conde de O'Reilly played a key role in directing public improvements and it was during this era that Cadiz developed into one of the country's most cosmopolitan cities and the sought-after destination for many of Spain's richest citizens. O'Reilly's six-year reign as Governor oversaw the construction of many of the beautiful and historic buildings in what is now the historic old city of Cadiz. A street in the old port, Calle del Conde de O'Reilly, still honours his memory.

O'Reilly was enjoying his retirement in the beautiful surrounds of Cadiz when in 1794 at the age of seventy-two, he was surprised to get a sudden recall to active duty. Ordered to take command of an army in the Pyrenees to oppose invading French forces, he was both honoured and delighted to be back doing what he loved the most. He set off in mid-March with great enthusiasm for the task that lay ahead, but sadly never got to fulfil his ambition of commanding an army one last time. He died unexpectedly under the warm spring sun in the village of Bonete in Valencia. He was interred in the presbytery of the local parish church.

During his lifetime he'd been Governor of Madrid, Cadiz and Louisiana, he'd been one of Spain's leading generals of the age, he'd rubbed shoulders with the King who'd personally made him a Count, he'd left a lasting and visible impression on the cities of Havana, Cadiz and San Juan in Puerto Rico

Despite his achievements, it would probably have

pleased Alejandro to find his final resting place in a small rural, farming village as it was into just such a community he'd been born. But in the course of his life, he'd come a long way from Baltrasna.

Albert D. J. Cashier
aka Jennie Hodgers

US Civil War Veteran

BORN AGAIN

It is estimated that over 150,000 Irishmen served as soldiers under the Union flag in the American Civil War. Of all those thousands, one Irish man in particular would make a unique contribution to the annals of that terrible conflict. He didn't win any medals of honour or rise through the ranks to become a general or anything of that nature. In many ways he was just an ordinary infantryman like thousands of others. But there was one great difference, one secret that Albert Cashier guarded from his fellow soldiers for the entirety of the war – he was, in fact, a woman.

Very few records remain of those born in Ireland during the famine or post-famine years, their memory washed away in a sea of starvation, death and emigration. In the turmoil of the time records were often haphazard at best, births and deaths frequently not recorded, and most of the official state records of the era that were made were subsequently lost in the flames of the Four Courts and the Custom House during the Irish Civil War.

So of Jennie Hodgers' childhood we know very little. It is likely that she was born in Clogherhead in Co. Louth, possibly on Christmas Day, 1843 or 1844. She herself claimed this was her birthplace and when she died, an administrator of her estate listed her parents as Patrick and Sallie Hodgers. Who they were exactly and what they did for a living is unknown, but a survey called Griffith's Primary Valuation conducted between 1848 and 1864 did show that there were six families called Hodgers living in Louth, many of these were probably closely related. An earlier report on people who had applied for a grant to grow flax listed a Patrick Hodgers, Senior, of Termonfeckin (just a couple of miles from Clogherhead) as having three spinning wheels. So it is possible that Jennie was born into a family of small farmers and linen-makers, spending her spring days planting flax seeds and pulling them and preparing them a few months later for her father to weave into thread. She would spend much of her later life working on a farm, so it's likely she chose this work based on her experience. We do know she didn't have much time for an education as she could neither read nor write when she arrived in the United States.

Louth lost almost one fifth of its population during the

famine and as much again to emigration in the decade to follow, thousands choosing the so-called 'coffin ships' over the grinding poverty of the land in Ireland. Jennie Hodgers was among them, relocating across the Atlantic aged about seventeen in 1862. Again accounts vary wildly about her journey, in some she is simply a passenger, in others a stowaway. Some versions have her donning male clothing during the voyage or alternatively the girl first becomes a boy in New York.

However she got there, it is likely she was in dire need of money. She was probably alone or in the company of an equally desperate younger sibling and there was one way to improve her chances of securing work.

At some point in the journey from Clogherhead to Boston, Massachusetts, Jennie Hodgers was reborn as Albert D.J. Cashier. Why she chose this particular name is a mystery, it may simply have been a spur of the moment thing upon seeing the word 'cashier' in some shipping office or train station. Interestingly the word 'cashier' also means 'to discard' or 'to dismiss a soldier from the army', and Jennie may well have overheard the word used in this context and chosen it as her own.

Why she chose to change her sex and remain that way is an even bigger mystery. Circumstances could have forced her, such as the improved chances of employment being a man presented. She was possibly a lesbian, although lesbians generally prefer the company of other women and Albert Cashier would spend many years almost exclusively in the company of men. The other possibility is that she was an eonist, which is a form of life-long cross-dressing, the term coined from the name of Charles Eon de Beaumont, a French courtier who was born a boy but spent most of his life as a woman. We will simply never know her reasons.

By 1862 Albert D.J. Cashier had arrived in America. And so had the Civil War.

A FIGHTING CHANCE

The chances of a woman being recruited as a soldier in the US Army in the nineteenth century were precisely nil. The only way a female could serve her country in the military was as a nurse, a cook or some sort of administrator. But as she grew in confidence about her male persona, Albert Cashier decided he could take a chance that his secret could literally be kept under wraps.

Albert decided to head west and a couple of months later turned up in the town of Belvidere in Illinois, almost two thousand kilometres away. He initially picked up some work as a handyman and then as a farmhand, clearly fooling the farmer who would not readily have chosen a girl for such manual work. Yet Albert was anything but muscular and manly in appearance, measuring only 5' 3" head to toe. And yet he outwitted employers repeatedly, clearly impressing them early on with his unfaltering devotion to hard work, learned in the muddy fields of Co.

Louth. But his jobs paid poorly and offered him no real long-term prospects.

The American Civil War had commenced in April of the previous year and the belief among the union states was that it would last only a few months. But in July 1861, in the first major encounter of the war, they suffered over two thousand casualties at the First Battle of Bull Run. This resulted in a major recruitment drive and the male citizens of the north began to sign up in their hundreds of thousands. Not all were motivated by the high anti-slavery ideals of Abraham Lincoln, indeed a large percentage of the Union Army was indifferent to the lot of the enslaved dark-skinned masses of the south. For many it was simply a matter of honour and loyalty to their country and for a great number of soldiers, on both sides, it was the attraction of the thirteen dollars a month wages. For some it was a combination of all of these factors.

Albert Cashier had been in America only a matter of months, so it's unlikely he had any great knowledge of the politics that lay behind the war. It was also probably too early for him to have developed any great loyalty to his new country, although he would have no doubt been exposed to many a patriotic discussion in his travels and among his work colleagues about doing one's duty. However, for a poor labourer, the possibility of earning good regular wages and the hundred dollars which was on offer simply for signing up, must have been a tempting inducement.

On 3 August 1862, Albert made the short journey west from the farmland around Belvidere to the recruiting station in the town of Rockford and joined the queue of men enlisting in the Union infantry at Camp Fuller. His petite size no doubt brought curious stares and sniggers from the others, but such was the need for new recruits that the officer in charge was happy to accept his services – after all, a short man can fire a rifle with as much accuracy as a giant. Unable to write, the officer recorded his name and Albert D.J. Cashier then signed his recruitment form with an 'X'. The Government records also note that he had a light complexion, blue eyes and auburn hair.

IRELAND'S HONOR

The medal of honor is the highest military decoration that can be granted in the United States of America. It is awarded for 'conspicuously by gallantry and intrepidity at the risk of his life above and beyond the call of duty while engaged in an action against an enemy of the United States.' Only 3,500 have been bestowed since its inception over two centuries ago. These men were born in over thirty different countries and Ireland by far leads the field of recipients, with 258. Germany is next with 128. Cork provided nineteen of these courageous individuals with Dublin and Tipperary supplying eleven each. Sadly, because the Medal of Honor demands such a tremendous act of valour, many of those were awarded posthumously.

Undoubtedly happy to have been accepted, Albert's heart must have sank in the next moment as he was ordered to report to a tent for a physical. Much to his relief this was cursory – eyes and hands were checked to see if he could shoot and feet to see if he would be up to the thousands of miles of walking that war in a country of America's scale demanded.

He was assigned to Company G of the 95th Illinois Infantry Regiment and despatched for two months' intensive training. He was the shortest and lightest person in the entire regiment.

MAN OF ACTION

He didn't have to wait long to try out his new army boots. The 95th was mustered into the Union Army in September and a few weeks later was marching the long road south to Grand Junction to join General Grant's Army of the Tennessee.

On that first long march Albert must have struggled somewhat to appear at ease while surrounded by a sea of testosterone. Whatever his sexuality, the challenge to maintain his secret was surely a mountainous one among a throng of men who openly used the side of the road to relieve themselves or shared huge, revolting open latrines in camp.

Albert was to get his first taste of action in the spring of

1863. In May of that year, General Grant ordered his army across the Mississippi and forced the Confederate forces to retreat to the garrison at Vicksburg. The thousand men of Albert's 95th Infantry Regiment were among those who would charge into battle and subsequently lay siege to the town for the next two months. During this campaign Albert was captured by the enemy and was sitting under

THE FIGHTING 69TH

As a means of bolstering Irish immigrant support for the union and sending a warning to Britain over her support of the Confederacy, the US Government decided to form an all-Irish brigade during the Civil War. The first commander of the Irish Brigade was Colonel Michael Corcoran who was actually being court-martialled for refusing to parade a regiment before the Prince of Wales, but such was the shortage of officers, he got the job anyway. The brigade fought heroically at the Battle of Bull Run and at several subsequent clashes, but Corcoran was unfortunately captured. Their new commander would eventually be Thomas Francis Meagher, the well-known Irish nationalist. The brigade suffered terribly at the Battle of Fredericksburg, losing over a thousand men, but fought so heroically that Confederate General Robert E. Lee dubbed Meagher's unit 'The Fighting 69th'. Reinforced, the brigade again served with distinction at Gettysburg. Eventually disbanded, a new 'Fighting 69th' would serve in WWI, earning a number of Medals of Honor, and again in WWII.

guard when the Confederate soldier turned his back for a moment. He quickly seized the man's weapon, prised it from his hands and knocked him to the ground with it. He then fled back to the safety of the Union lines to the cheers of his fellow soldiers.

On 3 July, the Battle of Gettysburg resulted in a victory for the Union Army which would prove the turning point of the war. The following day, with supplies and ammunition running low, the Confederates at Vicksburg surrendered, ceding control of the Mississippi River for the rest of the war. Albert Cashier and the 95th, although having suffered thirty-five deaths and with over a hundred wounded, had enjoyed their first taste of victory. By all accounts he had soldiered well, his fellow soldiers describing him as an excellent shot. So good in fact that he was regularly selected by his commanding officer to go out on the skirmishing line. Luckily for Albert, he also knew to keep his head low.

The 95th was engaged in several smaller battles over the course of that year but their next major engagement with the enemy would not come until March of 1864. It was fought along the banks of the Red River in Louisiana and involved over thirty thousand Union troops doing battle with the smaller Confederate force of twelve thousand. There would be no glorious end to this campaign for the Union. Over two months they fought a series of bloody engagements which cost them at least five thousand casualties, the 95th again incurring losses. Albert was not among the dead, despite an account of him rashly jumping atop a fallen tree trunk to taunt the enemy to reveal themselves and on another occasion clambering up a tree to replace a Confederate flag with the Union's colours. He was without doubt a courageous soldier, if displaying a little youthful foolhardiness.

Throughout these campaigns his deception continued to go undetected. He pretty much kept to himself and was considered shy. He avoided social contact and only engaged with the other men during marches or battle. It is recounted that because of his size his fellow infantrymen excused him heavy work, but that Albert repaid them by washing their clothes whenever the rare opportunity offered itself. This exchange of duties wouldn't have been unusual as many recruits were no more than teenage boys, some probably (illegally) enlisting as young as fifteen. It would have been common to assign these boys to uniform duties or cook's assistant while in camp. But as he entered his third year as a soldier, still nobody had any inkling that this particular boy was, in fact, a girl.

Under the scorching sun of a Georgia summer, Albert Cashier's depleted and weary regiment was ordered to the town of Jonesborough. Over two days, the Union army under General Sherman engaged the Confederate Army of Tennessee, who were defending the city of Atlanta. They successfully lured the Confederates away from their defences and seized the city. This battle is depicted in the famous fire scene in *Gone with the Wind*.

This was a key victory, which ensured the re-election of Lincoln and brought the end of the war within sight. The 95th saw further action in the pursuit and defeat of the fleeing Confederates and was involved in further battles in Georgia, Alabama and Mississippi. And as spring of 1865 turned to summer, the war was all but over. Albert Cashier continued to fight as well as any of his colleagues but remained mostly unharmed. Yet disease was rife in both armies and given the conditions in which they lived it is hardly surprising that death from cholera, infection and dehydration through diarrhea claimed more lives than enemy bullets. By the end of the war the 95th had lost over a quarter of her number with almost the same number wounded, some seriously. Yet of those who died, just eighty-four were killed in battle while over two hundred succumbed to disease of one form or another.

While Albert could evade detection, inevitably he couldn't accomplish the same with disease. In late spring he suffered a potentially disastrous bout of diarrhea and was forced to report to the camp infirmary, which was permanently filled with the wails of amputees or those in the death throes of some infectious disease. He pleaded with the doctors to simply give him some medicine rather than admit him, which he knew would result in his sex being revealed. Overworked and with impossible numbers to treat, they agreed and his secret survived, albeit at the cost of a few extremely uncomfortable days.

By the summer of 1865 the war had ended and on 17

August the 95th Regiment was mustered out of the army. The war had seen the end of slavery at a cost of one million lives, many of them Irish. Albert Cashier's name was not among the list of casualties.

THE MAN IN THE STREET

Albert returned to Belvidere for a couple of years, resuming his life of working at odd jobs on farms and as a general handyman. He then moved to the town of Pontiac and finally found a place he would call home for most of the rest of his life, Saunemin, which was a small country village south of Chicago.

He worked as a handyman, a lamplighter, a store attendant before again returning to the land, securing a job on a local farm. After the war he seems to have had no inclination to return to the persona of Jennie Hodgers and no one seems to have had any notion that he was a she. One side benefit of this was that in a state where women were at that time denied the vote, he made a point of voting in presidential elections.

He continued to work at the farm for the next forty years and also managed to retain his position as the village gas-lamplighter. He became familiar to all the residents, particularly as he often wore his Union uniform with pride while patrolling the street with his torch. His relationship with the farming family was such that the farmer eventually built him a one-room cottage on his land; the cottage is still in existence.

In 1907 at the age of sixty-four, Albert applied for a veteran's pension, which was granted. Albert is the only female veteran of the Civil War ever to receive this, although to the authorities at the time were completely unaware of the unique record they'd just set.

Then in 1910, the mask finally began to slip. He fell ill with stomach pains in his cottage one day and a friend, worried he hadn't been seen, called by and found him badly ill. She immediately called a nurse and in the course of her examination, gasped in shock at what she saw beneath the blankets. Albert pleaded with them not to reveal his true nature and they agreed. He recovered, and life went on as before.

Then the following year he was doing an odd job in the driveway of the local senator's home when the State Senator Lish reversed his car into Albert and broke his leg. A doctor was called and due to the nature of the injury, Albert's pants had to be removed. Inevitably, and in the presence of two men, Albert was revealed to be a woman. Once again Albert pleaded with them to keep the secret.

But Albert was now almost seventy years old and infirm as a result of the accident. The senator decided to admit him into The Soldiers and Sailors Veteran's Home in Quincy, Illinois. Whether through regard for his service in the war or through guilt at having caused the accident, the senator conspired to maintain the façade, making only a handful of doctors and nurses aware of the old soldier's femininity.

Albert lived among the other veterans for a couple of years, trading war stories and living a mostly peaceful life, none of the other veterans aware she was a woman. But eventually her mental health began to fade and she was transferred to the Watertown State Hospital for the Insane. Sadly this was the destination for many people who were probably in the first stages of Alzheimer's. Worse again was the fact that she was now forced to wear dresses, and she retained enough mental agility to rebel against this imposition, which was totally alien to her nature. As her mind began to fade so did her ability to protest the way she was dressed and she ended her days wearing female clothing for the first time in over sixty years.

In the course of her committal to the asylum, word finally leaked out to the press that she was a woman who had served in the war and there was a flurry of interest in her story. By now though many of her recollections, especially of her childhood, were confused and unreliable.

She passed away on 11 October 1915 at the age of seventy-one.

Albert D.J. Cashier was buried wearing the Union Army uniform of which she was so proud. She received full military honours and her coffin was draped in the American flag. Her grave is in Sunny Slope Cemetery, Saunemin. Her original headstone simply read: Albert D.J. Cashier

Co. G 95 Illinois Inf. In recent years a more fitting head-stone recorded her 'dual identity':

Albert D. J. Cashier
Co. G, 95. Inf.
Civil War
Born: Jennie Hodgers
in Clogher Head, Ireland
1843-1915

THE LAST POST

Albert Cashier did not command any regiments to great victories, he was a foot soldier, like thousands of other enlisted men. It was, in the main, these men who laid down their lives for their cause and battled with overwhelming fear to charge into the enemy's blazing guns. Many of their names were forgotten, trampled in the mud and blood of places like Gettysburg and Vicksburg.

Albert Cashier was one of those thousands of ordinary heroes of the American Civil War. Yet she was not the only woman who served in the war disguised as a man. There were over two hundred recorded cases of women who wished to serve in battle, but most were quickly discovered or killed in action. In this regard Albert remains unique as the only woman soldier to survive the entire war and to draw a pension.

Why did she do it? Was she simply an oddity with a curious sexual inclination? It's hard to judge her in the context of today when most of these issues are openly discussed and women's position in society, at least in the western world, bears no relation to those times. In the mid-nineteenth century, it was somewhat different. Men ruled the world and women, often as not, were reduced to a subservient, often thankless existence. Assessing her in the context of that era would serve her memory better.

The Board of Trustees of the Village of Saunemin where she lived most of her life are planning to restore her cottage as a national historic site and on the battlefield at Vicksburg stands a monument to all thirty-five thousand men who fought there. Among them you will find the name Albert D.J. Cashier.

On 6 November 1915, the *Irish Times* reported briefly on her passing:

FEMALE WARRIOR'S DEATH

The death is announced of the Irish woman soldier, known as Albert Cashier, whose real name was Hodgers, and who was a native of Clogherhead, Co. Louth. She distinguished herself in the American Civil War, and passed as a man up to two years ago, when her sex was discovered in a hospital. Her relatives are being inquired for by John E. Andrews, Superintendent Soldiers' and Sailors' Home, Illinois, USA.

In many ways that simple headline summed up the life of Albert Cashier aka Jennie Hodgers.

Mary 'Mother Jones' Harris

American Labour activist, social reformer and the 'Mother' of the U.S. Trades Union movement.

'Pray for the dead and fight like hell for the living.'
— Mary 'Mother Jones' Harris

THE POOR LAND

In the early part of the nineteenth century, two of the greatest leaders and campaigners on behalf of human rights in the nation's history emerged from rural backwaters in the south west corner of Ireland. One was Daniel O'Connell, The Liberator, who is rightly celebrated with monuments, statues and street names the length of the country. The other is almost unknown in the land of her birth. Her name was Mary Harris or, as she came to be called in the US, her adopted homeland, Mother Jones.

She cut a strange figure. A diminutive, motherly woman with a head of white hair, garbed in dark, workaday clothes standing at the head of an army of thousands of hardened miners, railwaymen and factory workers. But besides her unremarkable clothing, she often wore a steely expression that could cut through the massed ranks of her adversaries like a knife through butter.

When she would address her audience, Mother Jones at times spoke in the hushed tones one might expect from one's grandmother, and would then explode into an impassioned rage, striding about her platform, her voice carrying to the farthest reaches of her assemblage with a power and passion that belied her years. On one occasion when put on trial in West Virginia the District Attorney pointed at the frail old lady across the courtroom and declared, '*Your honour – there is the most dangerous woman in the country today!*'

But who was she and what forces moulded the woman who would become such a commanding and beloved leader of men?

In her autobiography she stated that she was born on 1 May in the year 1830, although she was into her nineties when this was written and her memory was possibly fading. Her birthday also coincided with May Day or International Workers' Day and its likely she 'created' this date for convenience, although that's not to imply there was anything generally untruthful about her character, it was simply a little political theatre to reinforce the notion of her destiny as a labour leader. May Day was also the day of the Haymarket Riot, one of the events that would shape her life, and she may have decided that she was truly born as a workers' champion on that day.

Many of the records from the nineteenth century were destroyed in the Irish Civil War, but surviving parish records would seem to indicate that her parents were married in 1834 in the village of Ballingeary in Cork. If her claimed birthday of 1830 was correct, it would suggest she was born four years out of wedlock, an event unheard of at the time. The more likely year of her arrival was 1837.

Her parents were Richard Harris and Ellen Cotter, both Catholics, he from the townland of Droumcarra and she from nearby Ballingeary. Richard was one of seven children of a tenant farmer and labourer who eked out a living on a mere four acres of land. Likewise Ellen Cotter grew up in a household of four siblings and two cousins; her parents toiled on a slightly more substantial twelve and a half acres. In the year of their marriage Richard was thirty-three and Ellen was just seventeen. It wasn't uncommon at the time for girls as young as fourteen to marry, the theory being that a young wife could bear lots of children to care for their parents in later life. Ellen would bear five children, of whom Mary was the second born.

The period was a time of great social upheaval in Ireland. The early 1830s had seen a 'Tithe War', when desperately poor families were forced to pay excessive tithes to the Church of Ireland, resulting in civil disobedience, refusal to pay and violent reprisals from the military. One of the most famous of these was the 'Massacre of Rathcormac' in Cork, when Archdeacon Ryder accompanied by a large military force attempted to collect his due tithe of forty shillings from the impoverished Widow Ryan. When the locals blockaded the farmhouse, the soldiers opened fire killing seventeen innocent people. Four sacks of corn were then collected in payment of the debt. Incidents such as this lived long in the memory and instilled a sense of injustice and rage that survived through generations.

When she was a child in the early 1840s, Irish tenant farmers were barely able to provide food and clothing for their families, let alone any comforts. High rents imposed by wealthy, often absentee landlords, reduced life for millions to a mere struggle for existence. Bailiffs hired by the landlords regularly carried our evictions with the assistance of the police or military, leaving entire families destitute. This continued even when the potato crop failed from 1845 to 1850, when a million people lost their lives. The terrible disparity between poor and rich and the power the wealthy wielded, using the instruments of the state to enforce their will, cannot have been lost on the young Mary. Many years down the road she would witness the very same misuse of power, but in an entirely different context. One can only imagine the rage that swelled in people's hearts at what they witnessed and the frustration of their powerlessness.

WORKING ON THE RAILROAD

At some point Richard and Ellen moved from their village to the northside of Cork city and it was here that Mary's youngest brother William, who would himself achieve a certain level of fame abroad, was born in 1846. By now the Great Famine was ravaging the country and like millions of his countrymen, Richard was forced to board a ship bound for the US in search of a life for his wife and children. Having spent a year in America he could now officially claim citizenship, at which point, by her own account, he then sent for Mary and the rest of the family.

The town of Munroe in Michigan was their first port of call, but when Richard secured work as a labourer on the massive railway building programme, he was forced to follow the tracks whose destination was Toronto in Canada. It was here Mary's family would settle and where she would receive her education in a public school. She progressed well and, not content to settle into the normal pattern of marriage and children, she decided to progress with her studies in what was called 'Normal School', which was a two year term in college to train as an elementary school teacher.

Her youngest brother William would remain in Toronto all his life, first joining the priesthood and eventually being appointed the Dean of St Catherine's Diocese. He became something of a celebrity in his day for championing the cause of education, not just for children, but for

their parents as well. He preached that for society to progress, immigrants must unshackle themselves from their
European origins and educate themselves to meet the
challenges of a new country and emerging technologies.
He spoke in favour of Home Rule in Ireland as a means of
bestowing civil rights on the people and was vehemently
non-sectarian. A prolific writer and a powerful public
speaker, the causes he espoused mirrored many of those
that would become his sister's passion when she was much
older and he undoubtedly was a powerful influence on her
and in all likelihood sowed some of the first seeds of social
activism in her heart.

Mary Harris believed in the maxim that 'the devil finds
work for idle hands' and she would certainly have her
hands full for the entire ninety-three years of her life.
While studying to be a teacher, she also trained as a dress-
maker and became quite proficient, ensuring her hands
were literally never idle. But it was to teaching she first
turned for a living, accepting a post with an elementary
school back in Munroe, Michigan. After a couple of years
she returned to dressmaking because she *preferred sewing
to bossing children.*

IN THE FAMILY WAY

Mary would always have itchy feet and in 1861 at the age
of twenty-four, she upped and headed south, returning to

teaching in Memphis, Tennessee. In the sultry heat of the southern town, Mary met and married a local man, George Jones and began to gain her first insights into the conditions and paltry rewards ordinary working men faced on a daily basis. George was an iron moulder, which involved pouring molten metal from a furnace into moulds, back-breaking work carried out in a stifling and dangerous environment. He was also a member of the Iron Moulders' Union and through him Mary began to gain her first insights into the methods and aims of America's nascent labour movement.

Although unions had been around in America for almost a century at this stage, they were mostly small groups limited to specific trades like cordwainers or cabinet makers and there was no overall organisation. Fear of retribution by employers also dissuaded many from joining or forming unions. Until an organisational framework was put in place many years later, the power of the unions would be severely limited.

During the next six years the couple had four children together but the joy of raising a family was to be snatched away from Mary Jones in the cruellest way possible. The events of 1867 were to have a profound effect on her for the rest of her life.

It crept upon the city slowly in the autumn of that year, like a mist rolling in from the ocean. One by one, people began to fall ill with muscle pains, shivers, headaches and vomiting. When victims became jaundiced, the cause was immediately clear – Yellow Fever. It wasn't the first time Tennessee had been hit by the plague and it wouldn't be the last, but it was claimed that industrialists deliberately failed to report incidents of the fever for fear that their factories would be closed down. With the poor intermingling in crowded workplaces the disease spread rapidly. Hospitals reported huge influxes of sufferers and the morgues began to fill up.

Mary Jones, young wife and mother of four, lost everything she loved in the world. Her memory of those days, written almost sixty years after the event, still imparts a terrible grief.

'In 1867, a fever epidemic swept Memphis. Its victims were mainly among the poor and the workers. The rich and the well-to-do fled the city. Schools and churches were closed. Across the street from me, ten persons lay dead from the plague. The dead surrounded us. They were buried at night quickly and without ceremony. All about my house I could hear weeping and the cries of delirium. One by one, my four little children sickened and died. I washed their little bodies and got them ready for burial. My husband caught the fever and died. I sat alone through nights of grief. No one came to me. No one could. Other homes were as stricken as was mine. All day long, all night long, I heard the grating of the wheels of the death cart.'

With her family wiped out, Mary applied for a permit from the authorities to nurse the sick in hospital and in their homes. She did this until the fever had burned itself out and the city was declared clean again. But the place no longer retained any hold on her heart, it was just a city full of memories of her dead. She would never marry or bear children again. Instead she would marry a cause and remain faithful to it her entire life.

FROM THE FRYING PAN INTO THE FIRE

The next phase of her life, though dramatic, was not quite so traumatic. She moved north to Chicago in 1868 and there re-entered the dressmaking business with a partner. Having struggled to raise a young family on a meagre wage, living in a run-down part of Memphis, Mary Jones would now be afforded a glimpse into how the other half lived.

Her dressmaking and sewing skills were sought after by the ladies who resided on the affluent Lake Shore Drive. Working in their houses she was shocked by the opulence they enjoyed while outside the window at which she sat sewing, she could see poverty-stricken wretches making their way towards the shore of Lake Michigan in search of work, or ragged women laden with children struggling towards the cooling water to escape the stifling, oppressive air of the tenements. Her employers seemed utterly indifferent to the seething masses of the poor who surrounded them. It was as though anyone outside their circle of wealth was either invisible to them or worthless.

At the end of one of those hot Chicago summers it must

have seemed adversity was stalking Mary. In October 1871, a small fire started in a backstreet in the east of the city, about a mile from where she had her business. Many of the buildings were constructed of wood at the time and were tinder dry after the summer heat. Fanned by an onshore wind the fire spread with terrifying speed, burning homes, public buildings, warehouses and even the ships moored in the river. Ninety thousand people were left homeless, among them Mary Jones, whose livelihood was reduced to ashes. Miraculously, only two hundred people died. Most of the homes burnt were the badly constructed wooden tenements formerly inhabited by the poor. To add to their burden, they now found themselves exposed to the horror of the approaching winter. Mary spent the night on the shore of Lake Michigan and over the coming days struggled to find food and shelter, eventually taking refuge in a church, which would be her home for the foreseeable future.

But the tragedy had stoked its own raging fire inside her. It was during those days when she lived among the huddling poor and shared their hopelessness that she first began to attend meetings organised by the labour movement. She joined the Knights of Labor, a group who originated in the south with the stated aim of abolishing industrial slavery. As the years passed she became more and more active, attending and organising meetings, sometimes in the crumbling, burnt out remains of public halls, sometimes in nearby woodlands so as not to provoke the ire of the powers of government.

She had her first experience of the abuse of that power during America's first ever nationwide strike, that of the railroad workers in 1877. Mary was drafted in to Pittsburg to help in the organisation. To control the massed gatherings, the city began recruiting deputies with little or no attention to their background. Many of them were drifters or men who'd previously been on the other side of the law, hired guns essentially. In the middle of the strike a huge railyard shed was set alight causing the destruction of one

MRS O'LEARY'S COW

One of the most colourful urban legends in American folklore is that of Mrs O'Leary's cow, the creature supposedly having been the culprit who started the Great Chicago Fire. It is almost universally known in the US and has been much referenced in popular culture, including Gary Larson's 'Far Side' and several popular songs. Catherine O'Leary was an Irish immigrant whose cow, Daisy, reputedly kicked over a lantern in her barn starting the inferno that would consume the city. Despite an inquiry that year that determined the cause was unknown, the unfortunate woman endured a lifetime of recriminations and reputedly died heartbroken. Twenty-two years after the tragedy a Chicago Tribune reporter, Michael Ahern, admitted he invented the story as it would make his recounting of the event more colourful. Daisy's fate is unknown.

hundred locomotives. In her autobiography, Mary states that it was common knowledge the fire had been started by the new deputies to help fan the flames of unrest and undermine their cause. There may be some truth in this although it's unlikely the rail company intended to destroy so much of its own property. Whoever was to blame, the city called in the militia and riots ensued, thousand of strikers were beaten and hundreds arrested, charged with arson and inciting riot. Many men went to prison for crimes of which they were innocent. Mary Jones came to realise that they weren't only fighting the wealthy but all the powers of the government. As she put it after Pittsburg:

'Came strikes. Came violence. Came the belief in the hearts and minds of the workers that legislatures but carry out the will of the industrialists'

THE HAYMARKET TRAGEDY

In the 1880s her commitment to the labour movement became her full-time job. Millions of immigrants were flooding into the eastern states of the country and into slums, grossly underpaid work and into degradation. Her home city of Chicago was the scene of countless strikes. Dock workers, lake seamen, railway workers, one after the other they sought salvation though mostly peaceful industrial action and were more often than not answered with violence from the authorities. As Mary Jones wrote:

'The workers asked only for bread and a shortening of the long hours of toil. The agitators gave them visions. The police gave them clubs.'

But a new group emerged among the baying poor. The agitators she refers to were European anarchists who had wormed their way into the consciousness of the desperate. The labour movement began to be tarnished by association with the anarchists, who were using the disenchantment of the poor as a vehicle to further their cause and who were seen as a direct threat to democracy and the government. When the anarchists began to call for an eight-hour day the industrialists bristled and denounced the notion as outrageous.

May 1 was to see the dawn of the eight-hour day and citywide protests and strikes were planned to underline the demand. At the McCormick Harvester Works the strikers gathered outside and when some workers didn't join them, bricks were hurled through windows and the owners informed the police that a riot was underway outside their factory. A large group of police arrived and charged the workers, killing several and wounding many more. This incident threw fuel on the fire of unrest that was smouldering in the city.

A couple of days later a meeting organised by anarchists was in full swing in Haymarket Square, in a desperately poor quarter of the city. The meeting proceeded peacefully until a column of policemen arrived and ordered the crowd to disperse. As they were addressing the workers, an anarchist extremist threw a pipe bomb among the policemen, killing several. Chaos followed the screams of the fleeing crowd. With the police in panic, they began firing randomly into the darkness, killing several more of their own men and an unknown number of workers. A *Chicago Herald* correspondent reported seeing at least fifty dead or wounded strikers.

Over the coming weeks and months, many anarchists were arrested, eight eventually being tried for murder. When seven death sentences were handed down there was outrage among the workers, especially as the man who'd thrown the bomb was never formally identified. Four were ultimately hanged, one committed suicide in prison. The result was that society in Chicago, and far beyond, was now more polarised than ever. To both sides, the incident had been a declaration of war on the other.

THE MOTHER OF ALL WORKERS

As she moved through the 1890s, Mary Jones came more and more to the coalface of industrial strife, leading striking miners, confronting industrialists face to face, being arrested and receiving death threats. She seemed fearless in the face of all of these and wherever she travelled she was instantly recognised by thousands of workers who were coming to idolise her. They gawped as she would stride up to gangs of hired thugs bent on breaking their strike, and their heads, and unleash a stream of invective against them from her tiny five-foot frame. They listened in awe as she mounted platforms and wagons and boulders and began to speak in a voice that surged like a wave and crashed over them with her unflinching war cries. *'Pray for the dead and fight like hell for the living'* she would exhort to tumultuous cheers. Once when asked about her humanitarian work she replied: *'I'm not a humanitarian, I'm a hell-raiser!'*

She liked to say that her address was her shoes; it travelled with her wherever there was a fight against wrong and on many occasions her shoes took her to Virginia to help lead a strike of coalminers. In the course of one of these visits several miners were injured and Mary spent the night helping to tend the wounds of the men. The story goes that one of them was so badly wounded he was barely conscious, mistaking the kindly face that was tending to him for his mother. The name stuck and from that night every place she visited she was addressed as Mother Jones.

Even the press adopted the name and politicians speaking of her actions in Congress (usually in a negative context) would refer to her as Mother Jones. It was a sobriquet she was happy to nurture, aware of the soft spot that even the most hardened men held in their hearts for their mothers. It would help win them to her side and the more new sons and daughters she could adopt, the greater the swell of the tide she hoped would one day wash away the injustice meted out to the poor.

In 1896 she and two socialist colleagues started a newspaper called the *Appeal to Reason*, with the stated aim of educating the working masses. The paper would survive for many years and become for workers one of the primary sources of information about their struggle for better conditions. It helped to spread news of events and reported every minute victory, every inch gained, encouraging other workers to strive to improve their lot.

And their lot was an extremely poor one. Employers specifically targeted newly-arrived immigrants as a group who could be hired for shamefully low wages. Having arrived penniless, most of these men had no choice but to accept the terms. Miners in particular were known to have to work as much as fourteen hours in brutal and dangerous conditions. They were housed in wooden shacks with no sanitation or recourse to any medical help. Thousands of people, children included, died of disease and malnutrition and no laws existed to prevent employers from forcing them to live and work in these appalling circumstances.

In 1899, Mother Jones travelled to Arnot in Pennsylvania to support miners who had been on strike for four months. When she arrived morale was fading, the mood despondent and the collapse of the strike seemed imminent. The company had started using 'blackleg' miners or strikebreakers and was under little pressure to concede anything. Her rallying calls to the men seemed to be falling on deaf ears so she decided on a new tactic, one that she would employ many times again in the future. There was one voice the miners wouldn't dare disobey – their wives. She appealed directly to the women to not only support their men, but to take direct action themselves. The wives responded in droves.

Hundreds of cheering women set off up the mountain trail armed with brooms, mops and buckets of water. On seeing the strike-breakers approach the mine, the women charged and beat the stunned men into a retreat to nurse their bruises. Over the coming weeks they maintained watch over the mine day and night, repeating their attacks if ever the company tried to bring in new workers. At the same time Mary Harris was travelling the surrounding countryside successfully encouraging farmers to stop supplying the mine owners with supplies. The company intimidated the owner of her lodgings into evicting her and when a miner put her up, he and his entire family were thrown out. This only had the effect of antagonising the workers even more. With mining at a virtual standstill, the company finally relented and all demands were conceded. It was a stunning victory and news quickly spread. Working men across the country began to realise that their cause wasn't in vain.

A few small steps had been taken in the fight for justice for the workers, but Mary Jones knew that there was still a very long road ahead. Over the coming years she would lead strikes in West Virginia, Alabama and Georgia, during which she witnessed conditions that amounted to little more than slavery. Children as young as seven were being forced to work in factories for twelve hours a day with little or no food, women employed in mills for a pittance were often mutilated by machinery because safety guards were deemed too costly. She saw entire families working twelve hours in a rope factory for just sixty cents a day. Disease was rife in many of the places she visited. Overwork and malnutrition left so many people so weak they couldn't fight off infection and hundreds of people were dying every day. To the government, it seemed these suffering masses were invisible.

In Alabama a powerful company successfully lobbied to have a law changed that would allow them to employ children under twelve. Mary urged workers to throw the state representatives responsible out of office at the next election. It seemed the workers had no voice in the corridors of power to espouse their cause. But she sought to bring millions of the defenseless together in the hope that their united voice would raise such a clamour that even the politicians, all the way to the White House, could not fail to hear it, and could not ignore it.

WOMEN AND CHILDREN FIRST

In 1902 Mary was arrested on trumped up charges of inciting striking miners to use violence against strike-breakers.

It was during the course of this trial (during which she called the judge a 'scab') that the defense attorney famously pointed at her and described her as *the most dangerous woman in the country*. It was a phrase much reported in newspapers and bolstered her image as an inspirational leader to the workers and a force to be feared by the employers and industrialists.

Seemingly tireless, she began to broaden the spectrum of her cause, which up until now had mainly focused on male workers. She began to organise meetings for groups of women who laboured in sweatshops making clothes or were employed as domestic servants. Though ahead of her time with regard to her campaigning for women's rights, she did still retain the traditional view of her time that women were better served staying in the home and caring for their children while at the same time supporting their husbands in their struggle for a better working life. Yet for those who had opted or were forced to work to scratch together a living, she campaigned vigorously for improved pay and fundamental rights in the workplace.

In the spring of 1903 she visited Kensington, Pennsylvania to support a strike of seventy-five thousand textile mill workers many of whom were women. But she was horrified to also see the vast numbers of children who toiled in the mills. It was estimated at the time that between one fifth and one sixth of all workers in America were children under twelve. The Kensington mills employed at least ten thousand children for pathetic wages and in hazardous environments. In her time there she witnessed children being brought to the union headquarters every day with hands, fingers or arms missing or crushed by machinery. Without exception the children were malnourished and many were suffering from infections.

Gathering a group of these unfortunates, she marched to the city courthouse where a huge crowd had assembled and there she addressed the lawmakers and politicians within. But they chose not to hear or to lay their eyes on the maimed children that she raised above her head. But several reporters did hear and quoted her widely that the mansions of Philadelphia's rich had been built upon the broken bones and hearts of children. The publicity inspired her, but she knew it would have to be more widespread and headline-grabbing to hold the attention of Washington.

The Liberty Bell, which had rang out in the name of freedom in that very city in 1776, was then on a tour of the country and attracting huge crowds. The bell had been adopted by abolitionists as a symbol in their fight against slavery and now it inspired her to a way of making sufficient noise herself to be heard from one end of the country to the other.

She asked the striking parents if she could 'borrow' their children for a couple of weeks to which they all readily agreed. Equipping them with knapsacks containing a knife, fork, cup and plate, she set off from Pennsylvania at the head of almost two hundred children supported by a handful of men and women strikers. It was to become known as Mother Jones' Children's Crusade. She intended to take the problem to the President's front door – literally.

The protest had been sent on its way by a vast mass meeting, thousands of striking workers and ordinary Philadelphians had attended, cheering the crusading marchers as they set off on their ten-day walk to President Theodore Roosevelt's summer home at Coney Island New York. The pattern was repeated all along the way, thousands thronging parks and squares to hear Mother Jones speak in the name of exploited children. In New Trenton, Jersey City and even Princeton University, the crowds massed as did the reporters, the crusade garnering the publicity she most desperately needed. Farmers came out and supplied food for free, the wives of workers gratefully clothed and washed the children, and village halls provided them shelter.

On reaching New York the police chief initially refused them permission to march, so Mary took herself to the Mayor's office where after a few well-chosen words – exposing him to the shame of child exploitation – his conscience got the better of him. They marched along the towering streets of the city and the children stared in awe, most of them never having set eyes beyond their own small town and its textile mills. They carried banners which read 'We want to go to school, not to work!' New

Yorkers gathered in droves on the sidewalks and cheered them on, the day culminating in a rally attended by an estimated twenty thousand people, a vast number at the time.

Then on to Coney Island where the children had a never before dreamed-of day among the amusements, before Mary Jones addressed another mass audience. She deliberately drew a parallel between the treatment of children in workshops and the fight against slavery, her words eagerly scribbled down by the reporters.

'Fifty years ago there was a cry against slavery and men gave up their lives to stop the selling of black children on the block. Today the white child is sold for two dollars a week to the manufacturers. Fifty years ago the black babies were sold C.O.D. Today the white baby is sold on the installment plan ... I shall ask the President in the name of the aching hearts of these little ones that he emancipate them from slavery.'

She describes in her book how she went to see a Senator Platt at his hotel to arrange a visit to the President. When she turned up with two hundred ragged children in tow the senator fled, so she arranged with the hotel manager to give all the children breakfast and charge it to the good senator's room. It was then on to President Roosevelt's house at Oyster Bay, this time taking just a handful of kids. But to her disappointment he refused to see her.

Initially there was gloom, but the Children's Crusade had brought so much publicity to the cause that the issue had been brought to the forefront of public and political consciousness. The following year the National Child

Labor Committee was formed with the aim of promoting *'the rights, awareness, dignity, well-being and education of children and youth as they relate to work and working.'* Congress would grant it a charter a couple of years later. Pennsylvania also bowed to the pressure, passing a law banning children under fourteen from working. And in 1909, the President, who had refused to open his front door to Mother Jones, decided to open the White House to help deal with the issue, instigating the White House Children's Conference, aimed at improving all issues of child welfare throughout the country. This conference would be held every decade for the next seventy years.

The march from Pennsylvania to New York had been just over a hundred miles long. But the campaign for children's rights had travelled a great deal further along the road.

REVOLUTIONARY

As if she hadn't enough on her plate in the United States, Mary Jones now became involved with Mexican revolutionaries, fighting to overthrow the dictator Diaz who had brought industry and modernisation into the country, but largely at the expense of human rights and liberal reforms. He was believed by the revolutionists to be in the pocket of businessmen, most of who were American.

When several of his enemies fled to California to carry

on their fight from afar, they were arrested and jailed on trumped-up charges and one of them, Sarabia, was actually kidnapped and brought back to Mexico, possibly with the connivance of authorities in the US. Mary Jones had heard of their plight and raised $4,000 to help in their defence. She also made representations to the Governor of Arizona to rescue Sarabia, which he duly did. The money raised to hire lawyers for the revolutionaries brought a good return. Having originally received lengthy sentences, the men were released on appeal after a couple of years.

When another Mexican rebel, Sylva, became ill in Leavenworth Prison, she appealed directly to the then President Taft, who agreed to meet her face to face. She pleaded with Taft to pardon Sylva on humanitarian grounds. Taft replied *'Mother Jones, I am very much afraid if I put the pardoning power in your hands, there would not be anyone left in the penitentiaries.'*

In 1911, at the age of seventy-four, she travelled to Mexico after the overthrow of Diaz where she met the new Mexican President, Madera, who brought her to his home and asked her to spend time in Mexico to organise the workers there. She was forced to decline because of her commitments across the border and because she was by now suffering badly with rheumatism. By the time she returned from her travels, she was exhausted.

When summoned as a witness before a Congress committee investigating incidents connected with the Mexican revolution which had taken place on US soil, she

gave a spirited account of the righteousness of her actions
in supporting the Mexican revolutionaries and even cited
events in Ireland:

*'As a patriotic American I never lost interest in the Mexican
revolution. I believe that this country is the cradle of liberty. I
believe that movements to suppress wrongs can be carried out
under the protection of our flag. The Irish Fenians carried on
their fight for Irish liberty here in America. Money was raised here
to send to Parnell, the Irish patriot.'*

THE WILD EAST

The conditions in the mines owned by the Paint Creek
Coal Company in West Virginia were among the worst and
most dangerous in all America. The wages were pitiful
and the miners were then forced to buy food from the
company, pay excessive rent, pay a 'school' tax and a
'burial' tax and also to pay 'protection' money, essentially
to protect them from a small army of company-hired
gunmen. When the miners went on strike these hired
guns drove them away from the mines where they established a tent city, barely surviving the filth, lack of food
and water and lack of fuel as the strike dragged on through
a bitter winter.

At the time Mary Jones had been touring in California,
giving lectures on human rights and campaigning for
changes in the law to protect workers. When she learned

of the situation in West Virginia she immediately cancelled all her engagements and boarded a train east.

In the summer of 1912 at the age of seventy-five, she made her way into the remote mountains of Virginia to the area at the centre of the strike, known as Cabin Creek, a remote, rugged area of rolling hills speckled with boulders and conifers. She was greeted with enthusiasm by the miners and their wives who pleaded for her to lead them. She warned them that there would be yet harder times ahead and that they must not flinch in the face of the enemy no matter how long the battle lasted and with that, made them swear an oath to join the union. Little did she know how dirty the conflict ahead would become.

As the months wore on violence escalated and there were almost daily reports of men and even women being attacked and beaten. The number of widows in the camp was testament to how far the company allowed its hired gunmen to go. They'd even supplied them with Gatling guns, heavy caliber machine guns that could fire three thousand rounds a minute. Mary Jones was enraged and sickened by the company's blatant acts of violence and disregard for the law. She led a march of several thousand miners to Charleston where the governor met them on the steps of government buildings. He conceded to Mary Jones wishes to disarm the gunmen and immediately imposed martial law in the area.

The military confiscated the gunmen's arms, but allowed the company to retain the Gatling guns that were guarding the mine and also allowed them to arrest and court-martial whoever they suspected of organising violence. Among those tried and sent to prison were many of the miners themselves. This further incensed the thousands barely clinging to life in canvas tents as the second winter of their campaign approached. Their only sources of food came from whatever the men and boys could hunt or gather or from the meagre donations from the union.

In early 1913, martial law was revoked and it immediately became clear that the gunmen had been secretly re-arming themselves. Mary Jones was asked by a group of miners to address the families in their camp and despite the danger of travelling in the mountains, she agreed. As they travelled along the mountain track, firing suddenly erupted and the men were forced to dive for cover. Mary Jones climbed off the trap and walked along the road to face the gunmen who had opened fire with a Gatling gun

SINGING HER PRAISE

The well-known, popular folk song, 'She'll be coming round the mountain', sometimes mistakenly believed to be of Irish origin, is in fact based on an old African-American spiritual song, but was re-written, it is widely believed, as a tribute to Mother Jones and her regular crusading visits to support striking miners in the Appalachian mountains.

without provocation. Despite warnings for her to stop, she coolly walked up to the gun and placed her hand over the barrel, calling for the miners to pass. Despite insults and threats, she refused to back down, telling then that if they '*harmed one of the white hairs on her head the creek would turn red with their blood*', as an army of five hundred armed miners were approaching around the mountain. Which they weren't, of course, but the gunmen believed her and backed off.

Unfortunately, she couldn't be there all the time to prevent bloodshed. She set off on a tour of cities to speak at rallies and campaign for the release of the imprisoned miners visiting Cincinnati, Columbus, Cleveland and Washington DC. She was influential enough to secure the release of all but two of the prisoners. But on the night before her return to West Virginia, company gunmen opened fire with a machine gun from a train which passed near to a miner's encampment, riddling the sleeping families inside. One miner and one woman were killed and several more were badly injured. A few days later a company mine guard was killed in a fight and the military were immediately brought back, arresting fifty strike leaders including Mary Jones. She and the others were charged with conspiracy to aid killers. This was punishable by death and given her age and reputation, the case aroused nationwide interest and almost universal condemnation.

Mother Jones was imprisoned despite the fact that transcripts of her speeches clearly demonstrated that she did not advocate violence, but rather respect for the law, force was only to be used as a last resort in the defense of one's family. She wasn't in good health and had been worn down by the lengthy campaigning in bitter conditions. The newspapers from New York to San Francisco fed every word to their readers and the public ate it up, causing an outcry at her treatment. Politicians, fearful of a backlash at the polls, convened a congressional inquiry. The plight of Mother Jones and the other prisoners was debated on the floor of the Senate. At one point during this debate a Senator from Clarksburg called her the '*The grandmother of all agitators in this country!*' When she would later hear of this she replied that she hoped to become the great, great grandmother of all agitators.

She had managed to smuggle a message from her prison cell, which a supporting senator read to the house:

'*From out the military prison walls of Pratt, West Virginia, where I have walked over my eighty-fourth milestone* (she was actually 'only' seventy-seven) *in history, I send you the groans and tears and heartaches of men, women and children as I have heard them in this state. From out of these prison walls, I plead with you for the honour of the nation, to push that investigation, and the children yet unborn will rise and call you blessed.*'

She won the day from her prison cell. A senatorial commission was appointed to investigate working conditions in the Paint Creek Company's mines. Mary was released soon after along with forty-two of the others and within weeks the company had backed down, giving in to almost all of the unions' demands and ridding the area of their hated enforcers. It had taken two years of abject hardship, cost many lives and left many others as cripples or widows or orphans. But it was a huge victory for Mary Jones and the miners and their sacrifice would ultimately benefit all the working men and women in the United States.

ROCKY MOUNTAIN MASSACRE

The lengths to which the mine owners in Cabin Creek had been prepared to go had indeed been shocking. But the events of 1913 to 1914 in the Colorado Mountains would ultimately horrify the entire country. What would become known as the Colorado Coalfield War was the most violent labour dispute in the history of the United States and at the heart of the battle was Mary Jones.

Underneath the rocky earth that covered the foothills of the Rocky Mountains ran a vast web of mineshafts constantly echoing to the sounds of men toiling for twelve hours a day, breathless from the dust as they hacked away with pickaxes at the rich deposits of coal. For many, the subterranean tunnels became their tombs.

On 23 September 1913, the miners decided to strike, making similar demands to those of their colleagues in Cabin Creek: an eight-hour day, better wages, abolition of the armed guard system, union recognition. John Davidson Rockefeller, Jr, member of the famously wealthy family, who were their principal shareholders, simply turned a deaf ear and the company refused point blank to negotiate.

Evicted from their shacks, the miners established several tent colonies; the largest of these was at a place called Ludlow, a name that would reverberate though the history of labour strife in the US.

The company employed the services of the Baldwin-Felts Detective Agency, who had a reputation for violently breaking strikes. Among their armoury was an armoured car mounted with a powerful Colt-Browning machine gun. The miners nicknamed this the 'Death Special'. Besides this, their 'detectives' frequently fired at random into the tent colonies at night, killing or wounding men, women and children, with the full blessing of the company. There seemed no limit to the barbarity of these men. To protect themselves from the sniping, many of the miners dug pits under their tents in which to shield their families from the bullets.

Mary Jones was in Washington when she first heard of the atrocities being carried out against the miners. Reading a newspaper one morning she saw an article declaring that the Governor of Colorado had barred her from entering the strike area. She hadn't actually said she had been planning to go, but this was like a red rag to a bull. Cancelling all her engagements, she immediately boarded a train for Denver from where she planned to travel to Trinidad, a town located at the heart of the dispute.

In Denver she was warned not to progress any further, but despite the presence of hired detectives and militia who constantly followed her, she outwitted them with the help of the likes of hotel porters and train conductors and much to their shock, arrived in Trinidad before they were even aware of it.

Her tiny victory was short-lived. She was arrested at her boarding house by a large company of militia and despite the protests of miners; she was brought to a military prison where she was held in solitary confinement for nine weeks. At one point a thousand women and children gathered outside the prison chanting for her release. The militia baton-charged them injuring hundreds. Legal moves were in hand to release her and the national press was reporting the imprisonment of an old woman. Eventually it was decided that holding her was causing more trouble than it was worth. But such was the fear of her influence, that when she was finally released it was done covertly, under cover of darkness with no announcement. They planned to simply escort her quietly out of the state. She was returned to Denver where she was brought before the governor. She openly told him she was returning immediately, despite his protests.

After a week in Denver, she again stole on board a train for Trinidad, was intercepted at a town called Walsenberg and arrested again. This time her confinement would be much more unpleasant than the relative comfort of the military prison. They put the seventy-seven-year-old woman in a filthy, freezing, damp cellar beneath the court-house. There was no sanitation and little light and she described having to fend off sewer rats with a beer bottle. The authorities were clearly out to teach her a lesson. But she stubbornly refused to submit and remained there for almost a month before lawyers hired by the union secured her release and, crucially, her right to travel anywhere in the state.

But she had other plans. The strike was being under-mined by the use of Mexican workers brought in by the company with promises of enormous wages, housing and medical care. They were transported in droves to the mines, which turned out to be simply dark pits of despair. Their pay and hours were even worse than the actual miners and having signed up they were forced to stay and work under the barrel of a gun. Mary Harris intended to put a stop to this flow of misery. She travelled to El Paso, which was the recruiting ground for the company and at a series of mass meetings she began to educate the Mexi-cans on the realities of working in the mines of Colorado. This she did for several months, seriously impairing the company's efforts to find the new blood it constantly needed, so much of it was spilled daily in the mines.

Mary Jones returned to Colorado and spent the follow-ing months travelling between the various miners' encampments, witnessing the suffering and deprivation of the families and attempting to lift their morale. All around her the battle went on. Some miners were being murdered and then others, having armed themselves for protection, would often retaliate. It was as though guerilla warfare was in progress, yet the strikers were severely out-gunned. The situation was deteriorating daily as the spring of 1914 approached. Mary Harris described her experiences in the tented villages in her autobiography:

'I nursed men back to sanity who were driven to despair. I solicited clothes for the ragged children, for the desperate mothers. I laid out the dead, the martyrs of the strike. I kept the men away from the saloons, whose licenses as well as those of the brothels, were held by the Rockefeller interests.'

On the morning of 20 April 1914, the company-controlled militia moved into positions on the other side of the train track which bordered the miners' tent city at Ludlow. Fearing an attack, the miners mustered what arms they had and took up defensive positions, sending their families into the pits beneath their tents for safety. Without provocation the militia opened fire with machine guns and rifles, shooting indiscriminately into the camp. Women ran screaming, babies clutched to their breasts, as the hail of bullets descended. Terrified children dived for what cover they could find amid the city of canvas. The miners grabbed their rifles and defended themselves as best they could. A lengthy firefight, which would last until dusk, began.

The militia was reinforced by the arrival of non-uniformed company gunmen and it seemed certain that hundreds would perish until a conscientious and courageous train driver brought his train to a halt on the track separating the militia from the camp. Many miners used the opportunity to flee with their families to the cover of nearby hills; many more boarded the train as a means of escape. But not everyone was so lucky. When the train pulled away the firing resumed, the militia using fire-bombs to set the tents ablaze. By nightfall the entire camp was in flames. But the true horror was not revealed until the morning.

In a refuge pit beneath one of the tents were discovered the charred bodies of two women and eleven children, burned to death when the militia had torched the tent above them. At least ten miners were also shot dead that day and hundreds wounded by gunshot or fire. A number of the militia had also perished. It was an atrocity that shocked the nation, receiving coverage in almost every major and minor newspaper from California to New York.

The miners rage at the massacre exploded into direct action. The United Mine Workers of America issued a call to arms which was eagerly answered. As many as a thousand miners armed themselves and began attacking mines, either driving off the guards or killing them and destroying all the surface buildings. Guerilla war ensued for two weeks before President Woodrow Wilson became directly involved in trying to negotiate a peace. He sent in the US cavalry to act as 'peacekeepers' between the opposing forces but all efforts to bring about calm failed, the company owners refusing to budge an inch.

Rockefeller meanwhile launched a huge publicity campaign to whitewash himself and his family of any wrongdoing. He misrepresented the conditions under which the miners worked and lived in a series of articles and leaflets, and in his later testimony before Congress.

With efforts at diplomacy at a stalemate, the President had encouraged the miners' union to redouble their efforts to get the public on their side and with this in mind Mary Jones and her union comrades set off an a nation-wide tour to drum up support. She addressed a whole series of what she described as 'monster meetings'

COURAGE UNDER FIRE

In 2007, the last known suvivor of the Ludlow massacre passed away. She was Mary Benich-McCleary and she was just eighteen months old when the attack happened. Her survival is now a much-recounted family legend. When the train stopped, her parents, like hundreds of others, saw their opportunity to flee. Her father hoisted up her three-year-old brother John and her mother lifted her new-born brother Tom, but in the chaos, neither realised Mary had been left behind. Luckily a courageous teenager heard her cries from a tent, scooped her up and fled to the sanctuary of nearby trees as bullets shrieked about his ears. Here they were found a few days later in some distress, but alive, and Mary would remain so until the grand old age of ninety-four.

(drawing inspiration from her countryman Daniel O'Connell), starting in Kansas and moving through a dizzying number of states including Chicago, New York, Seattle, Columbus, Cleveland and finally Washington. She also travelled to Canada to support a miner's strike there and garner their support for her cause and while there witnessed another tragedy first hand, a mine explosion that killed 119 men. The life of a miner was clearly cheap in any country.

Rockefeller eventually invited her and her colleagues to his office. The meeting was fruitless, Mary Jones describing him as *'a nice young man'*, but with regard to the needs of the miners *'he was as alien as is one species from another; as alien as is stone from wheat.'*

In fact, almost all her efforts were in vain, at least in the short term; the United Mine Workers of America eventually became drained of funds to support the strike. While refusing to recognise the union, Rockefeller put forward an 'Industrial Representation Plan', which included a so-called 'closed-shop union', agreed to provide a representative body for the mine workers and vowed to improve conditions at the mines. The strikers had no alternative. Desperate and defeated they voted to accept the plan and the strike was ended. Estimates at the total number of deaths in the Colorado Coalfield War ranged from sixty-nine to one hundred and ninety-nine.

Over the coming months and years a commission of investigation in Washington heard the testimony of hundreds of witnesses including Rockefeller and of course, Mary Jones. Their final report would lay the foundation for many labour reforms including an eight-hour day and a ban on child labour. If anything good emerged from Ludlow, this was it.

A monument today stands on the site where the tents of hundreds of miners and their families once lived, and died.

BACK TO WORK

Despite the defeat in Colorado, she was not disillusioned, believing that only continuous concerted action by every worker in every field of industry would eventually bring about the reforms she desperately craved. Her vision wasn't limited to the United States; the workers of America were drawn from a hundred different countries, including the country of her birth. This inspired in her a global vision of workers united against exploitation in every corner of the planet. To those who would brand her a communist, she would stress her patriotism and her belief in democracy, but with a strong sense of socialism at its heart.

Hardly had the sun had set in Colorado but Mary Jones was on her way to Chicago where a strike of textile workers had brought almost sixty thousand people on to the streets and where she would make a series of impassioned addresses to cheering crowds. A year later she would wage a campaign on behalf of streetcar workers in Illinois, a strike that would prove successful in securing their demands. In New York a similar struggle of streetcar workers had been in progress leading to riots. Although she arrived after these she was accused of inciting them and was arrested on numerous occasions for speaking in public without a permit. She was always released after a short interval; the publicity of keeping an octogenarian in prison bore no profit for the companies. By 1919 she was working to support striking steelworkers in Pennsylvania and through her efforts and those of her colleagues, over 100,000 men joined the union. Their strike would fail, again through intimidation, but in the future the new-found strength of the union would make change unstoppable.

In the 1920s she returned to Mexico, was greeted and feted by President Obregon and cheered by thousands of workers. She had developed an affection for the poverty-stricken Mexican workers during her visit seven years earlier, but beyond that this was a small step in advancing her cause of unifying workers across all the borders of the world. So enthusiastic was her reception that she would return again the following year and remain for several months.

But when she returned to the US in 1922, old age was finally beginning to catch up with her (she was now eighty-five). She was crippled with rheumatism and was forced to rest for two months, the longest period she'd been inactive her entire life. She had a falling out with the United Mine Workers, believing they were becoming too close to the industrialists they opposed and becoming too closely involved with politics and politicians, who she openly mistrusted. Her health continued to fail and she was hospitalised a number of times, but continued to make public addresses when she had the strength. Her final speech was in Ohio, in 1926, when she was the guest of honour at a Labor Day celebration.

The Autobiography of Mother Jones was published in 1925 and although it contained a number of factual errors, these were usually related to the timelines and precise locations rather than any deliberate attempt to manipulate the truth. Her memory and descriptions of the conditions and events were borne out by the testimony of many others present. And she was entitled to a few lapses of memory – she was, after all, eighty-seven at the time of writing.

Her rheumatism continued to take its toll on her body. She retired to live with Walter and Lillie May Burgess in Maryland where she celebrated her 'hundredth' birthday on 1 May 1930, (although she was in fact ninety-three). Among her birthday presents was the opportunity to make a final, fiery speech to a newsreel camera.

She died on 30 November 1930 and was buried in the Union Miners' Cemetery in Mount Olive, Illinois, along-side miners who died in the Virden Riot in Illinois of 1898.

Today, Mary 'Mother Jones' Harris is an icon of the American labour movement. Almost every American is aware of her name, if not her legacy, principally through a widely read, liberal magazine entitled *Mother Jones*, which you can find on virtually any news stand in the US. Several schools and university residences bear her name and historical markers denote many of the places where she brought her influence to bear.

A few years after her death, workers across America contributed to a fund to erect a monument at her gravesite, which was built by volunteer labourers. Fifty thousand people attended its dedication on 11 October 1936. The text on the monument reads:

When the sun, in all his state,
illumed the eastern skies,
she passed through glory's morning gate,
and walked in paradise.

Sleep the sleep of the noble blest,
for in life you sacrificed and gave.
We pledge to fill your last request,
'Let no traitor breathe o'er my grave.'

She was a woman ahead of her time, a leader who never flinched in the face of the most extreme threat. She was tireless and passionate in her support of the cause of fighting injustice and providing the men and women who built America with their bare hands the most basic of rights, that of the right to human dignity. Mary 'Mother Jones' Harris was a hero to millions in the most powerful country on earth. She said her home was her shoes and she went wherever they took her.

She had taken her very first steps on that journey in a tiny parish in Co. Cork.

ÉIRE 18

James Hoban White House Architect

BAILE ÁTHA CLIATH · 29.IX.1981 · ... D'EISIÚNA

James Hoban

The man who designed and built the White House – twice.

BUILDING A DREAM

It's an unfortunate aspect of the creative arts that in many cases the creator's work can overshadow his name, so much so that while his or her work is almost universally known, the person behind it is largely uncelebrated or even anonymous. Most people around the world have heard of *Gulliver's Travels*, for example, but have no idea Jonathan Swift was his creator. Likewise most people would be familiar with the iconic image of 'The Birth of Venus', but would struggle to name Sandro Botticelli as the artist.

Sadly, such is the case of the supremely-gifted architect of one of the most famous buildings in the world, the White House. It is seen on almost a daily basis by millions of people around the globe, yet mention the architect's name and most of them would shake their heads in ignorance. Even his own countrymen and women for the most part have no notion of his work, life and achievements.

We think of the White House and we think of names like Kennedy, Nixon, Clinton and Obama. None but a few devoted admirers would immediately associate the building with the name of James Hoban, who built a magnificent career for himself in Washington DC despite starting his life in Ireland on very uncertain foundations.

His father, Edward, was an impoverished tenant farmer on the vast estate of the Cuffe family, near the town of Callan in Co. Kilkenny. At the heart of the demesne stood Desart Court, an imposing edifice born of the era of Protestant ascendancy, when the Catholic majority of peasants were stripped of their land and power and the spoils were granted to wealthy English noblemen. This had resulted in a golden age for these landed classes when great estates and mansions sprang up all over Ireland.

For the tenant farmers who worked these estates however, it was less of a golden age and could, in some cases, more resemble a return to the stone age. They often provided their landlords with an income at the expense of any hope of escaping their situation – they more often than not produced barely enough to pay the rent and feed themselves.

Luckily for the farmers of Desart Court, their lord and

master was of a more enlightened disposition. Otway Cuffe, otherwise know as the First Earl of Desart, had been educated at Trinity College and would make some small contribution to the development of Kilkenny, standing as Mayor twice during which time he introduced the city's first street lighting and refuse collection schemes. His tenants were treated with reasonable fairness by the standards of the time and unlike many of his kind, instead of trying to control his charges by chaining them to ignorance, the Cuffe family established a school on the estate specifically for the education of the tenants' children.

It was into this world of great social inequity that James Hoban was born to his mother Martha in a thatched cottage in the shadow of the Desart Court mansion sometime between 1758 and 1762.

Initially the young James received a basic education in the estate school alongside his two brothers and his sister, and when he wasn't studying or helping his father in the fields, he must surely have often gazed up in wonder at the grand stately home, not in envy of the wealth of its inhabitants, but in admiration of its beauty and majesty. The beautiful Palladian design he admired as a boy would be echoed, years later, in his own remarkable architectural designs.

Besides the essentials of reading, writing and mathematics, the young James was also to learn skills that would no doubt prove useful in what it was assumed would be his future as a tenant or tradesman on the estate. And although no specific records exist to verify the nature of his training at Desart, based on his later business in the United States, he most likely learned the trades of carpentry, wheelwright skills and stonemasonry.

Whether in the schoolroom or in the workshop, it was soon noticed that Master Hoban had been endowed with a talent for drawing and design. Given his father's meagre income it's unlikely this talent would ever have been

THE BURNING OF DESART COURT

The magnificent mansion of Desart Court is widely believed to have been designed by another of Ireland's great architects, Edward Lovett Pearce and is said to have been one of the country's most outstanding architectural triumphs. In 1922 its owner was Ellen Cuffe, Countess of Desart, one of the first women to have been elected to Seanad Éireann and a member of the Gaelic League. That year anti-treaty forces issued an order to burn the homes of all Free State senators and in February a group of republicans with torches marched up the avenue to the house and torched the building. A truck carrying paintings and furniture that had been rescued was later stopped and its contents also burned. The house was rebuilt in 1926, but fell into decline over the next two decades and was eventually demolished in 1957 and its foundations grassed over. Today, cows and sheep graze over the empty space where once stood one of Ireland's architectural treasures.

brought to bloom unless James had received the patronage of Otway Cuffe. From his academic connections in Dublin, the Earl of Desart would have been familiar with the relatively newly-formed Dublin Society, which had been founded just a few decades earlier in rooms in Cuffe's old alma mater, Trinity College, to promote *'husbandry, manufactures and other useful arts and sciences'*. This it did by subsidising a number of schools in Ireland dedicated to the education of the country's most promising young students. In 1820 when George IV became the Society's patron, it would become known as 'The Royal Dublin Society', or RDS.

From the hushed, near emptiness of Kilkenny's fields, green with potato stalks and only the occasional bleating of a sheep or the groans of human toil to disturb the calm, James suddenly found himself amid the bustle of late-eighteenth century Dublin, newly emerging and ever-growing as it strove to make its name among the capitals of Europe.

GROWING TALL

If James Hoban had been impressed by his master's stately home, his own new home in Dublin must have overwhelmed him. The then Irish Parliament was housed in the impressive edifice that is now the Bank of Ireland on College Green. It was designed by Edward Lovett Pearce, reputed to have also been the architect on his own master's home, Desart Court, back in Kilkenny. Across the road, Trinity College looked proudly out along an emerging Dame Street, no doubt dreaming of the future luminaries it would send forth. The Wide Streets Commission was busy at work demolishing entire thoroughfares and new buildings were emerging skyward from the rubble. Beautiful Georgian squares like Fitzwilliam and Merrion were rising from land that once was home only to rabbits and birds. And Leinster House, the home of the Duke of Leinster, stood proudly aloof, its sweeping, majestic lawns then empty of the buildings that now house the National Museum and National Gallery. The contrast between Dublin and rural Ireland could not have been starker for the teenage Hoban. A reporter from the era wrote that *'There never was so splendid a metropolis in so poor a country.'*

His new surroundings clearly inspired him to greater things as he excelled at his studies over the coming years, garnering for himself the prestigious Duke of Leinster's medal for *The Drawing of Brackets, Stairs & Roofs* on 23 November 1780. This medal is now part of the Smithsonian Institution's collection.

By now Hoban was a young man, having come through an apprenticeship in the employ of Thomas Ivory, who had also been one of his tutors and was clearly aware of his potential. Ivory, a Corkman, was the headmaster of the Dublin Society from 1759 to 1786 and had originally trained as a carpenter, a trade he also shared with Hoban. A fine architect in his own right, Ivory is best known for designing the Law Society building in Dublin's Blackhall Place.

During his student years Hoban had the good fortune to gain experience working as a draughtsman, designer or possibly even a construction supervisor on a number of Dublin's finer buildings, some of which still stand today – and by which Dubliners casually breeze by daily without a thought to their origins. These include what was then the Newcomen Bank in Lord Edward Street and the then Royal Exchange, now City Hall (which has recently been restored as Hoban would have seen it in the eighteenth century). We know that Hoban was very familiar with the Royal Exchange, which was built during the years he was apprenticing; little did he know it, but he would later personally familiarise the First President of the United States with details of its materials and costs when estimating plans for the White House.

Hoban emigrated to the United States some time in the early 1880s. It is not known for certain when exactly, as most of his personal records were destroyed in a house fire long after his death, but it is a fact that at some point he found himself strolling the streets of another burgeoning city – Philadelphia, birthplace of the American revolution and of American independence. It probably seemed a natural choice for Hoban as at the time it was the second largest city in the world after London and the home to many of America's most influential citizens.

Hoban initially sought employment in the city, advertising his services in the *Pennsylvania Evening Herald* on 25 May 1785, an ad clearly intended to put his undoubted skills to use in the finer homes and establishments of the town – *'Any gentleman who wishes to build in an elegant style, may hear of a person properly calculated for that purpose who can execute the Joining and Carpenter's business in the modern taste. James Hoban.'*

Whether he had any direct contact with the glitterati of US politics at this point is a matter of speculation, but having a keen interest in his Irish compatriots, he would certainly have been well acquainted with the Irish signatories of the Declaration of Independence. And many of the Delegates to Congress also had direct connections to his homeland, particularly Pierce Butler, born in Kilkenny's neighbouring county of Carlow.

Butler had been a commander in the unsuccessful defence of the city of Charleston in his adopted state of South Carolina. The British artillery fire had virtually levelled every building and left the place a smoking ruin. The British would be gone three years later and when Butler returned as a politician, he urged reconciliation with former loyalists and enthusiastically supported Charleston's rebuilding, emotionally and physically.

Whether it was the prospect of plenty of work, the influence of his Irish peers in politics or simply a desire for a sunnier climate, Hoban saw his immediate future in Charleston, where we find his next documented appearance. In addition to his skills as a carpenter or architect, clearly he fancied himself as a bit of a mathematician, as he supplied an answer to a mathematical puzzle, which had been posed in the *Charleston Morning Post and Daily Advertiser*!

A couple of years later he'd definitely established himself, setting up a business and workshop with a business partner by the name of Pierce Purcell, listed as Purcell & Hoban Carpenters. The business thrived with the

THE FOUNDING FATHER
FROM A VILLAGE IN CARLOW

One of the signatories of the US constitution and regarded as a founding father of the US, Pierce Butler originally hailed from Co. Carlow. Born in Ballintemple in 1744 in a wealthy aristocratic family, he first went to the US as an officer in the British army. Having established a huge colonial estate in South Carolina, Butler, despite his wealth, was an outspoken advocate for the rights of the ordinary citizen (this didn't extend to the five hundred slaves he kept). When war broke out between Britain and the colonies, Butler found himself leading the charge against his former comrades and having chosen the winning side, went into politics after the Declaration of Independence, elected as the South Carolina delegate where he was one of the key people who framed the US Constitution. He was elected as a senator several times before his death in 1822 and was the creator of the electoral college system used in the election of American presidents.

constant demand for elegant homes for the southern state's wealthy elite. Within two years the men were advertising to recruit staff to meet their workload, placing a small ad in the *City Gazette & Daily* for *'carpenters who could finish work in an elegant style agreeable to drawings and directions given to them.'*

The abolition of slavery in the US was still over seventy years away and it was common practice for most people of reasonable means to own slaves. This practice even extended to members of the Christian churches and Hoban wasn't averse to keeping slaves himself. His practice was now established enough to train his own apprentices and among these he included his slaves, though there can be no doubt that this would also have increased their value. And he was certainly determined to retain what he clearly viewed as assets, exemplified by the notice he once placed in the press seeking a runaway: *'a slave carpenter named Peter, 5' 7' or 8' well dressed in a brown coat, corduroy britches and a three-cocked hat.'*

Hoban also established an evening school to train young artisans in architectural drawing and among these was Robert Mills who has been described as the first professional architect to have been born in the US and who would later go on to design the Washington Monument.

Although proud of his Irish roots, Hoban was keen to officially embrace his new nation in full. In 1790 an Act decreed that immigrants would be required to wait a year before becoming naturalised. James Hoban became a US citizen virtually the day after the year expired. This may have been through some new-found patriotism, but also Hoban was a shrewd businessman and mixing as he was with the gentry of the fledgling country he must also have been aware that being an American could do his prospects no harm at all.

Hoban would leave his mark on the city of Charleston in the form of many fine homes and public buildings, including the Charleston County Courthouse and the plantation-style William Seabrook House, a magnificent wooden structure that stands to this day.

But he'd also left his mark on the memory of many of his fellow-citizens and could number among his friends and acquaintances many of Charleston's most eminent politicians and businessmen. These included Henry Laurens, a wealthy rice merchant, soldier and political leader who happened to be a close personal friend of George Washington, and when the President visited the city in 1791, James Hoban was granted an introduction.

The government had decided that a newly-constructed showpiece capital was needed (replacing Philadelphia) to properly symbolise the emerging nation and the Irishman was lucky enough to spend some time in the company of George Washington. He clearly made a deep impression, as the President would recall him from memory a year later. No doubt much of their discussion centred, if Hoban had anything to do with it, on the newly-agreed site for the country's capital on the Potomac River and the architectural possibilities it presented.

WASHINGTON DC IS BORN

That same year Washington appointed a French-born architect and civil engineer, Pierre L'Enfant, to design a layout for the capital city under the supervision of three state-appointed commissioners. His plans were truly impressive with a sweeping Mall at either end of which would stand the Presidential House and the Capitol building – pivotal points about which the entire city would revolve. He envisioned a vast, palatial Presidential home that was four times the size of the one ultimately built.

Unfortunately for L'Enfant, his vision extended way beyond the budget and he had repeated yelling matches with the commissioners. Eventually he would be removed from the project and it was decided that the design of the Executive Mansion (as it would be called) and the Capitol building would be decided by separate competitions to be held in 1792. L'Enfant's dream was partially realised, particularly in the eventual building of The Mall and he deservedly received the recognition due for his contribution with a monument on his gravesite in Arlington National Cemetery on a hill overlooking the great capital.

One can imagine the enthusiasm with which James

Hoban set about his task. He must surely have been aware that if his design was chosen, it would most likely stand for centuries as a symbol of his adopted country. It was an architect's dream.

In seeking inspiration Hoban cast his mind back to the buildings he'd seen rising from the muddy fields bordering the River Liffey, to the work of his mentor, Thomas Ivory, that of Edward Lovett Pearse and especially to the designs of Richard Cassels who had created Leinster House, now the home of the Irish Parliament.

Leinster House was designed as a 'country residence' for the Duke of Leinster in 1745 to 1748. This would seem almost laughable to anyone who knows Dublin today, Leinster House virtually sits at the very core of the city, but seen in that light it does bear a striking resemblance to many of the fine rural mansions that speckle the Irish countryside and of course, similarities are immediately apparent with the façade of the White House. By co-incidence James Hoban's chief source of inspiration, Leinster House, would later become the headquarters of the Royal Dublin Society, who had provided the inspiration and education he'd needed to become a major architect.

Leinster House and several other major buildings in Dublin from the era were designed in the Palladian style – derived from the sixteenth-century work of the Italian architect Andrea Palladio. His designs in turn were inspired by the classical temple architecture of the

Ancient Greeks and Romans. To Hoban's mind the classical grandeur of the ancient world seemed to perfectly convey the statement he wanted to make with his Presidential building. Indeed this association with ancient Rome would continue to be a theme that inspired many other public buildings throughout the USA – and would also inspire many of their governmental practices.

Hoban submitted his design some months later as did many other aspiring architects of the day. Among these was Thomas Jefferson who although ultimately unsuccessful, would later console himself by becoming the third President of the US and having the opportunity to reside in the building his rival would design.

'GET ME THE IRISH GUY'

The story goes that when George Washington reviewed the designs of the various architects, he immediately favoured Hoban's. Having met him in Charleston the year before, he had clearly been impressed by Hoban as someone with whom he could work. He did have difficulty recalling his name though and reputedly said something of the nature of *'Get me the guy from Charleston … the Irish guy'*. In a letter written to the commissioners Washington also wrote that the architect *'has been engaged in some of the first buildings in Dublin, appears a master workman, and has a great many hands of his own.'*

The 'Irish guy' duly obliged and with great enthusiasm met with Washington soon after. Though impressed by Hoban's proposal he wasn't entirely satisfied, believing the initial design wasn't large or ornate enough. Hoban didn't believe this in any way compromised his creation or at least if he did, he never expressed it, and at the President's behest redesigned the building thirty per cent larger and with an impressive reception room, which today is known as the East Room.

The cornerstone of the building was laid without ceremony on 13 October 1792 by George Washington. A brass plate under the stone bears James Hoban's name, where it rests to this day. Over the next eight years would rise a building of pale sandstone, of two stories, with a hundred rooms within. (The original plan had envisioned three stories, but the local quarry ran out of stone.)

Initially the commissioners granted the task of carrying out the work had tried to recruit labourers newly arrived from Europe, but the numbers fell far short of their needs. So ultimately much of the labour was carried out by a mixture of enslaved and free African-Americans. In fact the state of Washington now exists on land ceded by the states of Virginia and Maryland, both of which were so-called 'slave states'. (The US at the time was divided into either 'free states' where slavery was banned or 'slave slates' where slavery was legal.)

Most of the skilled work, that of the stonemasons, carpenters and so on, was carried out by a limited number of immigrant artisans. Hoban singled out Scottish workers to build the walls as they were familiar with working with sandstone, a very common building material in their homeland, as anyone who has ever been to Glasgow or Edinburgh can attest. The brickwork, carpentry and plasterwork were performed by Irish and Italian men.

As the work progressed the paid workmen and slaves alike came to view Hoban as a strict but fair taskmaster. He garnered a reputation as a leader of men and in time would earn the sobriquet of 'Captain Hoban' due to the military-style authority he enforced, the discipline he employed and the loyalty he commanded. In particular he enjoyed the respect and trust of the Irish workers, for whom he naturally held an affinity and when the building would ultimately be completed he continued in his efforts to help newly-arrived Irishmen and their families.

James Hoban was, if nothing else, a practical man, epitomised by the fact that he approved the building of a temporary church on-site while at the same time also allowed, encouraged even, the opening of a brothel just a stone's throw away. He was actually the landlord of this establishment and employed an Irish Madam called Betsy Donoghue to run the place. This apparently didn't conflict with his own deeply-held religious views. He simply recognised that many of the men were here alone in a strange land, far from their wives and families. At the time men outnumbered women in the area by about six to one and many of them would have to endure an enforced celibacy for years at a time. If satisfying some of their more basic needs contributed to a more efficient worksite, he was only too happy to oblige.

At one point, short of skilled artisans, Hoban ran the following advertisement:

$2.00 per day will be given for good carpenters and joiners, at the President's House and in proportion for those less skilful, to be paid daily or weekly, as may be required.

A man working six days a week could earn twelve dollars, considered generous in those times. By standards back home this was a small fortune. A good proportion of this was sent home to families in Ireland, Scotland or Italy and unbeknown to their God-fearing folks back home, another large proportion was spent in the company of Betsy Donoghue's girls or in the temporary drinking houses that dotted the area. Conscious also of the fact that the workers regularly drowned their sorrows in alcohol, he often distributed rum or whiskey on the basis of how high a man was prepared to work on the walls. No doubt the after-effects of such inducements contributed to a few of them breaking their necks over the years.

Tough he may have been – he needed to be, as he was charged with bringing order to a building site populated by hundreds of mostly illiterate, often intoxicated men speaking a multitude of languages – but James Hoban was generally viewed, particularly by his peers, as a quiet and modest man. This is evident in a newspaper article written by a Charleston reporter in 1792, in which he relates

James Hoban's success with no little pride. *'On this occasion we think it but justice to observe that Mr Hoban as a man of ability is unassuming and diffident. When a mere boy he received a mark of distinction from the Royal Society of Dublin which none else could then achieve. When the President of the US honoured this city with a visit last year, Mr Hoban was introduced to him as a man of merit and of genius under the patronage of General Moultrie and Mr Butler and we may safely add that it is no small matter of universal satisfaction to the citizens of Carolina that their fellow citizen Hoban has succeeded in this enterprise.'*

MORE THAN ONE STRING TO HIS BOW

With the construction of the Presidential House ongoing, James Hoban also dedicated himself to a number of other enterprises which he regarded as his civic duty towards the development of a city still in its infancy. In 1793 he established a Masonic lodge – Federal Lodge No. 1 – which is still in existence today. Freemasonry was multi-denominational, in religious terms demanding only a declaration of belief in a Supreme Being. This again seemed to rail against his strict Catholic beliefs, Freemasonry having been condemned for centuries by the Catholic Church for *'teaching a naturalistic, deistic religion in conflict with church doctrine'*. Clearly though Hoban was a man who greatly respected the religious views of others. In the new

America he'd rubbed shoulders with so many creeds, it's likely to have seemed the perfectly natural thing to do. Being a Freemason would also, of course, keep him in touch with all aspects of public and business life in the new city.

While he was busy establishing the Federal Lodge, he was also nurturing the growth of Catholicism in Washington, designing the city's first Catholic Church, unsurprisingly called St Patrick's, and persuading a priest he is likely to have known and conversed with in Dublin, Father Patrick Caffrey, to migrate to America and tend a somewhat wayward flock of mostly Irish immigrants.

It is interesting that in 1794 Bishop Carroll, who was the first archbishop in the United States, serving the Archdiocese of Baltimore, and also the founder of Georgetown University, issued a letter in relation to Papal probationary edicts on Freemasonry, stating that they would not be enforced in his diocese. It is undoubtedly the case that he knew Hoban and his work for the Catholic Church and it is possible that the Irishman had some influence on this particularly liberal decision. Whatever the case, a number of prominent Irish Catholics and Scottish Presbyterians founded Washington's first Masonic Lodge and Hoban was appointed their First Worshipful Master. Future members would include President Washington himself, future Presidents Theodore Roosevelt and Andrew Jackson, Director of the FBI, J. Edgar Hoover, William P. Ross, the Chief of the Cherokee Nation and many other influential politicians and public figures.

By 1799, with the exterior of the Presidential House nearing completion, Hoban was firmly established as a leading figure in the capital. He was aged about forty and it was only then that his busy schedule allowed him the opportunity to cast his eye over the eligible ladies about the city. His gaze came to rest on a lady by the name of Susanna Sewell, a Catholic girl from a wealthy family in Maryland. He was relatively old to be considering marriage as the average life expectancy of anyone surviving childhood around then was about fifty. Yet the match was agreeable to her father, revolutionary war hero and property developer, Clement Sewell, and the couple were married on 13 January of that year.

Their life by all accounts was a happy one and if James had found difficulty finding time for romance up to now, he certainly made up for it over the coming years as Susanna provided him with no less than ten children. It is not certain how old Susanna was but its safe to assume she was a great deal younger than her husband, given her undoubted fruitfulness. Among their offspring their sons Edward and Francis became successful US Navy Officers, Henry became a Jesuit Priest and James Hoban Junior became an accomplished lawyer and renowned orator who regularly gave impassioned speeches supporting Irish independence from Britain. James Junior was also apparently the spitting image of his father. Their family was not without tragedy unfortunately, and within a space of one year, 1822 to 1823, James Hoban lost his wife and his teenage daughters Helen and Catherine all to a common killer in those times, tuberculosis, or TB.

Susanna was a formidable character herself and just before their marriage James discovered that he wasn't the only one with an interest in architecture. He had been provided with a relatively modest house by the City Commissioners, but Susanna decided immediately that it *'was not suitable for entertaining'*. She demanded that her husband insist the commissioners provide funds to extend, in particular to provide a much more substantial kitchen. His request was greeted with frowns by the tight-fisted group, but clearly more afraid of his wife-to-be than his employers, he made his case with such vigour that they reluctantly agreed. Over the coming years Susanna would have her wish to be the proud hostess to many of Washington's dignitaries.

POLITICIAN, MILITIAMAN, BUSINESSMAN, CIVIC LEADER

By 1802 the work on the Executive Mansion was almost complete, but James Hoban's work on laying the foundations of a living, breathing city Washington was only beginning. By now he was not only one of the state's leading architects, but also a Captain of the Militia Company which was the forerunner of the police department, a

AMERICA'S FUTURE
PLANNED IN A PUB!

In 1799, Rhodes Tavern was officially opened and the hostelry (a block from the White House site) quickly became the city's unofficial town hall. Presidents, senators, business leaders, newspapermen and of course James Hoban, frequently met there to discuss and plan the development of the burgeoning city and the new-born country. Press reports of meetings regarding the civic and political development of Washington and beyond frequently feature Hoban's name as the meeting's chair. The pub was the polling centre for the city council elections, the boarding house for congressmen, it was where citizens successfully lobbied Congress for representation and the building would witness every presidential inauguration for almost two hundred years. Sadly, despite efforts to preserve the building, in 1984 a developer brought in bulldozers in the middle of the night and razed it to the ground. A historical marker is all that remains to remind citizens of the spot where much of their country's future was planned. The names of Presidents Roosevelt, Taft, Wilson and Jefferson appear on the plaque, after that of James Hoban.

census taker, an elected member of the local Washington City Council, which had been granted the right by Congress that year to have some say in their own affairs. And he was also a prosperous property developer. Although extremely negative connotations immediately spring to mind nowadays when one hears that term, it seems Hoban was quite the opposite of the image of the greed-driven, champagne-sipping types that are so familiar now. Instead he donated a great deal of his own time and money pursuing causes that would advance the development of the community as a whole.

Keenly aware of how his own father's employer had granted him the opportunity to further himself with an education, he decided others should have the same chance. When Hoban had first arrived, the area was little more than a few muddy tracks and worksites populated almost exclusively by male labourers and the only women to be found came at a price. By now families had begun to descend on the area in their thousands, eagerly migrating to the potential employment the building of a new city brings. James Hoban saw their children running untamed and ignorant with their only future prospect being one of hauling bricks or digging the earth from dawn to dusk. So he initiated a private fund to recruit school teachers and build schools in the area, putting a great deal of his own money into the venture as well as persuading other wealthy individuals to contribute.

Many of the newly-arrived families he saw were fellow

Irish men and women struggling to find their feet on their new land or, for those with no skills, struggling for their very survival. James Hoban often used his position as a councilman to promote causes for their betterment and also founded an organisation called the Sons of Erin, whose primary mission was to help the needy Irish find housing, work, medical help and to encourage them to become naturalised citizens. This brought benefits for the newly-arrived Irish, but it has to be said, it also wouldn't have harmed James Hoban's chances of getting re-elected when these new citizens got the vote. He was nothing if not a practical man.

While George Washington *et al* may have been the founding fathers of the United States, James Hoban can truly be counted among the founding fathers of the city of Washington. As a politician he repeatedly pushed for infrastructural development and was frequently turned down due to lack of funds. He persisted nonetheless, aware as he was that infrastructure was the key to the making the city truly habitable for its citizens and to bringing it economic success. He was among the influences that ultimately saw the city begin to stretch its arms in every direction, reaching out to embrace the nearby city of Georgetown and bridging the chilly waters of the Potomac. As the city grew Hoban grew with it and he was appointed the Superintendent of all of Washington's public works in 1798. Besides the Executive Mansion, his hand in one way or the other helped to shape some of

Washington's iconic buildings. He was one of the main supervising architects on the US Capitol Building, oversaw the construction of the original Treasury Department Building and he designed the famous Blodgett's Hotel, a regular meeting place of the US's founding fathers, but sadly no longer in existence.

But he was also a businessman and working on public projects was relatively poorly paid. He continued in his private practice, the main thrust of which was building homes for the burgeoning middle classes and he was the architect behind many of the fine single and two-storied houses of the day. His most famous private residence was that of President James Munroe. Accounts vary as to whether this was designed by Hoban or Thomas Jefferson, but Hoban clearly had a hand in it – the design echoes the Palladian style he had favoured for the Executive Mansion.

THE PRESIDENT MOVES IN

Sadly, the man who had instigated the building of the Presidential Residence, George Washington, never had the opportunity to reside in it, as he died in 1799, just one year before the exterior was completed. When originally conceived, the Executive Mansion was to be of sandstone, which clearly is not white in colour. The original white appearance arose because the stone had to be coated with lime-based whitewash during construction to protect the porous stone from damage caused by freezing, although it would be a long time before the name 'White House' would catch on.

The first President to live there was John Adams, second President of the United States, who moved in on 1 November 1800, when the government was officially relocated from Philadelphia to Washington. Although the building appeared complete from the outside, most of the interior consisted of undecorated rooms which would echo to the sound of hammers and carpenters for a further two years. Soon after he wrote to his wife Abigail:

'I Pray Heaven Bestow the Best of Blessings on This House and All that shall hereafter inhabit it. May none but Honest and Wise Men ever rule under this Roof.'

Abigail herself arrived a couple of weeks later and was horrified at the conditions under which she was expected to live. Her observations were less philosophical than her husband's:

'There is not a single apartment finished. We have not the least fence, yard, or other convenience outside. I use the great unfinished audience room as a drying room for hanging up the clothes.'

It is amusing to think that the room Abigail refers to, now the East Room, and today the location of entertainments for foreign dignitaries and for press conferences, was once filled with clothes lines of sodden petticoats, bloomers and pantaloons.

Despite poor Abigail's lack of conveniences, they remained in the residence until John Adams completed his term, by which time the finishing touches had long since been put to the interior. With the exception of George Washington, it would be home to every US President in American history.

THE DESTRUCTION OF
THE WHITE HOUSE

In 1812 a war began between the US and Britain which would last for three years. The causes were many, among them British trade restrictions and their support of native Indians as well as the press ganging of Americans to fight in the British navy. When it was over, both sides ended up with pretty much what they'd started with, with the exception of course of the twenty-five thousand men who had died in action or through disease as a direct result of the war.

One of the other casualties was the White House itself. The British entered Washington on 24 August 1814 and with US forces occupied elsewhere, found the city essentially defenseless, President James Madison having been forced to flee at the last moment. The British reputedly seized the Executive Mansion where they helped themselves to a dinner that had been just prepared for the President. Their bellies full they torched the place, a fire that would destroy everything except the exterior walls. They then set off down the Mall and did the same thing to the Capitol. In an hour, the ten years of work of James Hoban and thousands of others had been reduced to a smouldering shell.

President Madison was adamant that the Mansion be reconstructed exactly as it had been and Congress quickly appointed James Hoban to rebuild the structure. And that is what he literally had to do. The intense heat of the fire had been suddenly doused by a storm, the rapid cooling causing much of the stonework to crack. As a result the exterior walls had to be disassembled stone by stone. All that remained of the original building was the basement, although sections of the beautifully carved ornamentation did survive and would be re-used.

With the building razed to the ground, congressmen and commissioners began to wonder if the public purse was deep enough to accommodate such a mammoth rebuilding project. Hearing the rumours, Hoban, determined to see his iconic structure rise again and being ever-practical, quickly amassed as much of the materials he could find to commence the work and had them piled in mountainous stacks around the site. He hired skilled masons to carve the new stone and set carpenters to cutting beams by the hundred. With so much of the money already now committed because of Hoban's efforts, the opposition faded. Yet he was still fearful that the new incoming President might have other plans, so when the construction work did actually start he hired over thirty stonemasons (a huge number for one project) and had everyone work extra long shifts.

The upshot of this extraordinary effort was that the rebuilding was complete inside three years, an amazing feat considering the original work had taken a decade, and President James Munroe moved in with his family in 1817. However, to achieve this deadline, Hoban this time had used timber supports instead of brick on some interior walls. They bore up well – for one hundred and thirty years – but eventually would have to be reconstructed during the reign of Harry Truman. Some scarring still remained on the new building as some of the stone and decorative ornamentation was re-used, and to conceal this the entire building was painted with white lead paint instead of the original whitewash. Many people believe that this is where the name 'White House' originates, however the lighter whitewash of the original building had already given rise to the nickname. In 1812 a Congressman Bigelow wrote to a friend 'There is much trouble at the White House, as we call it, I mean the President's'. But the term didn't actually become official until 1901 when President Theodore Roosevelt had the term *White House – Washington* added to the stationery.

THE FINISHING TOUCHES

By the time he had finished building the White House for the second time, James Hoban was nearing his sixties. Yet his enthusiasm for work and the various causes in which he'd become embroiled did not dim in the slightest. He continued to speak at Council for the many thousands of Irish families who constituted a huge proportion of the population of Washington DC (one writer at the time claimed the Irish made up half the city's numbers, but this is most likely an exaggeration), and he continued to embrace his first love, designing private and public buildings throughout the city.

Despite his apparent humanitarianism which had included organising schools, housing, employment and medical care for the poor, he seems to have had a contradictory attitude towards slavery. As his family expanded to huge proportions, the number of slaves he owned grew almost in proportion; at one point he was master to nine. After his wife and two daughters died and other members of his family flew the nest, he reduced the number to just two. Then in 1828 he did a curious thing – he signed a petition calling for the abolition of slavery in the District of Colombia, yet failed to free his own remaining slaves. His only concession to them was that he stipulated in his will that when he died they be sold to someone within the city, this to prevent them being returned to the much harsher conditions of the plantations.

Just a few short years later, that will would be put into effect when James Hoban died peacefully on 8 December 1831. It probably would have pleased him, a devout Catholic, to pass away on an important Catholic holy day, The Feast of the Immaculate Conception.

In his will, he left the not inconsiderable sum of $60,000, the equivalent today of roughly $1,500,000.

Initially he was buried on the old graveyard of the church he'd designed, St Patrick's; he was reinterred at a family plot in 1863 at the Mount Olivet Cemetery in Washington DC.

REMEMBERING JAMES HOBAN

In 1880 a fire in Hoban's family home destroyed all his personal and business papers so our knowledge of him comes from the remembrances of others, from a few letters, official records and newspaper articles and advertisements. In fact, beyond his own lifetime, nobody even knew what he'd looked like until 1959 when his great-great-grandson produced a wax-bust portrait, made from life around 1789. This and an etching of his son, who reputedly bore a striking resemblance, provide us with at least a glimpse of the face of James Hoban.

In honour of his lifetime of work for the city of Washington, there have been a number of tributes and monuments in his name, among them a street in the Georgetown area named in 1931, a World War II ten thousand-ton troop ship called the *James Hoban* and in 1981 the United States and Ireland jointly issued stamps to mark the one hundred and fiftieth anniversary of his death. In 1992, to commemorate the two hundredth anniversary of the beginning of construction of the White House, the US Mint issued a silver dollar, which featured an image of Hoban on the reverse side.

In August 2008 a group of American architectural students from the Catholic University in Washington DC spent a number of weeks at Desart in Kilkenny, working with local craftsmen and stonemasons constructing a memorial they had designed to honour James Hoban. A large structure of stone and glass, the memorial contains a simple stone wall, which gradually changes to one that is highly refined – essentially a metaphor for Hoban's life from that of a poor uneducated child to one of the founding fathers of America's capital and creator of one of the world's most famous buildings.

But the greatest memorial to James Hoban can be seen on our television sets or in our newspapers anywhere in the world on any day of the week. It is the White House itself, which will always stand as an elegant monument to one of Ireland's most unsung, yet greatest, architects.

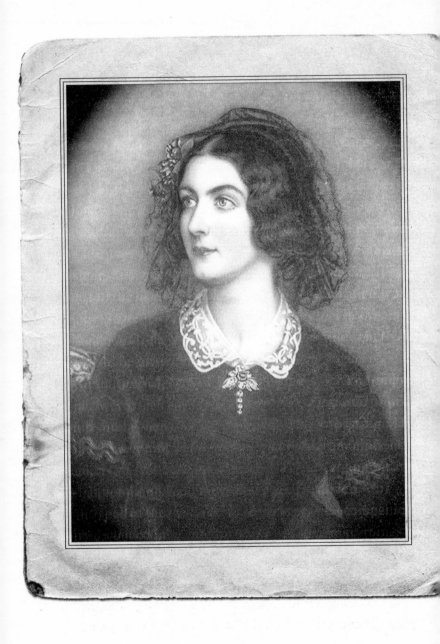

Lola Montez

*Courtesan, Countess of Landsfeld, scandal of the Victorian age,
dancer, writer & lecturer*

THE APPLE DOESN'T FALL FAR FROM THE TREE.

I n the northern Sierra Nevada in California there is a hiking trail called the 'Lola Montez Trail'. Walking it you will experience some steep inclines and declines, sometimes it is easy underfoot and other times it can be rocky and quite treacherous. In winter, temperatures can drop to a biting minus 10 degrees Celsius and as high as 30 degrees in the summer. But whatever the time of year, one always enjoys a sense of natural beauty – and of wildness. It is not a particularly long hike, a few miles, so sadly the experience is short lived.

It's actually hard to imagine a more appropriate metaphor for the life of Lola Montez. No statue or painting could more accurately capture her life. Glorious highs and ignominious lows, fiery hot temperament and icy cold moods. Famed for her beauty and at times utterly wild. And tragically short-lived.

Her life was always the subject of gossip – much of it malicious – and her own tendency to exaggerate or, in many cases, tell blatant lies in order to aggrandise herself didn't help. The one thing we can say with certainty about Lola is that almost nothing is certain.

Eliza Gilbert was born on a winter's day in the tiny village of Grange in Co. Sligo in 1821 under the shadow of the great, flat-topped expanse of Ben Bulben. At the time of her birth Queen Victoria was just two years old and the female infants could not have had a more marked divergence in their attitudes to society and how women in particular were expected to behave. In fact Eliza would later in life describe herself as having been born of a *somewhat combustible compound*.

Her mother was Elizabeth Oliver, who was the illegitimate daughter of the MP for Cork and Limerick, Charles Silver Oliver, a wealthy British landlord who owned an estate of twenty-thousand acres and had once famously had a United Irishman, 'Stalker' Willis, hung, drawn and quartered and then had his head placed on a spike outside the local market hall. Not that Elizabeth's mother moved in the social circles of wealthy English landlords, more likely she was seduced by his position of power, his wealth and ultimately by Oliver himself.

Elizabeth was trained as a milliner, one of the few professions open to a girl at a time when girls were simply expected to wed and mind the home. And when Edward Gilbert, a low-ranking British Army officer walked into her life when she was just fifteen, she married him at the drop of a hat, so to speak.

One year later, along came Eliza, born into a poor home to an immature mother and a father with few prospects, in a remote and damp corner of Ireland. It was hard to imagine how such a tiny flower could survive, let alone thrive.

PASSAGE TO INDIA

Early in 1823 Ensign Edward Gilbert was recalled to base in England and it was here, on 16 February, that his daughter was baptised Eliza Rosanna Gilbert, in St Peter's Church in Liverpool. Gilbert was a member of the 25th Regiment Light Dragoons who, over the previous twenty years had served for the most part in India, so it was inevitable that at some point he and his young family would make the long journey east and to new horizons. Unfortunately the sun set prematurely on Eliza's hapless father as he'd barely set foot in India when he contacted cholera and died leaving his now nineteen-year-old bride alone with a baby daughter in a strange land.

Elizabeth's period of grieving was as short as her supply of money and displaying a practical trait she would bequeath to her daughter, she married another officer, this time moving up a notch to a Lieutenant Patrick Craigie. Elizabeth was still in her teens and already on husband number two, Eliza at the age of four, must surely have been taking notes.

Patrick Craigie took a liking to the child and doted on her somewhat, but she seemed spoiled and given to severe tantrums, more ferocious than would normally be expected from a child of her age. It was decided that she would never receive the discipline she required while living in India. She needed the self-command and cultivation that they believed only an education in Britain could bring.

Eliza turned six during the voyage to Britain and her initial port of call was Lieutenant Craigie's father who lived in Montrose in Scotland. Undoubtedly Eliza's dark complexion, acquired under the burning Indian sun, set her apart among the pale locals of northern Britain, but what really distinguished her was her temperament. She was described as a *'queer, wayward little Indian girl'* who was frequently in trouble, on one occasion shocking the townsfolk by running through the streets naked. The attention this act earned her was clearly savoured by the rebellious girl.

She lasted about five years in Scotland until, undoubtedly to the relief of Mr Craigie Snr, his daughter Catherine Rae opened a boarding school in Monkwearmouth, on the river Wear in north-east England. Quickly packing Eliza's bags she was dispatched south to the care of Mrs Rae and her husband. She would only last a year here, but she did leave an impression, both good and bad, on the staff. Almost two decades later her art teacher, a Mr Grant, in response to a query about the famed 'Lola Montez', would recall the young Eliza in some detail in a letter to the *Sunderland Herald*. His description of her was uncannily reflective of the reports of Eliza in adulthood. He would write:

'(She was) symmetrically formed, with a flowing graceful carriage, the charm of which was only lessened by an air of confident self-complacency – I might almost say of haughty ease – in full accordance with the habitual expression of her else beautiful countenance, namely, that of indomitable self-will – a quality which I believe had manifested itself from early infancy. Her features were regular, but capable of great and rapid changes of expression. Her complexion was orientally-dark, but transparently clear; her eyes were of deep blue, and, as I distinctly remember, of excessive beauty, although bright with less indication of the gentle and tender affections of her sex than of more stormy and passionate excitements.'

It wasn't all good news however. He added:

'It was impossible to look at her for many minutes without feeling convinced that she was made up of very wayward and troublesome elements. The violence and obstinacy, indeed, of her temper gave too frequent cause of painful anxiety to her good, kind aunt.'

Once having punished her with *'solitary durance'* the

rebellious Eliza was released only to storm out like *'a little tigress just escaped from one den to another!'* This behaviour would, at the time, have been severely frowned upon had it been perpetrated by a boy. For a girl, it was simply inexcusable.

And escape was indeed part of Eliza's plan in the not too distant future. Having been sent further south to complete her education in Bath, the sixteen-year-old learned of her mother's plans to marry her off to a wealthy sixty-four-year-old judge, Sir Abraham Lumley. Eliza herself judged the notion repulsive and turned for comfort to a friend of her mother's, Lieutenant Thomas James, who rapidly fell under her spell. They eloped back to Ireland and were married in Co. Meath on 23 July 1837. Her mother immediately washed her hands of her wayward daughter.

But Eliza soon discovered that her hasty marriage was no honeymoon. She later wrote that her days in rural Ireland consisted of hunting, eating, more hunting and more eating. *'I wished for nothing more intensely than to be abducted once more, but this time not by a potential husband but by anything or anyone who would rescue me from this deadly monotony.'*

It was hardly the glamorous life she imagined for herself and to placate her, James' solution was to transport her from the damp fields of Co. Meath back to the dusty soil of Bareilly, about 150 miles from Calcutta, in India. But as Eliza would observe, *'runaway marriages, like runaway horses, are almost always sure to end in a smash-up'.*

Discordant accounts describe how Lieutenant James was either violent to her, unfaithful or simply boring. One account has Eliza suspicious of her husband's desire to take so many early morning rides. Following him, she finds her husband in the arms of a Mrs Lomer. Fuming, she returned home in a rage and banished him from the house. The scandal, if such a scene ever took place, reputedly shook the regiment and was the tittle-tattle that danced across the tongues of the British community for months after. Many of the ladies would not have been too reserved in spreading or indeed embellishing accounts of Eliza's spell in India, as she was described by an observer as looking *'like a star among the others who were all plain'.*

Her mother was outraged, somewhat hypocritically believing that her daughter's behaviour in leaving her husband had brought great shame on her family, conveniently forgetting that she'd been no shining angel herself in her youth. Her mother wanted her to leave India immediately and for once, she and Eliza found a point of agreement.

But scandal followed Eliza like a loyal dog. Still only nineteen, her first marriage had ended in miserable failure but, like her mother before her, Eliza wouldn't be long replacing the man in her life. Thomas James accompanied her half-way down the Ganges and left her in the care of Capt and Mrs Larkins and a couple of American friends, Mr and Mrs Sturgis. No sooner had he disembarked, than

Eliza would embark on an affair that would further outrage society.

The ship docked at Madras and up the gangplank strode a dashing army officer called Lieutenant Lennox. Both Eliza and her mother seemed to be particularly drawn towards men in uniform; as the voyage progressed, Eliza was shameless in displaying her affections towards Lennox and he apparently was equally shameless in receiving them. Her guardians were shocked at her behaviour and eventually disowned her, leaving her and Lennox to enjoy the life of sin on the ocean wave, all the way back to Portsmouth. And beyond.

DIVORCE & TONGUE-WAGGING

It is truly amazing how quickly salacious gossip spreads. And the bawdier the story the more quickly it travels, whirling at breakneck speeds to the eager ears of people on the other side of the world. And this is in the days before mass communication. Eliza and her lover barely had their feet on dry land when her husband James, back in far flung India was yelling 'divorce'.

The details of the whole affair were subsequently laid bare for an avid public, deprived of any regular form of titillation in the highly conservative society of the time. The *London Morning Herald* of 18 December 1842 keenly reproduced extracts from the testimony presented in the divorce court, evidence that must have had many a Victorian eye popping from its socket.

Initially the evidence consisted of other passengers on the ship from India having observed a strong intimacy between Eliza and Lieutenant Lennox, which consisted of sharing the same table at dinner and walking the deck together. For a society that was, outwardly at least, sexually repressive in the extreme, such behaviour was considered grossly improper. But things were to get much, much worse. It seems Eliza and friend managed to arrange adjoining cabins and it was noticed that they occasionally entered the wrong door. It was alleged that *'great and indecent familiarities passed and in many instances were seen to pass between them.'* A cabin maid testified that she had personally witnessed Lennox lacing up Eliza's stays and also claiming Lennox was present when Eliza was pulling up her stockings. When confronted about her behaviour by her chaperones, Eliza gave them plenty of lip about their illiberal attitudes and informed them she was her own mistress.

Undoubtedly she was; she was also clearly Lieutenant Lennox's, as the testimony revealed further scandalous evidence about their relationship. As soon as they landed, the pair had the audacity to share a room in a lodging house in Portsmouth, called of all things, The Star and Garter. From thence to the Imperial Hotel in Covent Garden where they *'retired on the night of said twenty-first of February to the said Bedroom in the same and there lay naked and alone in one and the same bed there being but one bed in the said Bed Room and there had the Carnal use and knowledge of each others Bodies and committed Adultery together.'*

This was jaw-dropping stuff and despite Eliza's counter-claims that her husband had already committed adultery with Mrs Lomer in India, the judge dismissed this as pure invention on Eliza's part (which it possibly was) and granted the divorce, remarking that Eliza had been *'guilty of behaviour at which a crocodile would tremble and blush'*. Under the terms of the divorce neither party could re-marry while the other was alive. This was to prove troublesome for Eliza down the line.

The publicity surrounding the divorce scandalised London society and Lieutenant Lennox quickly disappeared from the scene. His father, a prominent peer, is likely to have exerted considerable pressure on his young son to distance himself from Eliza's evil ways.

Finding herself alone and virtually penniless, Eliza spent a brief time with a relative of her stepfather in Edinburgh before she hit on a plan that was as outrageous as the reputation she now enjoyed, or endured.

If anything positive had come out of her romantic liaison with Lennox, it had been that an American passenger called Mrs Stevens had remarked on her grace while dancing with her companion on board the ship. Clearly less troubled by the intimate nature of the goings-on than her British counterparts, Mrs Stevens had suggested she might pursue her talent in some form. As Eliza lay alone in her bed in Edinburgh she dreamed of the fame of her contemporary, the world-renowned Austrian ballet dancer Fanny Elsser, and all the wealth and attention such a life could bring to her.

THE BIRTH OF LOLA MONTEZ

Soon she was on her way to Spain to train as a dancer and three months later Eliza Gilbert was no more. When she set foot back in London it was not as the daughter of humble Irish parents, but as the offspring of Spanish nobility. Her dark blue eyes, tanned skin and dark hair

A VICTORIAN PASSION

The double standards of Victorian society make the 'outrage' at Lola's behaviour all the more laughable. It was an open secret than a great many men of 'society' kept mistresses and were frequent visitors to the brothels dotted around most cities. According to The Lancet in 1857 there were six thousand brothels and eighty thousand prostitutes in London alone! Ireland was not immune to this; in 'The Monto', Dublin's red light district, Ireland's capital 'boasted' what was the largest red light district in Europe. In fact legend has it that Prince Albert Edward, who would later be King Edward VII, lost his virginity in the dark, dingy streets of The Monto.

fitted perfectly with the deception, which she crowned with a dramatic new name – Maria Dolores de Porris y Montez – or Lola Montez for short.

Using her charms on the unsuspecting manager of Her Majesty's Theatre in London's Haymarket, Lola secured a run of her 'show' in which she hoped she would enthrall her audiences with her new-found skills. The impresario fed the following line to the *Morning Post*: '*On Saturday next a new danseuse makes her appearance. She is a Spaniard, with black eyes, taper ankles, and a clear olive complexion, which realise all our fantasies of the pure Andalusian beauty.*'

She stepped out onto stage in 3 June 1843 and must have thought she'd found the pot of gold at the end of the rainbow. The critics bought the Spanish persona hook, line and sinker. The *Morning Post* was in raptures:

'*The dancing of the fair Senorita was so novel that, for a time, the audience, in their surprise, forgot to applaud. Her wonderfully supple form assumed attitudes that were not dreamt of – the line of beauty being still preserved, in spite of the boldness of her movement.*'

The *London Evening Mail* likewise:

'*The haughtiness with which she stepped, the slow play of the arms, the air of authority with which she once stopped with the hands resting on the hips – all gave an air of grandeur to the dance.*'

And likewise the *Observer*, *The Spectator*, *The Weekly Chronicle*, *The Examiner* were all fulsome in their praise. And as she awoke the next morning to read the reviews it must have given her particular pleasure to peruse the words of the *Morning Herald*, the paper that had so eagerly reported on the scandal of her divorce:

'... *and then the commanding figure of Dona Lola Montez is revealed in all its glory to the view. And a lovely picture it is to contemplate.*'

But like most things in Lola's life, the success was to be short-lived. Having spent a joyous few days dining at the tables of enraptured noblemen and their families and speaking in practised broken English of her Spanish heritage and her dance training in the Teatro Reale in Seville, Lola was suddenly on the back foot. Inevitably, she was eventually recognised as the divorced Mrs James.

She wrote letters to the press issuing denials and even personally visited the homes of influential members of society whom she had impressed in a vain attempt to convince them of her authenticity and noble Spanish bloodline. But it was fruitless. The manager immediately cancelled her remaining performances, embarrassed at the amount of negative press she was generating for the theatre, and also clearly feeling like an idiot for having been so easily fooled by her 'Spanish beauty'.

For Lola Montez, so briefly attaining the glory she sought, it was time to pack her bags again. But along with her Spanish outfits and her dancing shoes she packed her determination to succeed at any cost. And she knew exactly where she was heading.

LEADING EUROPE ON A MERRY DANCE

It may have been the worst of times in London for Lola, but she was determined to have herself the best of times by travelling to Paris, a city where her identity was still a secret.

The first door she knocked on was that of a renowned ballet master in the Rue de Pelletier in early 1844. She was smart enough to know that her Spanish twirling would not be enough to fool the glitterati of the Paris theatre, which was renowned at the time for its classical dance. However, she must have had some innate talent, as she impressed enough to secure an appearance at the Paris Opera on 30 March 1844.

Reviews were mixed. *La Presse* was generous and it's probably no co-incidence that its editor would become Lola's future one true love. Mostly the rest of the press reviews were either indifferent or antagonistic. Whatever effect it had on her career as a dancer, her appearances and her indisputable beauty propelled her into the limelight and into the company of some of the most famed members of Paris's bohemian society.

It is said she came to know the writer George Sand quite well and although there is little evidence for this, the fact that they were both women living under pseudonyms and both had the capacity and willingness to shock their respective societies, it seems like they might have had a lot to talk about.

A couple of bohemian types she definitely did mingle with were the composer Franz Liszt and the writer Alexandre Dumas. And Lola certainly knew how to mingle.

Her relationship with Dumas isn't particularly well documented. It seems to have been a sort of 'one night stand' affair, though in Lola's case this lasted several days. Unlike the hero in his novel *The Count of Monte Cristo*, Dumas may have counted himself lucky to escape Lola's attentions after such a short time. Liszt on the other hand was not so lucky.

Two biographers of Liszt offer us a picture of Lola, or a picture of one part of her in particular; one asserts that *'everything was false about Lola Montez, except perhaps her ample bosom'*, while another salivates over the fact that *'Lola's beauty, particularly the spleandour of her breasts, made madmen everywhere.'*

Whatever the attraction, she proved initially irresistible to Liszt. Securing a dancing engagement in the Royal Theatre in Dresden, Lola was fortunate to have the famous Hungarian in the audience. Still just twenty-three, Lola was at the peak of her beauty and Liszt was captivated by her dark charms. They made a pretty pair as Liszt toured Europe displaying his stunning skills as a pianist, he with a long mane of fair hair and hawkish good looks, her with the dark, almost Mediterranean looks.

While Liszt's nimble fingers found a willing subject in Lola, her charms would not be enough to save the relationship. Over the course of the following year Liszt increasingly found himself distracted from his work by Lola's demands for attention. And when it wasn't forthcoming her fiery temper often boiled over leaving him scurrying out of her path.

Liszt was also involved with another woman, the French author Marie d'Agoult, who also happened to be the mother of his three children. She became incensed at the sight of Lola cavorting openly with her lover and dumped him that year, telling him that she was happy to be his mistress but didn't relish the idea of being one of several. The following year she published *Nelida*, purportedly a novel, but unashamedly identifiable as an account of her years with Liszt, including a couple of not too complimentary observations about the central character's lovers.

The following summer Liszt was invited to unveil a statue of Beethoven in Bonn amid great celebrations and feasting. During the festivities, fuelled by copious amounts of German beer and French champagne, an argument arose as to whether proceedings should be carried out in French or German. Lola, who had accompanied the great man to the unveiling decided to take things into her own hands, or rather, her feet, by leaping on the table and giving the audience an impromptu display of her dancing skills, twirling on the table top and sending bottles and glasses flying in all directions. The composer was horrified.

The story of the ending of their relationship is in all likelihood apocryphal, as is so much of what has been written about her. Yet it is too colourful to omit from any account of Lola's life, and besides, her life often seemed stranger than fiction, so it's just possible there is some element of truth in it. The story goes that having decided to dump Lola, Liszt couldn't simply find the courage to tell her face-to-face, scared not only of a tongue lashing, but also of a physical one. Sharing a hotel room with Lola while on tour, he quietly awoke and crept from the room early one morning. Proceeding to locate the hotel proprietor, he handed over a substantial sum of cash, an amount he estimated would more than cover the damage that Lola would inflict on the unfortunate hotel room when she learned of his departure. The legend goes that the fiery Sligo *cailín* raged and rampaged in a tantrum of destruction for a full twelve hours before finally burning herself out. The love affair with one of Europe greatest composers and pianists was also extinguished.

A curious footnote to the affair was that despite the tempestuous nature of the relationship and his decision to finally part from Lola, who – frankly – had become an embarrassment to him, he would later speak of King Ludwig (Lola's greatest conquest) as being one of the luckiest of mortals. He would write: '*She is the most perfect, most enchanting creature I have ever know ... one can understand everything that King Ludwig has done and sacrificed for her! Everything!*' Clearly time had filtered all the unpalatable residue of their affair from Franz's memory.

TRUE LOVE

A friend of Alexandre Dumas was Alexandre Dujarier, the co-editor of *La Presse*, a newspaper that often serialised his novels. On his invitation, Dujarier had attended a performance of one of Lola's shows (presumably before she and Dumas fell out) and the unfortunate newsman was smitten. There is another version of the story of their meeting (there's always another version when it comes to Lola) in which she stages a fake horseriding accident, along comes her white knight and helps her and Lola gets access to the largest circulation paper in Paris as well as guaranteed rave reviews, while Dujarier gets access to Lola. She *had* actually been in a horse riding accident (involving the Emperor of Russia no less), but this had actually taken place a couple of years earlier.

Yet apparently Dujarier did have some positive influence on her life and Lola did care for him greatly. He is reputed to have educated her in liberal politics allowing her to more easily mix in the cafés and restaurants haunted by the bohemian society of Paris.

The couple became a feature of the Paris social scene and were often seen strolling hand in hand around Montmartre.

Yet Dujarier had to endure the taunts of fellow

pressmen about his favourable treatment of Lola in his newspaper. He bore the verbal barbs despite his loss of credibility and was actually rumoured to be engaged to Lola, the marriage to take place the following spring.

But there was to be no fairytale ending in Paris in the spring. The following March, Dujarier was either at a party, in a bar or a card game depending on your source, when he became involved in an argument with a Monsieur de Beauvallon, who was a rival critic or and old enemy or simply a loud-mouthed drunk, depending on who you want to believe. Much wine having been consumed by both parties, De Beauvallon insulted Dujarier about an old affair of his at which point Dujarier challenged the man to a duel. This was a truly bad move on the editor's part as he had no duelling skills whatsoever and his opponent was an expert. And naturally by the time word of the duel spread, Lola was the apparent woman whose honour had to be defended. By all accounts this was nonsense, but Lola seemed to be a magnet for that sort of gossip.

The next morning Dujarier made a will and clearly having no confidence in his duelling skills, wrote a goodbye letter to Lola:

'My ever dearest Lola: I want to explain why it was I slept by myself and did not come to you this morning. It is because I have to fight a duel. All my calmness is required, and seeing you would have upset me. By two o'clock this afternoon everything will be over. A thousand fond farewells to the dear little girl I love so

much, and the thought of whom will be with me for ever.'

The following day the two men met on the duelling field, pistols at the ready. Dujarier fired and missed by a mile. De Beauvallon fired and hit Dujarier in the heart, also shattering Lola's heart in the process. A sketch from the time shows a distraught Lola throwing herself across her dead or dying lover as he reclines on a bed.

Her grief seems to have been genuine and the life of gay Paris suddenly held no more charm for her. Within weeks she'd bid the city *adieu*. But her travels would soon take her right to the top of European society.

FIT FOR A KING

Her first brush with royalty was a brief affair when she somehow won her way into the heart of Prince Henry LXXII of Ruess-Lobenstein-Eberdorf, a tiny principality in Germany. Besides his brief encounter with Lola, the Prince's main claim to fame is that at LXXII or seventy-two, he holds the world record for having the largest regnal number of a monarch. He probably also holds the record for the shortness of his relationship with Lola Montez as she quickly upset many of the royal household and staff with her arrogant attitude and antipathy for royal etiquette. The story goes that she liked to take a short-cut across the Prince's beloved flower-beds and when reproached by a gardener she physically assaulted the unfortunate servant. Again this may or may not have a grain of truth to it, but whatever the facts, she did earn the title 'The Fair Impure' among the community and ultimately Henry is quoted as telling her to *'Leave my kingdom at once. You are nothing but a feminine devil'*.

Far from being discouraged, Lola headed for Munich where her debut performance at the Hof Theatre was attended by the sixty-year-old King Ludwig I of Bavaria. The most famous anecdote concerning her meeting with Ludwig recounts the King's admiration of her famed bosom. Once again, depending on who you listen to, this took place in the theatre after her performance, at a gala dinner in the palace or in the King's bedroom, but the likelihood is that it never took place at all. Still, it's wonderfully titillating and probably the most famous Lola anecdote. As he spoke to the beautiful 'Spanish' beauty, old Ludwig repeatedly found his eyes drawn southward, eventually asking blatantly if her bosoms were real. Completely unruffled, the bold Lola rapidly undid her bodice and pulled the garment apart revealing the genuineness of her breasts to the shocked on-lookers.

True or otherwise the public would soon be profoundly shocked at how quickly Ludwig fell under the spell of the young enchantress. Lola soon found herself ensconced in the Royal Palace and her influence began to grow almost immediately. Ludwig was used to having mistresses (to go with his wife and eight children), but none had a hold on him quite like Lola. He spent much of his time writing love poems to her and awarded her an annual allowance that was more than twice the amount a cabinet minister received. He commissioned a portrait of her, which is the only real glimpse we have of the beauty that put a spell on the hearts of so many men. This painting is still on display in the Munich Museum.

As the months passed Lola increasingly came into conflict with the Catholic Church, the Jesuits in particular. They viewed her illiberal ways as utterly shocking and were horrified at the way in which Lola was bringing her influence to bear on the King to dismiss conservative politicians and society elders in favour of more broad-minded individuals. Lola, in her Spanish guise, had been passing herself off as a Catholic whereas in actual fact both her parents were Protestants and she had also been baptised as one. But religion was not going to be an obstacle for the ever-pragmatic lady, although she later developed a lifelong hatred of Romanism and of Jesuits in particular.

Ludwig seemed to indulge Lola's every desire, renovating a house for her at massive expense, lavishing her with clothes and jewelry, issuing state decrees at Lola's whims. This reached the point where the cabinet became known among the populace as 'The Lolaministerium'. What Lola gave in return seems to have been very little, considering the length of time she spent with Ludwig. It is said she only ever slept with the old man twice and that he had to content himself with sucking her toes, a favourite pastime of his, by all accounts.

The effect her toes and other attributes had on Ludwig was astonishing. Less than a year after walking into his life, Ludwig decided she was to become a naturalised citizen of Bavaria. When his ministers refused, the King gave them twenty-four hours to think about their careers. Not surprisingly they relented. But more was to follow. Now a citizen, Lola could now be officially afforded a title, which would completely cement her position in the royal household of Bavaria. And against massive ministerial and public opposition, on the 14 August 1847, Lola Montez became the Baroness of Rosenthal and Countess of Landsfeld.

All during this time, Lola had been courting the attentions of a group of university students. These young men responded to the click of Lola's fingers like panting dogs. They ran her errands, accompanied her on her walks about town, defended her vigorously from any slights directed her way and even serenaded her. They were frequent visitors to her home and sure enough rumours began to spread like wildfire that her home had become a place of orgies, the flames doubtlessly being fanned by the church. It seems likely that Lola was intimately involved with one or more of these young men, but Ludwig turned a deaf ear to the tales and continued to content himself with kissing her portrait every time he passed it and the occasional toe-suck.

In 1848, two years into her sojourn in Bavaria, things began to come to a head when Lola finally pushed things too far, convincing the King to dismiss a Jesuit Professor of Philosophy. Lola and His Highness began to endure constant haranguing from the general student body; only her own few loyal students remained at her side. The situation grew more and more tense, with Lola publicly remonstrating with the raging students. Enraged herself, she berated the embattled Ludwig for allowing the insults and insolence to continue. Unbelievably, Ludwig bowed to her wishes and decided to close the university for a year. The entire city of Munich was in shock. The news actually received widespread coverage in the press all across Europe.

The City Council dispatched a deputation to the King begging him to reverse his decision. There were daily reports of students rioting across the city and the talk in the bars and cafes in every back street was of revolution. Windows were smashed and banners raised bearing the words *'Down with the concubine!'*

Ludwig may have lost his heart at the sight of Lola, but now he was fearful he might actually lose his head in a re-run of the French Revolution, so ugly was the mood of the city. He had no choice. While still declaring his eternal love for Lola he decided to completely reverse his decision and re-open the university.

While the city celebrated, Ludwig realised he'd become a laughing stock. His position was now completely untenable. Any decree he might issue would be met with the same hostility and who knew where it would stop the next time? Five weeks later, on 21 March 1848, he abdicated in favour of his eldest son, Maximilian.

It was also the end for Lola, at least the end of a chapter. She was expelled from Munich with immediate effect on the grounds of having had improper influence on the Royal household and the state, and stripped of all the possessions she'd acquired through Ludwig's benevolence. Distraught, she fled to Switzerland with a couple of the students who'd remained at her beck and call. There she waited for Ludwig to join her but he never arrived. He would end his days alone in Nice.

Lola was also officially deprived of the title that the King had bestowed upon her, but officialdom had never been a problem for resilient Lola. She would continue to refer to herself proudly as The Countess of Landsfeld for the remainder of her days. And she still had a lot to pack in.

BIGAMY AND ARREST

Late in 1848 Lola found herself back in London and within months returned to her first love, not dancing, but men in uniform. George Trafford Heald was an army officer and came from a wealthy and influential family. He caught Lola's eye while she was walking through Hyde Park on a spring day in 1849. Learning of his background she quickly dispatched a note introducing herself as 'The Countess of Landsfeld' and inviting him to a soirée with some friends in her London apartment.

Heald willingly accepted and the moment he stepped through her door he was transfixed, not realising he'd crossed the threshold of a world of trouble. Lola exuded sexuality and left Heald's head in a spin. Within weeks he'd proposed and Lola had happily accepted, omitting to mention to her new fiancé that the terms of her divorce precluded her from re-marrying while her husband was still alive. This inconvenient legality she blithely ignored and strode down the aisle on 19 July.

Heald's wealthy family were outraged, so much so that his aunt started to dig deeply into Lola's past. And she'd barely put her foot on the investigative shovel when she turned up Lola's previous marriage to Lieutenant James. The honeymoon barely over, two detectives from Scotland Yard arrived on the newlyweds' doorstep in August and promptly arrested Lola for bigamy.

When she made her court appearance soon after, the aisles were packed with voyeuristic Victorians keen to catch a glimpse of the woman they saw as an infamous harlot. Once again Lola was the talk of all of London. The judge remanded her to reappear at a future date and she left the court in a tumult of attention that one would expect from a modern day pop star. Unfortunately not all the attention was of an adoring nature.

Heald was, it appears, unperturbed by Lola's failing to mention her ex-husband, and to escape the clamour of the press and anger of his family, the pair fled England for the sunnier climes of the south of Spain, her supposed birth-place.

Clearly having forgotten her own dictum about runaway marriages ending in crashes, this one, like her first, hit a wall at full speed. The pair argued incessantly and the relationship, if there ever was one, lasted less than two years.

They went their separate ways and he ended up a few years later in Lisbon, by which time he'd developed a great fondness for alcohol. While boating under the influence one day his skiff overturned and he drowned. The *Cork Examiner* reported his death seemingly at Folkestone, but this is probably the port to where his body was returned. His death notice did manage to have a small swipe at his ex-wife.

DEATHS
June 20, at Folkestone, George Trafford Heald, Esq.
This gentleman was formerly an officer in the 2d Life
Guards, and was one of the persons stated to have been
married to the notorious Lola Montes.
The Cork Examiner, 2 July 1856

Lola meantime, had headed off to pursue the American dream.

THE BIG APPLE

Before heading west, Lola returned briefly to Paris where she brushed up on her dancing with lessons from the well-known instructor Jardin Mabille, who reputedly had an understanding of the type of act that would go down well in the still-youthful nation of the United States.

Her time in New York was, as one might expect, a roller-coaster. The reviews of her performances were mixed, but many of her mostly-male audiences cared less about her artistic skills as a dancer and more about her alluring shape and suggestiveness. Her outfit on her debut was described as 'flattering', but the performance left a lot to be desired and she seemed out of breath a great deal of the time and unable to maintain tempo (Lola smoked incessantly throughout her life which was a likely contributor here). She actually claimed that a Jesuit had been planted in the orchestra to throw her timing! Often when confronted by a hostile audience, the entertainment for the audience would be found not in her dancing, but in her on-stage explosions of temper. She would round on them to roars of laughter calling them every name under the sun. But the shows weren't all disasters and many of the reviews did praise her ability, almost without exception they would say something to the effect that her lack of skill is more than compensated by her beauty and grace.

She often made the headlines for reasons other than her stage performances. In May 1852 while entertaining a number of guests in her hotel, she became embroiled in an argument with an Italian prince who had slighted an acquaintance of hers. Enraged, and probably a little drunk, Lola grabbed the prince's moustache and yanked. Expelled from her room he met a fellow Italian downstairs and the pair headed back with renewed courage. Whatever Lola did the Italians ended up tumbling down the staircase causing a great ruckus, half the hotel being awoken and eagerly giving eye-witness accounts to the arriving press.

At one point Lola, incensed at the coverage she was receiving in the New York press wrote an outraged letter in which she claimed her character had been slandered and vilified. *'If all that is said of me were true, if half of it were true – I ought to be buried alive.'*

When she departed New York, *The Herald* was sad to see her go as their readers would be deprived of all the *'fun, drollery and scandal'*.

CALIFORNIA GIRL AND THE SPIDER
DANCE

Lola arrived in San Francisco in 1853 and her performances brought much better press, particularly her infamous Spider Dance. There seemed to have been a number of variations on this, but essentially it was designed to titillate and tease her audience.

The Spider Dance consisted of Lola arriving innocently on stage in a dress made of layers of chiffons, supposedly representing a spider's web. At first playing the role of a country girl on a cheerful afternoon stroll, she begins to realise that her dress is inhabited by spiders. As the dance progresses she pirouettes faster and faster to the quickening beat, tearing at the layers of her dress to shake loose the spiders, which she then crushes with her foot. Eventually little of the dress remains (by 1853 standards) and the audience is in raptures at being afforded a glimpse of her slender legs and ankles.

During one daring performance for the benefit of the city's firemen, a number of the uniformed audience had thrown their hats on stage during the Spider Dance, the hats made of a stiff cloth material and being conical in appearance with a wide brim. Crushing many of the hats as though they were spiders Lola then proceeded to the final hat and pulled her petticoats over it, squatting down, a foot planted either side of the hat, in what was a blatantly erotic addition to the routine. She finally sprang skyward and stamped on the hat to great applause.

It was during one of these shows that she came to the attention of husband number three. Patrick Purdy Hull was an Irish-American newspaperman of some wealth. Like military men, those in the publishing industry seemed to have an attraction for her. As usual she was only months in the city when the wedding was announced and the pair were married in a Catholic ceremony in Mission

Dolores Church on 2 July 1853, Lola again neglecting to inform her husband, or the priest, that she wasn't actually a Catholic.

Once more the marriage floundered with the couple arguing constantly and often publicly. At one stage after an argument, a screaming Lola threw his clothes out of the upstairs window of a hotel, much to the amusement of passers-by in the street below. Hull did accompany Lola on a tour of cities in western USA, but her appeal was beginning to wane, perhaps in direct proportion to her fading beauty.

GRASS ROOTS

Lola withdrew from the stage and also from high society. She and Hull moved to a small goldmining town called Grass Valley, then in California, now in the state of Nevada. She purchased a house in the town's main street and settled down to a quiet life, she hoped. But within months of her arrival her marriage was over and she threw Hull out on the street.

One story recounts how Lola maintained a menagerie in her backyard consisting of monkeys, coyotes and, of all things, a bear. When Hull shot her bear, whether by intent or accident, Lola banished him from her home and her life. While the tale of the menagerie seems to have some foundation, Hull's encounter with the bear and subsequently Lola are probably an exaggeration.

With Hull gone, Lola would remain in Grass Valley for a further two years, her notoriety bringing some attention to the town and giving the locals something to gossip about, and her home, now rebuilt, is listed as one of the state's historical landmarks.

She largely lived a quiet life in the town and came to love the local children, among whom was a small girl called Lotta Crabtree, who, with Lola's help, would go on to become one of America's most celebrated singers. She also helped to care for injured miners and tended to sick children. An indication of the change in Lola came when a preacher described her in a sermon as *'a shameless devil in the guise of a beautiful dancer'*. In past days she probably would have trounced the man, but instead she visited him and made such an impression she stayed for dinner with him and his wife.

But the old fire wasn't gone yet. In November 1854 the editor of the *Grass Valley Telegraph* wrote another in a series of articles lambasting Lola for her previous reputation. Lola maintained that the editor, Henry Shipley, had been a regular uninvited visitor to her home, seeking to gain her attention and her favours, and often in a drunken state. His denials of this couldn't protect him from her rage when she read his latest disparaging attack on her character.

Seizing a horsewhip, she set off along the main street of the town until she found Shipley drinking with his friends

LOLA'S STAR IN THE MAKING

When Lola first began to encourage little Lotta Crabtree in her singing and dancing, she couldn't possibly have imagined what a colossal figure the tiny girl would become. Lola is said to have wanted to take Lotta with her to Australia but her mother, who turned out to be a shrewd businesswoman, refused to let her go. Instead she took her daughter on a tour of mining camps where the child soon became a star, dancing and singing ballads for the miners. By the time she was twelve, they'd moved to San Francisco and were already considerably wealthy. Her mother famously didn't trust banks (and who can blame her) and carried countless wads of thousands of dollars in cash around in trunks, until she eventually began to invest it in real estate. Lotta was by now touring in New York, Chicago, Boston and all over the Midwest under the banner 'Miss Lotta, San Francisco's Favourite'. Her star didn't fade as she matured, in fact over the next twenty years it burned so brightly she became one of the wealthiest performers in US history. When she died in 1924 her estate was valued at a then astronomical $4,000,000, most of which she left to war veterans and animal causes. Those first few steps she'd learned from Lola had certainly taken her a long, long way from Grass Valley.

in the Golden Gate Saloon. Bursting through the swing doors, to the astonishment of the clientele, she began swirling the whip above her head landing a cutting blow on Shipley before he managed to seize the whip. She still managed to get a punch in, cutting his cheek with a ring before, according to Shipley, resorting to her most fearsome weapon, her tongue. Her language was enough to make even the assembled miners blush.

DOWN UNDER

At the age of thirty-four, Lola decided to give her dancing career one last shot. And her target was another emerging nation, Australia. She'd become involved with a young actor called Noel Folland, who had left his wife and children for her. She appointed him her manager and on 6 June 1855 she and Folland sailed for Sydney on the *Fanny Major*.

A series of performances in Sydney, Melbourne and Adelaide brought mostly condemnation from the audiences who were largely made up of ex-pat Englishmen and their wives, as susceptible to outrage as their Victorian cousins back home. The *Sydney Morning Herald* described her performance as *'the most libertinish and indelicate performance that could be given on the public stage'*. While in Australia she acquired the nickname 'La Grande Horizontale' and it was claimed that in her performance at Melbourne, she raised her skirts so high that it was obvious she was wearing no underwear, though this is probably the result of an over-active imagination rather than reality, as Lola frequently wore flesh-coloured tights.

She sought a more appreciative audience in the gold-mining towns of the Australian outback and quickly found it, at one point performing her Spider Dance to four hundred gold diggers who reputedly cheered rapturously and rewarded her performance by tossing gold nuggets on the stage.

Having performed in the mining town of Ballarat, she was not rewarded so generously. The editor, Henry Seekamp published a cutting editorial on her lack of moral character so, in a reprise of her reaction to negative publicity in Grass Valley, Lola decided to respond with the cutting riposte of a riding crop. In a famed incident in Australia newspaper folklore, she burst into Seekamp's office and began flailing him with the crop, chasing him into the street and whipping his backside as he ran. Seekamp's agonised cavortings are said to have been the inspiration for a musical composition by Albert Denning entitled 'The Lola Montez Polka'.

Yet overall, the comeback tour was a failure. It may have brought her some earnings, but it didn't bring her the praise she so desperately sought. It was also to end in tragedy when on the return journey, the young Folland fell overboard and was lost. There were as usual a variety of discordant reports to cover this incident: he had fallen over when drunk, he had committed suicide, and naturally, that Lola had pushed him overboard in the course of a fight, although there was no evidence of this whatsoever.

LOLA THE WRITER, LOLA THE LECTURER

Her dancing career most certainly at an end, Lola returned to New York where her career took an unexpected twist. She began to write at first on the subjects with which she was completely familiar – beauty and fashion. Her book *Secrets of a Lady's Toilet with Hints to Gentlemen on the Art of Fascination* written in 1858 contains many tips on beautifying oneself that could have been written yesterday, encouraging the use of purely natural products and the avoidance of cosmetics, which she regarded as poisonous (many beauty treatments in those days literally were extremely poisonous). She would also write her autobiography, which the best you could say about it, is that it is chronologically accurate for the most part. Lola had a tendency to exaggerate greatly or if it suited her, lie blatantly.

She also embarked on a lecture tour, which included a visit to the Rotunda Rooms in Dublin, now the Ambassador. Many of her lectures and writings attacked the Catholic Church, an institution to which she'd developed a strong aversion during her time in Bavaria. She praised the Church initially for its contribution to civilisation around the world, but would then launch into lengthy streams of invective, calling it *'an enemy of progress'* and claiming it had *'tied bands of iron around the expanding hearts of freedom.'* Contemporary accounts tells us she spoke with authority and passion and despite the controversial nature of her subject matter, she often received better reviews for her lectures than she did for her dancing.

In her final years, Lola underwent a spiritual transformation and actually found religion herself. She became a frequent visitor to prisons in New York, but especially frequented Magdalen Asylums for so-called 'fallen women'. These institutions had been founded in Ireland and had now spread to Britain and the US and conditions within them were incredibly harsh. Lola was both an Irishwoman and a fallen woman who somehow had managed to stay on her feet, so she had a particular empathy for the unfortunate girls condemned to live in these horrendous places.

THE CURTAIN FALLS

On 30 June 1860 Lola suffered a sudden stroke, which left her partly paralysed. In December she came under the care of a Reverend Francis Lister Hawks, an Episcopal Minister, and during her time with him she came to be truly repentant for the life she now believed she had wasted. Her mother visited her during this time, but they were by now too far apart to find a meeting of minds. Unwelcome, she left after a brief visit and never saw her daughter again.

Many stories claim that Lola died of syphilis, but these simply follow the pattern of malicious gossip that followed her. In reality, weakened by her stroke, she contacted pneumonia after taking a short stroll on a winter's afternoon and died a few days later, repenting to the end and clutching a bible in her hand. Reverend Hawks later described her final moments: *'I do not think I ever saw a deeper penitence and humility, more real contrition of soul, and more bitter self-reproach, than in this poor woman.'*

Lola was buried in Greenwood Cemetery in Brooklyn with a handful of friends in attendance and the Reverend Hawks officiating at her graveside.

The legend of Lola Montez still survives today. Her character has appeared in many films, television series and novels through the years. She has been the subject of plays, inspired a song entitled 'Whatever Lola wants, Lola gets' and even been the subject of an Australian musical based on her life story. Over a thousand websites are devoted to Lola Montez. In Nevada she has a mountain named after her – Mount Lola, along with a lake and the aforementioned Lola Montez Hiking Trail.

In many ways she was a woman ahead of her time. Of course her behaviour was shocking and she was vain, arrogant, temperamental, selfish and even violent. But driving much of it was Lola's indignation at not being allowed the same personal freedoms as men. This subject is still debated in today's supposedly liberal society. A century and a half ago such a desire was unthinkable. And for simply acting on that belief in the face of such opposition, Lola Montez demands our admiration.

The last word must go to the writer Aldous Huxley, who though not a contemporary of Lola, is quoted in Horace Wyndham's biography of her as having said *'her reputation automatically made you think of bedrooms'*.

Argentinean national hero. Founder of the Argentine Navy

STILL WATERS RUN DEEP

For the Irish emigrant in the eighteenth and nineteenth century, South America would not usually come to mind as a place to establish a new home. The US, Australia or Britain were far more likely to attract Irish settlers keen to escape the grinding poverty of their country of birth. Yet a small proportion of Irish (still in their tens of thousands) did opt to cross the equator to the vast unexplored lands of tropical rainforests and Latin tongues. And though relatively few among the teeming masses of Spanish, Portuguese and native South Americans, the Irish had a completely disproportionate representation among those who were to become the heroes and legends of independence and freedom from their colonial masters.

Among the most renowned of these was William or Guillermo Brown, as he came to be called. Yet the deeds and name of Guillermo Brown still remain foreign to many people in Ireland. And even those who know of him may be surprised to learn that the Irish-Argentinean figure may not quite deserve the near-sainthood to which he has sometimes been elevated.

The only thing that we know for certain about the early life and character of William Brown, the 'Father of the Argentinean Navy', is that it is as fathomless as some of the seas upon which he would gain immortality in his later life. He was the son of a poverty stricken farmer, he was the illegitimate son of an aristocrat, his father worked in a mill, Brown wasn't his real name, he was a deserter from the British Navy, he was an agent of the British, he was fortune hunter and mercenary, he was an Irish and Argentinean patriot, *he was a pirate* … take your pick.

History is a matter of perspective. To the British, Oliver Cromwell is a champion of liberty, one of the top ten Britons of all time. To the Irish he is little more than a butcher. To the British in Argentina, Guillermo Brown was a brilliant British naval strategist doing battle on behalf of the crown against one of Britain's greatest enemies, Spain. To the Irish nationalist and Irish-Argentineans, he was an Irishman through and through who carried the spirit of Irish patriotism to his new home which infused him with the passion to defeat another powerful and oppressive

Above: A sombre sculpture to the memory of Charles Yelverton O'Connor by sculptor Tony Jones. Depicting a man on a horse just beyond the breaking waves, the monument is near the spot in Fremantle where the great engineer took his own life.

Right: A portrait of Charles Yelverton O'Connor taken in 1897, when he was fifty-four.

Above: A bronze sculpture of Paddy Hannan in Burswood Park, Perth, depicting the grizzled and weather-worn prospector hard at work.

Below: A sign marking the street named in honour of Alejandro O'Reilly in Havana. The plaque below, in Spanish, Irish and English, reads: 'Two island peoples in the same sea of struggle and hope. Cuba and Ireland.'

Right: Jennie Hodgers aka Albert Cashier (right) taken during the Civil War, with an unknown fellow soldier who has no idea his comrade is a woman.

Left: One of a number of stamps issued by the Argentine postal service in honour of their country's greatest naval hero, Guillermo Brown.

Top: A US newspaper article honouring the fearless workers' champion, Mother Jones, on her '100th' birthday.

Centre: Mother Jones heads a protest march through heavy snow in Denver in 1914.

Bottom: A stamp jointly issued by Ireland and the U.S. in 1981 to mark the 150th anniversary of James Hoban's death.

'Mother' Jones, Fearless Strike Leader, Celebrates One-hundredth Birthday

Veteran of Many Labor Battles Led an Eventful Life; Faced Thugs and Gunmen; Defied Injunction Judges; Is Loved by Thousands of Workers in All Sections of America

By BUDD L. McKILLIPS

"Mother" Jones, militant labor leader who braved thug-manned machine guns to organise miners' unions, led protest marches of strikers' wives over wild mountain ranges, defied Rockefeller's gunmen in Colorado and West Virginia, and took an important part in every major strike of the last six decades in the United States, celebrated her one hundredth birthday Thursday, May 1.

Since last fall she has been living with some friends on a quiet little farm in Maryland a few miles from Washington, D. C., and the farm house was gaily decorated for "Mother's" party.

Flags and bunting literally covered the house. A large arch, bearing the word "Mother," curved over the driveway leading from the main road.

Governor Ritchie and Staff

Cars started arriving early in the morning and continued to come until almost sundown. Governor Albert Ritchie of Maryland and his staff were among those who drove out to greet "Mother."

Twenty-seven men, who, that morning, had stood in the bread-line for their breakfast, walked all the way from Washington to pay their respects to the woman whose life has been devoted to waging war on industrial evils.

A band from the National Soldiers' Home arrived at noon and furnished music for the party during the balance of the day.

Men and women who were boys and girls in the labor movement when "Mother" was even then a veteran, came to add their felicitations to those contained in congratulatory

the bosses' thugs shoot down men and women who only ask for a chance to live like human beings," she told the writer.

"We had lots of strikes, and lots of times our people were shot and killed in cold blood," she continued.

"Take that Ludlow massacre—that was a murderous, bloody affair . . ."

Faced Machine Guns

One can easily imagine "Mother" Jones inspiring a crowd of discouraged men and women to carry on under great odds.

She is a natural leader—a sort of Joan of Arc. One of my friends insists that if she had been a man and an army officer "Mother" Jones would have become a world-famed colonel of cavalry—that she had an uncanny sense for detecting the weakest point in an enemy's force and attacking there with a vim and daring that carried her through to victory.

Pleaded With Presidents

During her career she frequently visited the White House to plead organized labor's cause or to demand that some injustice be stopped. And it was not often that her pleas were refused.

President Taft pardoned 14 Mexican revolutionists who were about to be extradited to President Diaz and certain death at the hands of a firing squad.

Twelve Union Pacific railroad strikers, jailed for violating a Federal injunction, were freed by President McKinley at "Mother" Jones' request.

She spent little time in jails herself. Although she was frequently arrested it was almost impossible to keep her locked up. If she got a chance to talk to those in authority she usually succeeded in convincing them that they were wrong.

and said: "You can't talk here," I asked him if he was fool enough to think he could do what all the men in the world hadn't been able to do since creation—keep women from talking—and we marched right into the mine, past the guns and bayonets of the militia and every man there came out on strike."

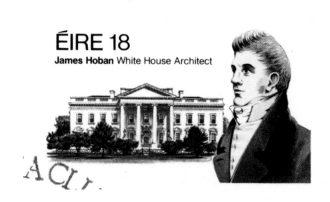

ÉIRE 18

James Hoban White House Architect

Above: This portrait by Joseph Karl Stieler, painted for King Ludwig I of Bavaria, captures the allure of the young Lola. It currently hangs in Schönheitengalerie in Munich which appropriately means the 'Gallery of Beauties'.

Left: A smiling George 'McIrish' McElroy poses beside one of the planes that brought so much fame yet claimed the lives of thousands of young men in World War I, including his own.

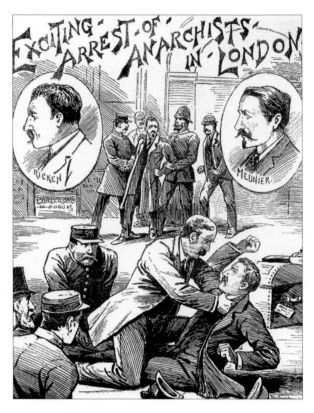

Above: The arrest of French anarchist Théodule Meunier at Victoria Station in 1894 by William Melville, as portrayed in *The Daily Graphic*. Meunier reportedly tried to drag the detective under the wheels of a train.

Left: Monsignor Hugh O'Flaherty demonstrates his golfing prowess as a young man. His path would ultimately lie along a completely different course.

Above: John Holland's so-called *Fenian Ram* or *The Holland II*, on display outside the Paterson Museum, New Jersey.

Right: John Holland in the hatch of one of his early submarine designs prior to a trial run.

McGRATH

Above: Spectators look admiringly at the colossus that was Nenagh-born Matt McGrath, winner of an Olympic Gold medal in Stockholm in 1912.

MARTIN SHERIDAN

Left: Mayo-born Martin Sheridan as he appeared on a Mecca Cigarettes trading card in 1910. Sheridan was once described by The New York Times as 'The world's greatest all-round athlete'.

colonial power. To the locals he may have been born else-where, but he is one hundred per cent Argentinean, a courageous and fearless genius who would have given his life for their present day freedom.

The truth probably lies somewhere in between.

LANDLUBBER

His destiny would eventually bring him to sea, but it was far from the smell of the ocean that Guillermo Brown was born. On the question of his nationality there is no doubt. He was born in Foxford in Co. Mayo on 22 June 1777. He was therefore definitely Irish. But of course Ireland was part of the British empire then, so he was also definitely British, depending on your point of view. It's also quite likely he was born into poverty; his home in Foxford was a small, whitewashed cottage on Providence Road.

The curious thing is, it was his mother and not his father who was a Brown and it would have been unheard of to take one's mother's name, unless of course there was perhaps no father in the household. There is a story that his uncle was a priest called Gannon who was arrested for taking part in the 1798 rebellion who escaped and spent years on the run, surviving with the support of locals. This rebellious, familial link seems to imbue Guillermo Brown with a nationalist, anti-British spirit. There is also a story that Gannon, whoever he was, was the young William's father which would make him William Gannon. Whatever the truth, it is said that as an adult he refused to discuss his early life, which seems to suggest there was something he wasn't exactly proud of in his lineage.

The uncertainty about those childhood days continued when he emigrated to the US at the age of nine. Some versions say his family emigrated. In others he was alone with his father when they arrived in Philadelphia in 1786. Legend has it that a friend of his father offered them the hospitality of his home, then unfortunately caught yellow fever and died, bequeathing a dose to William's father before he passed on. The father soon succumbed to the same fate leaving the nine-year-old orphaned and alone in a strange land. Wandering along the banks of the Delaware River, an old English or American sea captain spotted him, took pity on him and offered him a job as a cabin boy. Young William had barely set foot on the gangplank when he'd found his sea legs. He set sail for a career as a merchant sea man that would see him quickly scale the rigging to become captain within a decade.

Whether any of this is true is anyone's guess. But as a beginning, at least it does have a certain romanticism befitting of the future naval hero. However he began his naval career, he certainly thrived on it and did rise through the ranks to become a captain. His ship, flying a British (or an American) flag, sailed mainly between Britain and South America and by some accounts he was a simple merchant, by others he was a gun-runner, happy to sell weapons to either the insurgents or the colonials in the struggle for South American independence. His only interest was in making money. While there is possibly some basis in this, it seems unlikely that a man who would literally risk his life in later battles would do so without any true cause other than that of accumulating wealth.

What happened next is that his ship was press-ganged into the service of the British Navy. Or was it? Another story says that his ship was seized by the French Navy during the Napoleonic Wars of 1803-1814. Alternatively his ship was captured by an English ship which in turn was captured by a French ship!

This particular adventure saw him a prisoner of war in France from where he escaped disguised as a French officer, possibly, or else he formed a friendship with an English officer and both escaped to Germany, or England.

One thing he most definitely did take the time out to do was marry an English girl called Elizabeth Chitty from Kent on 29 July 1809. She would later bear him two children, one of whom would die tragically.

The myriad strands of half-truths, exaggeration and lore all sprinkled with a few facts which constituted his 'life' up until this point now finally begin to merge into something upon which most historians agree – well, almost!

THE IRISH IN SOUTH AMERICA

Many other Irish people made a significant contribution to the history of the countries of South America. These include military men, politicians, engineers, doctors, and publishers to name but a few. These panels give a brief summary of the achievements of a handful of these men.

JOHN THOMOND O'BRIEN – ARGENTINE GENERAL & ENTREPRENEUR

Born in Baltinglass, Co. Wicklow in 1786, John Thomond O'Brien moved to Buenos Aires in 1812 to engage in trade. As the war of independence gained momentum, he enrolled in the army and quickly rose to be aide-de-camp to Jose San Martin, the key leader of the rebellion. Repeatedly decorated in battle, O'Brien was ultimately promoted to general. After the war he was granted the lease of a silver mine by the Peruvian government for his services to the cause of freedom. During his civilian lifetime he achieved some notable civil engineering feats including digging a 600-metre long canal through a mountain complete with nine locks, laying a railroad and also transporting an entire railway engine across the Andes! A street in Buenos Aires bears his name, as do a rural train station and an Oberon Class submarine (the O'Brien S22) in the Chilean navy.

MERCHANT OF FORTUNE

By 1809 he was certainly back at sea. He travelled to Montevideo where he became part owner of a merchant ship which he named after his wife. The *Eliza* traded between his new home port and Buenos Aires, but unfortunately ran aground and had to be abandoned. He did manage to rescue the cargo (possibly of munitions) and sell it and his venture had been profitable enough to provide him with funds to purchase another ship. He moved to Buenos Aires and purchased a schooner called the *Industria* with which he opened the first regular sailing packet service between Uruguay and Argentina.

His first direct involvement in the war of independence was less an act of rebellion than one of commercial practicality, and probably revenge. Buenos Aires was a flourishing port and when the city ousted the Spanish and installed its own government in 1810. The Spanish reacted by blockading the port entrance. Upon approach, Brown's ship was commandeered by the Spanish and he reputedly reacted by organising a raid on one of the blockading ships, which he captured and returned to the city in glory. This left no small impression on the newly-installed authorities in Buenos Aires.

In 1812, Brown moved permanently to Buenos Aires with his wife and two small children. His sailing exploits continued to impress and by now he was regarded as a mariner with supreme skills.

With Spanish ships continuing to attack Argentine ports and ships, the insurgent government in Buenos Aires decided to take decisive action to protect its coasts and trade. Their 'navy' was tiny having been commissioned just four years earlier, standing at just seven ships of varying sizes and capabilities. They offered Brown the rank of Lieutenant Colonel and the opportunity to take command of the forthcoming battle. He accepted despite the knowledge that he was both outnumbered and outgunned.

The sparking point of the conflict would be the tiny fortified island of Martin Garcia about thirty-five kilometres north east of the city in the middle of the River Plate. His ships were crewed by a mixture of nationalities: Argentine insurgents, and a great many Irish and English mercenaries. His initial attack on 11 March was repulsed by the Royalists under the command of Jacinto Romarte. Brown suffered heavy casualties, his own ship, the *Hercules*, taking considerable damage. But he was not to be outdone. Hastening repairs and recruiting fresh crew, he returned on 15 March and attacked again, this time succeeding in completely reversing the outcome. Some versions of this battle say the decisive victory came on St Patrick's Day, but this may or may not be a way of bolstering the legend of the Irish rebel leading the charge for freedom.

But the conflict was not over. Romarte fled with his fleet of ten men-o-war and made for the port of

Montevideo, being reinforced *en route* by three armed merchant ships. In early April, Brown went in pursuit and succeeded in blockading the Spanish into the port. Four thousand insurgents had meanwhile surrounded the landward side of the city leaving Montevideo completely

DANIEL FLORENCE O'LEARY — BRIGADIER GENERAL IN WARS OF INDEPENDENCE, VENEZUELAN DIPLOMAT, HISTORIAN.

Born in Cork city in 1802 he joined the British Legion at the age of sixteen. The British were keen to support the rebellion in South America as it opposed their centuries-old foe the Spanish, so soon after, the teenage O'Leary's regiment found itself in Bolivia. O'Leary quickly learned the language and was soon in Guyana training under Simon Bolivar himself. He repeatedly distinguished himself in battle and was appointed aide-de-camp to Bolivar. By the age of just twenty-eight he had been promoted to Brigadier General. In 1834, the now Government of Venezuela appointed him their consul to Europe and he spent the next six years in Paris, London, Madrid and the Vatican. During this time he visited his only surviving sister in Cork. When he returned to Venezuela he wrote a history of the South American wars of Independence which extended to thirty-two volumes! After his death his body was re-interred in the National Pantheon in Caracas, next to that of Bolivar. 'Daniel Florencio O'Leary' Plaza in downtown Caracas is named in his honour.

surrounded and facing the threat of starvation.

With little choice, on 14 May the Spanish sortied with their thirteen ships and there ensued a three-day running battle off the coast of Montevideo. During the conflict, Brown, commanding the flagship *Hercules*, was struck by a

THOMAS CHARLES WRIGHT – FOUNDER OF THE ECUADORIAN NAVY

Born in Drogheda, Co. Louth in 1799, Wright trained with the British Navy from the age of twenty-one. Wright returned to Ireland an officer in 1817. Influenced by the French Revolutionary ideals, he soon set sail to join the forces of Simon Bolivar, the inspirational leader of the rebellion in the north west of South America. Wright played a key role in several battles for which Bolivar promoted him to lieutenant colonel and personally praised his skill and courage. Sent to Guayaquil in Ecuador to marshal a fleet of ships, his subsequent actions saw him promoted to Commodore of the Pacific Squadron. He eventually settled in Guayaquil and founded a naval school that is still in existence today. By the time independence was achieved, Wright had become something of a luminary in Equadorian society and eventually married the President's niece. He was appointed governor of Guayaquil and Commander of the Naval Forces. He died in 1868 and in 1999 a stamp was issued in Ecuador to mark the two-hundredth anniversary of his birth.

cannonball and his leg shattered, yet he continued to bellow orders over the roar of cannonfire. Ultimately his tactical brilliance resulted in the capture of most of the Spanish fleet and the burning of two Royalist ships, the remaining few fleeing back to port. The Spanish-controlled city of Montevideo fell a few weeks later with the capture of seven thousand prisoners, an arsenal of munitions and ninety-nine merchant ships.

General San Martin, one of the prime leaders of the revolution called it *'the most important event for the American Revolution until now.'* Brown was showered with honours and made Commander-in-chief of the Argentine Navy, ensuring his name would gain immortality in the annals of the country's history. His flagship, the *Hercules*, was presented to him as a personal reward for his victory, which proved to be the thin end of the wedge in prising away Spanish dominance of the region.

During the following years he successfully led an attack on the Spanish-held port of Callao in Peru and another stronghold at Punta de las Piedras in Ecuador. By 1818 the Argentine War of Independence had merged with that of Chile's struggle for freedom and decisive land battles had effectively ended Spain's threat. But Admiral Brown's battles were not complete. During the next decade he would be called upon again to face a completely new enemy.

BATTLE OF WITS

Physically, Guillermo Brown was described as being tall and powerfully built with a brow that resembled the rolling waves on which he sailed, and with passionate, burning eyes. In private life he was said to be softly spoken and extremely private, yet on deck he commanded with a powerful, projecting voice and a fair but firm treatment of the crew, who reputedly regarded him with awe. He was also said to be personally courageous in battle, often to the point of rashness, the wounds he suffered during his career a testament to the fact. Whatever he had, it brought out the best in men and inspired them to greatness, something they would need in the months ahead.

In 1825 a dispute arose between Argentina and Brazil over an area then known as the Bande Oriental or the Eastern Strip, which is essentially present-day Uruguay. In December of that year, war was declared and Admiral Brown organised another fleet inferior in numbers, but far superior in training. Yet the odds were against him.

Initially Brown concentrated on attacks on naval vessels and ports along the Brazilian coast. It was during raids like these that he earned himself something of a reputation as a privateer, a plunderer or even a pirate, unashamedly taking the spoils of his captures as a reward for himself and crew. Piracy and privateering were closely linked up to the end of the nineteenth century, eventually both were made illegal. 'Privateering' was the hiring of naval men and ships to fight on behalf of a state, their reward being that they could plunder whatever they captured. To the winning side these men were privateers, to the defeated state they were pirates.

But with a Brazilian blockade of Buenos Aires in place, he was drawn into a direct confrontation with the Brazilian

WILLIAM BULFIN — WRITER AND NEWSPAPER EDITOR

Born in Offaly in 1864, Bulfin emigrated to Buenos Aires aged twenty, but soon felt the pull of the pampas. He began to write much-admired articles for the leading English-language newspaper, The Southern Cross (which was owned by Michael Dineen from Cork) that colourfully painted pictures of the vanishing way of life of the gauchos. He eventually re-located to the city and became the proprietor and editor of the newspaper. His writings were subsequently published in the New York Daily News and in book form as 'Tales from the Pampas'. He was a fierce advocate for the rights of newly-arrived immigrants and a keen Irish nationalist. He returned to Ireland for several months in 1902 and wrote a renowned account of a cycling tour of Ireland. Rambles In Eirinn gives us great insights into Irish rural society of that time. His nationalism rubbed off on his offspring, both of whom ended up as republican activists in Ireland. He died in 1910.

navy in what became known as the Battle of Juncal, taking place in the broad mouth of the River Plate.

As a rallying call to his men Brown uttered what would become a line learned by generations of Argentine school-children over the next two centuries: *'Comrades! Confidence in victory, discipline and three hails to the motherland.'* To great cheers the crews manned their seven ships and eight tiny, one-gun launches then raised sails to engage the Brazilian fleet of seventeen warships. Argentine-Britons contend that Brown always sailed into battle with the Union Jack flying from the mast, Britannia's reputation for ruling the waves supposedly instilling fear into the hearts of the enemy. Argentines dispute this, as (naturally) do the Argentine-Irish. While Brown did definitely have British Navy connections, it does seem unlikely that he would call for 'three hails to the motherland', meaning Argentina, and then hoist the flag of another nation above his ship.

The battle took place over two days from 8 to 9 February and the weather was stormy, hot and humid making maneuvering difficult for both fleets. The key differences were Brown's ability to adapt to the poor conditions, the fact that his fleet was equipped with longer-range cannon and the accuracy of his Argentine gunners. He repeatedly allowed rough seas to force the Brazilian ships into the error of getting too close, at which point the Argentine guns could easily pick them off. One by one the enemy fell and at the end of the second day twelve ships had been captured, three burnt and just two escaped. The Brazilian

AMBROSIO O'HIGGINS — GOVERNOR OF CHILE AND VICEROY OF PERU

Born in 1720 in Ballynary, Sligo, the son of peasant farmers, at age thirty Ambrose travelled first to Spain and eventually to Chile where he enrolled in the army at the age of thirty-eight. Despite his late start, his rise through the ranks was spectacular, finally resulting in his appointment as Governor of Chile. A love affair with a noblewoman resulted in the birth of a son, Bernardo O'Higgins, who would gain legendary status as The Liberator of Chile. On a gruelling journey across the Andes, Ambrose conceived the idea of a series of mountain shelters, leading to the country's first ever postal service. He was also responsible for a significant infrastructural development of the then undeveloped colony. Ambrose was further promoted to the post of Viceroy of Peru, which then comprised Chile, Bolivia and a large part of Brazil, which was the pre-eminent colonial post in the Spanish empire. He died aged eighty-one in 1801. Many towns and ports bear his name to this day. The Chilean city of Vallenar, is also a hispanised version of his birthplace, Ballynary.

commander had also been captured and Brown had not suffered a single loss. It was an outstanding victory and severely damaged the Brazilian fleet.

Brown also commanded the fleet in the Battle of Los Pozos. This took place within sight of Buenos Aires and again the Argentines were vastly inferior in numbers with just eleven ships to the Brazilians thirty-one. During this battle he uttered another of his most repeated quotes: *'Open fire! The people are watching us!'* The victory was not as decisive, but it was a victory nonetheless with the Brazilian fleet routed.

The conflict continued on land for months with Brazil essentially defeated, but Argentina not having sufficient resources of men or arms to take full advantage of their victory. The conflict itself was finally resolved the following year when Uruguay was recognised by both combatants as an independent state at the signing of the Treaty of Montevideo, with Admiral Brown acting as Argentine Commissioner at the proceedings.

But Brown's victories were not gained without great personal loss. During one particular engagement on 8 April 1827, the Argentine ship *Independencia* was hit by enemy fire, killing Sergeant Major Francis Drummond, who was the fiancé of his daughter Eliza. Worse was to follow. Upon hearing of the news Eliza committed suicide by throwing herself into the River Plate. For Admiral Brown, memories of the battle would forever after be bitter sweet.

By now, Guillermo Brown was recognised as the greatest naval leader in Argentine history and the most popular man in the entire country. He was appointed Governor of Buenos Aires in 1828 and remained in that position for a year, but political wrangling wasn't to his taste and he soon returned to private life and business.

ACROSS THE OCEAN

It would be over a decade before he was to become involved in another major naval battle. In 1842, Civil War had broken out in Uruguay and a former commander of Brown had sided with one of the warring sides. Admiral Brown, now sixty-five, led the Argentine fleet to victory over his own former officer, John Coe, in three separate engagements close to Montevideo. That same year he was again victorious in the Battle of Parana when he defeated a Uruguayan fleet led by the famous Italian Guiseppe Garibaldi, who would eventually lead Italy to reunification. Brown is reported to have said of Garibaldi in the aftermath of the battle: *'Let him escape, that gringo is a brave man.'*

Political changes in Argentina resulted in many naval and military officers being discharged. Yet Brown, now with legendary status, was retained and eventually retired to his villa, Casa Amarilla in Barracas, home to some of the wealthiest individuals in the country. From his terrace he could look out over the river upon which he'd enjoyed his greatest victories and which, tragically, had also claimed the life of his beloved daughter.

In 1847, aged seventy, in the company of his second daughter, Admiral Brown decided to undertake the

JUAN MACKENNA – CHILEAN HERO OF THE WAR OF INDEPENDENCE AND MILITARY ENGINEER

Born in Clogher in Tyrone in 1771, McKenna was a nephew of that other famous Irish-Spanish general, Alejandro O'Reilly. Aged seventeen he joined the Irish Brigade in the Spanish Army, rose through the ranks quickly and by twenty-four he was a captain in the Royal Regiment of Engineers. Eventually migrating to Chile, he became a key military strategist for the insurgent forces under Bernardo O'Higgins and was eventually promoted to general. He was ultimately appointed Governor of the province of Osorno and was responsible for countless infrastructural developments, many of which are still in use today. Tragically, he died in a duel aged just forty-three. His grandson, Benjamín Vicuña Mackenna would become one of the most influential writers and historians in Chile.

arduous journey across the Atlantic Ocean to Ireland and in particular to his native town of Foxford in Co. Mayo. What spurred this return to his homeland is uncertain. It may have been out of a sense of nostalgia and a wish to share with his daughter his childhood experiences. He must certainly have been aware that Ireland was at that time in the throes of the greatest catastrophe in her history, the Great Famine, as it was widely reported in newspapers which would have reached South America through the frequent merchant ships or those of the British Navy. And Mayo in particular was one of the most badly affected regions, with hundreds starving to death or dying of cholera every day. Perhaps, as a wealthy man, he had come purely for altruistic reasons, to see if he could provide some help to the town where he'd been born. Perhaps he'd even come to seek out relatives still living in the area and maybe to finally bury the illegitimate skeleton in his closet. Whatever his motives, it can't have been a pleasant stay as it would have been near impossible to shield his daughter's eyes from the starvation and disease-ravaged countryside.

He returned to his Buenos Aires home where he was to continue to enjoy a long retirement. He died ten years later, on 3 March 1857, at the age of eighty. At his funeral in Recoleta Cemetery, General Bartolome Mitre, who five years later would become Argentine President, stated in his eulogy *'Brown in his lifetime, standing on the stern of his ship was worth a fleet to us'.*

MONUMENTAL LEGACY

There are 1,200 streets and plazas named after Guillermo Brown in Argentina and countless naval vessels and institutes – and four football clubs – also bear his name. The monument in Recoleta Cemetery that marks his final resting place is something of a shrine in the country and a favourite visiting place for natives, busloads of schoolchildren and tourists alike. Buenos Aires boasts an imposing statue of him and there are many more scattered throughout the country. A statue also stands outside Admiral Brown House in Foxford and in recent years an Irish naval vessel sailed to Argentina to take part in commemorations marking the 150th anniversary of his death, returning with a bust of the Admiral, which now stands on Dublin's docklands. So highly was the Irishman regarded in his adopted homeland that Argentina became the first country to officially recognise the Irish Republic when it was declared during the Easter Rising.

There can be no doubting the impact he had on Argentina and the legendary status afforded him since his death. But was he a true patriot or a man who sought to use his skills and the advent of war to his own advantage? He certainly did reap the spoils of war, of that there is little doubt. But his patriotism for his adopted land cannot be doubted either. Nor his courage.

The one thing that can be said with absolute certainty about Guillermo Brown is that he was a master mariner and naval strategist of the highest order, to rank alongside the greatest of such men throughout history. For that the people of Argentina have been eternally grateful to this son of Foxford, Co. Mayo.

George Henry 'McIrish' McElroy – One of the greatest 'aces' of World War I.

FLIGHTS OF FANCY

George McElroy was born in 1893, ten years before the Wright Brothers took to the sky for man's first flight in 1903. And by the time he first climbed on board a plane in 1916, only thirteen years had passed since that day at Kitty Hawk, when 'The Flyer' first broke free of gravity for just twelve seconds and climbed to an 'altitude' of ten feet.

So to state that powered flight was still in its infancy when World War I broke out in 1914 is an understatement. If powered flight was in its infancy, armed air combat hadn't even been born. So it's no exaggeration to say that the men who would take to the skies to do battle with each other over the next four years showed a level of courage that is difficult to conceive.

George Edward Henry McElroy was not just one of those men, he was among the greatest of them, his name sitting comfortably with the likes of the legendary Baron von Richthofen or Edward 'Mick' Mannock.

His parents were Samuel and Ellen McElroy, a middle class Church of Ireland couple living in the then rural part of Dublin known as Pembroke East, or more specifically Donnybrook. Samuel hailed from Roscommon and Ellen from Westmeath and together they ran a small school at Beaver Row beside the river Dodder, the school also serving as their residence. They married in 1892 and in the spring of the following year along came the first of eight children, all of whom would survive infancy, which was quite unusual for the time. That first child was George, born on 14 May 1893.

Samuel's profession was 'National Teacher' and when the Census of 1911 was carried out, Ellen listed herself as a 'work-mistress' who 'had education', which is probably the early twentieth-century term for 'housewife'; her education meant she was likely also to have assisted her husband in his teaching duties.

Among his neighbours in Donnybrook at the time, George McElroy could have counted four cow-houses, two stables and a piggery, the owners of which are likely to have sent their children to the McElroy's school down the road. The Dodder, which flowed quietly by outside their front door, was a rural backwater on the outskirts of Dublin and the present-day chaos of traffic and concrete was an age away. No passenger jets thundered overhead and the only thing that flew across the skies above Donnybrook were the birds.

When George came into the world, Ireland as a nation was in the throes of being born. Home Rule was the political issue of the day being hotly debated in the newspapers, on the streets and in the pubs. For nationalists this was a sellout, falling well short of their dreams of a country free from British control. Politicians and people alike were divided on the debates that raged, indeed many were torn between a natural love for the land of their birth and a loyalty to the King. But for some, the British Empire was now something that demanded not only loyalty, but servility, and their simmering resentment of their British rulers would boil over within little over a decade, an event that would have a direct influence on George McElroy's life.

THE GREAT WAR

It's likely George McElroy was home from college in June 1914 when word first appeared in the newspapers of the assassination of Archduke Franz Ferdinand of Austria by a Bosnian-Serb nationalist; the fuses lit by this event would engulf Europe in the flames of war for four long years.

Within a couple of months, posters started appearing on

the walls of shops, pubs, police stations and post-offices all over Ireland. Lord Kitchener's finger pointed demandingly out at the viewer, telling him that his 'country needed him' or that he should 'join his country's army', signed off with 'God save the King' as a further appeal to men's patriotism. While many believed it was patriotic to oppose the very King who called for their support, thousands of other Irishmen answered Kitchener's call. George McElroy was one of the first to answer the call, proud to be an Irishman, but also of the belief that it was his duty to help prevent a defeat by the Germans and their allies. He wasn't slow about signing up, putting his name to his enlistment form on 2 August 1914, less than three months after he'd celebrated his coming of age.

He joined the Royal Irish Regiment, which was entirely raised and garrisoned in Ireland and spent the next couple of months in training. It wouldn't be long before he saw action. He was shipped initially to France and then on to Belgium and the town of Ypres, or what was left of it. Clearly comfortable at the controls of mechanical vehicles, he was assigned the task of courier, hurtling between command posts with vital communications when telephone contact was lost, something that happened every other day.

In April 1915 the Second Battle of Ypres commenced and McElroy's battalion was among those to be assigned the task of holding the front line. This battle is infamous as the first in World War I in which poison gas was used on

KERRY'S KITCHENER

Almost everyone is familiar with the image of the very British-looking mustachioed military officer pointing out from the WWI poster proclaiming 'Your country needs you!' Most people don't realise the man, Lord Horatio Kitchener, was actually a Kerryman. Well, sort of. His parents were very English and had just bought land in Kerry when out popped Horatio. His military career was one of stark contrasts – renowned for his humanitarian treatment of Muslims in the Sudan, yet reviled for his murderous campaigns against the Boers, in which he, and the British government, introduced the concept of the concentration camp to the region, and in which thousands of Boer women and children perished in brutal conditions. He was appointed Secretary of State for War during World War I and correctly predicted a prolonged war that would require millions of men, thus the famous recruitement campaign. He died when the ship on which he was travelling was sunk in 1916. Conspiracy theories abounded after his death – it was the work of a Boer and German spy, it was planned by the British Government who wanted him out of the cabinet, it was a Jewish conspiracy or finally the ship was blown up by Irish republicans who had planted explosives against the hull. Then again it was probably just a lucky shot by a U-Boat.

a large scale. It was not the more commonly known mustard gas, but chlorine gas. At first when the soldiers in the trenches saw the yellow-green cloud drifting across no-man's-land they believed that the Germans were advancing on them behind a smokescreen. So they held their positions and prepared for the attack, unaware that the onslaught would be on their lungs. They noticed a strange odour, a cross between pepper and pineapple and a peculiar metallic taste in their mouths.

Before they realised what was happening, all the men began to experience severe burning at the back of their throats and in their chests. They began to flee from the sinister cloud, many coughing violently and vomiting, their eyes burning as they stumbled half-blind across the muddy, pock-marked terrain. Hundreds of men, having taken just a few breaths of the gas, fell clutching their throats and never rose again. George McElroy reached safety, but not before he'd had severe exposure. His respiratory system badly aggravated, his time at the front was over almost before it began. Unable to cope with the vast numbers of wounded, the army decided to ship thousands home for treatment. By the time George McElroy departed for Dublin in May 1914, seventy thousand of his colleagues and thirty thousand of the enemy were dead, wounded or missing in action.

RISING

He spent months in treatment, much of it simply resting as any form of exercise after his exposure to chlorine gas quickly led to exhaustion. He was keen to return to service, and as soon as the toxins had been washed from his system he was reassigned to his regiment and waited for the call to return to the front.

But for the soldiers stationed in Dublin in early 1916, battle was a great deal closer than they could have imagined. On Easter Monday, 24 April, word began to filter through of a number of disturbances around Dublin. Nationalist rebels had seized certain strategic points around the city and the following day the soldiers were called upon to quell the insurrection. George McElroy marched out with his fellow soldiers sharing an air of confusion about what exactly was going on. But when he realised the enemy were his own countrymen he drew the line. Risking serious retribution from his commanders, he refused to fire on his fellow Irishmen, even if he disagreed with their politics.

He got off relatively lightly, probably because the army's losses at the front were already so great they couldn't afford to put too many of their own behind bars. Instead he was refused permission, at least for the moment, to return to active duty and sent to the British Military Garrison in Tipperary Town, where four thousand men were sitting and waiting for the call to action and their chance to fight the German Army. Yet the next time he went into battle would not be on his feet or riding a motorcycle, but in a machine that most people of the era had never even seen.

ACES HIGH

By 1916, the battle for control of the skies was in full swing. But these men were no ordinary soldiers. The image that was proudly painted of them was that of knights of the air, doing solitary and deadly battle with each other against the immense canvas of the sky. Newspapers eagerly recounted their heroic deeds, dramatic sketches showed them diving and looping as they blazed machine guns at each other, children even swapped trading cards adorned with images of the different planes in action. Governments on all sides used these images as promotional tools to sell war bonds, those who lived long enough would sign autographs for adoring girls and excited children, publishers sought them out to write books about their derring-do. In contrast to the grim, bleakness of the trench warfare, the battle of the skies filled peoples' minds with romantic images of heroism and chivalry.

For the previous decade the fascination of flight was to most young boys and men akin to the present day prospect of travelling into space. To be able to climb into a machine and take to the skies, soaring high above the earth and whirling like a bird filled many an imagination day and night. Children with their arms outstretched horizontally ran around schoolyards everywhere miming the drone of the early aeroplane engines.

But in the early days of World War I, aerial combat was little more than a joke. Planes were first used purely for reconnaissance, enemy aircraft often passing each other as they went to take a look at the other's troop movements, the pilots often known to have waved at one another in greeting; that didn't last long. They soon resorted to carrying handguns, manoeuvring close enough and then trying to shoot a hole in a propeller or a fuel tank. Buffeting winds and the vibration of the early engines made any success next to impossible.

Machine guns were fitted to the aircraft, but again they had limited success as the key angle of fire was straight ahead and the guns couldn't shoot in this direction as they'd hit the propeller. The solution came in 1915 when the Dutch aviator Anthony Fokker, who owned an aviation company in Germany, invented a mechanism that allowed the gun to fire synchronously through the whirling blades. In the first weeks of its use, the British pilots were shocked when they realised that the German planes could simply point the nose of their aircraft at them and fire with deadly effect. The Allies nicknamed his mechanism The Fokker Scourge and eventually developed a similar design of their own.

By 1916 the names of many of the aces (pilots with five

victories) had entered the public consciousness. The likes of Edward Mannock, Rene Fonck of France and of course Baron von Richthofen, the famous Red Baron of Germany, were chatted about in pubs, factories and over the family dinner table. Dads regularly read out the tales from newspapers and magazines to the pricked ears of his gathered family. And soldiers garrisoned in barracks pored over the same articles, often bemoaning their prospects in the filth and horror of the trenches while these fly-boys got all the glory and the girls.

The stories fascinated George McElroy as he lay in his bunk in Tipperary Garrison, dreaming of what it would be like to soar into combat. The fact that the life expectancy of a new pilot was a mere eleven days didn't trouble him unduly. The possibility of entering this entirely new frontier of battle overcame any qualms he might have had.

REACHING FOR THE SKY

In late 1916, McElroy put in a request to transfer to the newest division of the British armed forces, the Royal Flying Corps. Clearly his previous indiscipline had been forgotten, as much through necessity as actual forgiveness. The Germans were taking down planes almost faster than the British could build them and with each aircraft lost it inevitably meant a life lost. The chances of surviving a crash during a battle were preposterously low.

The ongoing Somme offensive was a huge drain on manpower, including trained pilots, and that summer they even decided to drop the requirement that recruits to the RFC should have a flying licence.

The British needed new blood and they needed it fast.

McElroy was transferred to Upavon Airfield in the south west of England, about twenty miles from the cathedral town of Salisbury. Upavon is known as the birth-place of the RAF as this is where its forerunner, the RFC, had its main base and training school.

He would receive just a few months' training. All the pilots agreed that the initial part of training was a total waste of time. The men spent anything up to a month sitting in classrooms learning the inner workings of their engines, how to repair their weapons (this was totally impossible in flight) and how to stitch the canvas, which might have been helpful if they ever got to take a camping trip, but wasn't going to serve much purpose when engaging an enemy, guns blazing, at high speed in mid-air.

George McElroy passed these initial tests with flying colours and was officially granted a cadetship. He began his flight training in an Avro 504, the standard trainer plane throughout the war.

The first few flights were simply as a passenger, indeed trainees were observed keenly in these to see the psychological effect of leaving the earth behind, an experience to which humans were completely unaccustomed until a few years beforehand. If they seemed to handle the strange and sometimes frightening sensation reasonably well they moved quickly on to dual handling of the flight. Pilots often froze at this stage and the instructor commonly solved the problem by hitting them on the head with whatever was handy, like a wrench, rapidly jerking them back to life, albeit with a thunderous headache.

After as little as two hours dual flying time, the pilots were expected to go solo, staying up for as much as twenty minutes circling the airfield. Getting airborne was the easy bit, landing was precarious. One of the Avro 504's design features was a type of 'ski' or 'skidder' that ran between the wheels, its purpose to prevent the plane nose-diving during landing as so many trainees landed with the tail too high causing the propeller to hit the ground, destroying the plane along with anyone who happened to be in the trajectory of the rapidly-dismantling bits of propeller.

The casualty numbers among cadets were astounding. Twenty crashes a day at each airfield were common and five cadets died daily along with many others being seriously injured. During the course of the war, eight thousand cadets were killed.

Having completed his basic training, (twenty hours flying time and thirty landings) George McElroy was moved on for 'higher training'. This could involve climbing to altitudes of seven thousand feet in aircraft constructed mainly of wood and canvas and could only reach speeds of 100 mph. Gunnery training also commenced, with pilots expected to shoot at a canvas targets pulled by a tow-plane, many of which regularly returned with holes in their rudders as testament to the inaccuracy of the trainees.

But by August, McElroy was judged proficient enough to be awarded his wings. He would cross the English Channel for the first time in two years. On his previous visit he'd been riding a motorcycle. This time he'd be riding his luck in a flimsy bi-plane thousands of feet above the ground.

NUMBER 40 SQUADRON

His destination was Camblain l'Abbé Airfield near the town of Bruay, which was just a few miles from the Belgian border. It was the current base of 40 Squadron under the leadership of the famous Edward Mannock, Britain's highest scoring ace of World War I.

Mannock immediately took McElroy under his wing, from which he undoubtedly benefited enormously, as his flying skills on arrival were basic, to say the least. He was given a French biplane fighter called a Nieuport 17, a popular plane with the pilots, but not one that he took to. With Mannock as formation leader, 40 Squadron made several successful sorties over German lines, but McElroy failed to score a single victory. He told Mannock that he found the Nieuport unresponsive and lacking in stability.

THE ACE FROM BALLINCOLLIG

Although George McElroy is officially Ireland's greatest WWI fighter pilot, Britain's highest-scoring ace, Edward Mannock, was probably born in Ballincollig in Cork to British parents. In fact his Irish roots are why he earned the nickname 'Mick'. From a working-class background, his parents moved to India when he was young and then to England. As an adult he was a passionate socialist and member of the Labour Party, which didn't initially sit well with the middle-class background of most of his comrades. But his skills as a pilot, his courage and his eventual leadership soon changed all that. He admitted to being terrified in battle, particularly of burning to death, and carried a pistol in the event he needed to finish himself off. He hated the Germans deeply and was initially merciless, revelling in their horrific deaths. Later, on a visit to the front, seeing their charred bodies changed his view. He was credited with sixty-one victories (some versions claim seventy-three) before his plane was hit over German trenches and burst into flames. He never had to use his pistol – in an effort to survive he leapt from the plane before it crashed. Sadly, his body was never definitively identified, although the remains of a downed British airman who was possibly Mannock were buried in a spot close to the crash site and later re-interred in Laventie Cemetery in northern France. During his career he was awarded the Distinguished Service Order medal with 2 Bars, the Military Cross with Bar. He was also awarded the Victoria Cross posthumously.

His squadron leader obviously had faith in his protégé as he persisted with him throughout the autumn of 1917, but still without success. Finally he was assigned a new plane, this time an S.E.5a, a British plane that would be instrumental in regaining superiority in the skies. This aircraft was much preferred over the well-known Sopwith Camel, which handled so poorly that pilots said it had been responsible for more deaths than German fighters. The S.E.5a was much faster than any plane available, including the German planes, which gave it a crucial advantage. Its handling was also far superior to earlier models, its engine more reliable and it gave the pilot almost unimpeded vision.

When McElroy climbed on board the single-seater plane and took off, it was like sitting back into his favourite armchair. He felt completely at ease at the controls and as Christmas 1917 drew near, George McElroy finally had the gift he'd dreamed about for over a year.

METEORIC RISE

Just a few days after sitting down to his Christmas dinner, McElroy went in search of the enemy in his new plane. He didn't have far to look. Flying over Drocourt, just ten miles from base he spotted and engaged a German plane on a bombing run, making several hits before the plane plummeted to the ground at 11.20 am on 28 December.

One of the great skills he possessed was his marksmanship and it would be estimated later in his career that on average he would fire only 130 rounds per mission, a tiny number for a machine gun.

A fortnight later he destroyed a Rumpler Taube, a common German aircraft, and then had a second success before the month was out. His confidence was growing at an exponential rate, as were his aerial kills. Early in February he brought down three more two-seater German aircraft and could officially call himself an 'Ace'. His comrades had another term for him – 'Deadeye Mac'. He was so christened due to his extraordinary marksmanship and his fearlessness in combat.

His skills, courage and aggressive tactics drove him still further. By 18 February he had chalked up a total of eleven victories including a remarkable eight successes inside a week. Two of his victims were German observation balloons, a key target for the British and their allies as they operated as today's equivalent of satellite intelligence, easily reporting troop numbers, positions and movements. At first glance they were an easy target, but the reality was quite the opposite as the baskets suspended beneath them were equipped with powerful, long-range AA guns concealed behind an armoured screen. The gunner could easily hit an incoming plane long before the aircraft's guns were in range.

On 19 February McElroy was transferred to 24 Squadron which only employed single-seater aircraft, designed exclusively for combat, making it the world's first aerial fighter squadron. His talents and record suggested he would fit in well with his new comrades. He was also promoted to Lieutenant and given the responsibility of patrol leader. It took him two days to prove his worth, taking down an enemy single-seater Albatros.

His tally began to grow at an impressive rate, audacious sorties among enemy aircraft, displaying fearlessness and often recklessness as he swooped and twirled amid the chaos of screaming engines and thundering machinegun fire. In his brief six weeks with 24 Squadron he brought down thirteen single-seater German fighters as well as five observation two-seaters. His bravery and his results did not go unnoticed and on 26 March his was awarded the Military Cross for 'conspicuous gallantry and devotion to duty' and for 'setting a magnificent example of courage and initiative'.

Then on 7 April his career very nearly came to an abrupt end. On approach to the airfield while returning from a mission, the wheels of his plane struck the top of a tree sending the plane in a near dive towards the earth. He managed to pull up enough to avoid a direct nosedive, but his plane crash-landed and he was wounded seriously enough to require two months convalescence, an eternity for these pilots.

It may have been some consolation to him that while recovering in hospital he was awarded the Military Cross First Bar for among other things, attacking a squad of four enemy planes and bringing one down and on the same mission engaging another plane and sending it crashing to earth in flames.

Towards the end of June he was passed fit to return to duty and re-assigned back to 40 Squadron where he would renew his friendship with Mick Mannock, who by now had christened him George 'McIrish' McElroy. He simply took up where he'd left off, destroying two balloons and a fighter in a few days and bringing his tally to thirty. He was now among the most talked-about aces in the war.

At a dinner attended by most of the squadron in June, a fellow pilot recalled Mannock berating his friend for flying too low when carrying out low-altitude operations, where planes became an easy target for ground fire. It's unlikely the young Irishman took his advice on board, but the irony is that Mannock seems to have ignored the very warnings he was dishing out.

THE FINAL DAYS

The summer days of July were upon him. But George McElroy would never see August. On the first day of the month he destroyed three more planes and continued in a similar vein over the coming weeks. His courage and leadership were again officially recognised when he was honoured with the Distinguished Flying Cross, the citation noting that he 'never hesitated to engage the enemy regardless of their being, on many occasions, in superior numbers'.

He had another close call on 20 July, when in mid-combat his engine started to vibrate violently and he was forced to break off his attack. Smoke started to stream from the plane and in seconds flames began to burst from under the engine hood. Desperately trying to prevent the fire spreading to the fragile timber and canvas, he attempted a downward spiral at high speed but this was ineffective and he was forced to pull up and carry out another crash landing. His skill saved him yet again and he was thrown clear of the burning aircraft, miraculously escaping with only scratches and minor bruising. He was badly shaken, but had been handed a clear warning, one which his often foolhardy nature would force him to ignore.

A week later he received a terrible emotional scar to add to those he'd gained in battle when he heard the news that his closest friend and mentor Edward Mannock was missing in action, presumed dead. It was commonplace to lose fellow pilots, often before anyone even had a chance to get to know them, but no previous loss had inured George McElroy to his friend's demise. He was heartbroken.

By now George McElroy's tally was up to forty-six, having gained sixteen victories in July. This achieved in just forty weeks' service and was a record that was never surpassed. He was also awarded a Second Bar Military Cross, one of only ten pilots to receive this in the course of the war.

On the last day of July he took off on what would be his final mission, attacking and destroying a German Hannover C over the village of La Chapelle-d'Armentières, which was in German hands. His tally had now reached forty-seven and would climb no higher. Having returned briefly to base to refuel, he set off again to the same region, apparently flying low over enemy positions and attacking the ground troops and artillery with machine gun fire. Whether he was in search of some form of atonement for the loss of his friend, nursed a death wish, or was simply carrying out another audacious act of courage, his final low-level flight almost precisely mimicked Mannock's. He never returned.

A couple of days later a German plane flew over the British lines and the pilot dropped a note confirming that George McElroy had been killed by ground fire. Two days later he would be decorated for the fifth time, but on this occasion his medal would be awarded posthumously. The citation that accompanied the Bar to the Distinguished Flying Cross would commend his 'brilliant achievements, keenness and dash have at all times set a fine example and inspired all who came in contact with him.' Ironically, it would also praise his courage in attacking at low altitudes.

It was said of George McElroy by a fellow pilot that, 'He truly stands as a leader and is worthy of being remembered as the hardest fighter of the "fighting Irish".'

IRELAND'S GREATEST FIGHTER PILOT

George McElroy was buried in Laventie Cemetery; his grave is in the same row and just a few metres away from the probable grave of his best friend, Edward 'Mick' Mannock. His simple white tombstone bears the inscription:

> *In Memory of*
> *Captain G. E. H. McELROY*
> *M C and 2 Bars, D F C and Bar*
> *Royal Air Force*
> *who died age twenty-five on 31 July 1918*
> *Son of Samuel McElroy, B.A., and Ellen McElroy, of Donny-brook School, Dublin.*
> *Remembered with honour*
> *LAVENTIE MILITARY CEMETERY, LA GORGUE*

There are no memorials to George McElroy in Ireland. Like many of those who fought on the British side in World War I, the bravery of this Irishman from the south was ignored for generations by successive governments. Only in recent years has the courage and sacrifice of the Irish who fought in World War I been acknowledged at memorial ceremonies. Also in recent years, the War Memorial Gardens at Islandbridge in Dublin have been beautifully restored. In the granite bookrooms within the gardens you will find inscribed the names of all 49,400 young Irish men who died. Among the finest of them was George 'McIrish' McElroy.

William Melville

Famed detective and the first 'M' – MI5's first Spymaster

SNEEM AND BEYOND

The statue of the Egyptian goddess Isis, presented to the tiny, picturesque village of Sneem by the people of Egypt, seems a little out of place as she stares out over the village, resplendent in the warm summer light. Nestling at the head of a small inlet on the southern side of Kerry's Iveragh peninsula and almost surrounded by rugged mountains on the landward side, the village is immediately engaging, not least because of the warmth of its welcome, but also because of its vividly colourful buildings and its equally colourful inhabitants, past and present, among whom was one William Melville.

Two squares joined by a bridge over the Sneem river seem to bustle constantly during the summer months with visitors come to admire its undeniable charms, belying the fact that its population totals just 279 people. Any of its hospitable pubs like Dan Murphy's Bar would seem at night to account for half this number. Like many of the other buildings in the village, Dan Murphy's bright pink exterior seems to have been one of the many the beneficiaries of a travelling paint salesman who unloaded all his stock of vivid, eye-popping colours at half-price.

Outside the pub sits 'The Stone Outside Dan Murphy's' worn smooth by the bottoms of countless courting couples over the decades and itself now famed in song.

> *Those days in our hearts we will cherish*
> *Contented although we were poor*
> *And the songs that were sung*
> *In the days we were young*
> *On the stone outside Dan Murphy's door*

From courting couples to Egyptian goddesses, everything in Sneem seems to have some memorial or sculpture to its memory. The village actually boasts the largest display of outdoor sculpture in Ireland. One commemorates Former President Cearbhall Ó Dálaigh who lived locally prior to his death in 1978 – Sneem was the venue for his state funeral. Isis stands near a sculpture park called 'The Way of the Fairies' recalling Ireland's megalithic heritage. A large, two-ton Panda sculpture donated by the People's Republic of China vies for attention with a tall steel 'cactus' presented by the Israeli President Herzog. In the grounds of St Michael's Church stands a large bronze statue of the risen Christ, in the north square sits a huge rock with a bronze plaque commemorating the visit of General de Gaulle in 1969 and in the south square stands the imposing figure of Sneem's Sean 'Crusher' Casey, the undefeated wrestling champion of the world, 1938 to 1947.

Yet nowhere it seems can one find any memorial to one of Sneem's most famous sons, William Melville, who would become one of the most famed and recognised detectives of his era in London's great metropolis and eventually become Britain's first spymaster and head of its secret service bureau, the first ever 'M' in fact, renowned from Ian Fleming's James Bond novels and the subsequent movies.

Melville's upbringing and family life provide few clues to the career that lay ahead. Born at Direenaclaurig Cross near Sneem on 25 April 1850, William was the eldest of three sons of James and Catherine Melville who owned a pub and bakery; the original building still operates as a popular pub, called the Blue Bull. Baptised in St Michael's Catholic Church, Melville attended the local national school and in his teenage years was reputedly one of the area's finest hurlers.

Sneem, like much of Ireland in those days, had lost many a son and daughter to emigration. And while these were enforced exiles, as he approached his twenties and despite his undoubted love of his hometown, William was beginning to feel like a big fish in a small pond and longed to escape the limitations of a life working in his father's bakery.

His departure from Sneem and his first steps into the world of police work have an aura of mystery about them befitting his later career – the story goes that he climbed aboard his pony and cart for his weekly journey to Killarney to collect supplies, waved farewell to his family and then simply vanished. The pony and cart were eventually noticed idling outside Killarney train station some hours later, by which time William was undoubtedly many miles away, staring out at the fields as the steam train chugged towards the port of Cork or Dublin, dreaming of a life of adventure wherever the wind in the sails of his ship would take him.

BAKER TO BOBBY

William Melville would eventually resurface at the age of twenty-two working as a baker in Lambeth, which in all likelihood wasn't the fulfillment of the dreams he'd imagined. Likely though that following in his father's footsteps was initially the only work he could find to sustain himself until an opportunity presented itself for betterment. London at that time must have seemed almost overwhelming to him, a vast metropolis that was considered one of the most important in the world with an ever-growing population of over three million people, in stark contrast to Sneem's tiny community.

London's burgeoning masses presented him with his first opportunity to make a career for himself as the growth in numbers brought with it the inevitable growth in criminality and in turn the need to combat this with a larger police force. While he'd been working as a baker, the Metropolitan Police had just endured its first ever police strike, its forces clamouring for better pay and conditions and more police – they were being overwhelmed in some areas and simply couldn't cope. Melville seized on the chance and joined up immediately after the strike's successful conclusion.

For his first six months he was stationed at what was probably the city's most famous station, Bow Street, which was subsequently to become the site of the premier London Magistrates' Court. He was assigned to patrol an area from Covent Garden to Holborn armed only with a truncheon and a whistle. His beat took him through the more upmarket Strand, which was then (and still is today) packed with theatres, many of them long since vanished like The Vaudeville, The Strand Musik Hall with its risqué burlesque show or The Olympic Theatre, which in 1872 featured a performance of one of Gilbert & Sullivan's early collaborations called 'Trial by Jury'.

The strains of light opera would have long faded from his ears by the time he reached Covent Garden and its bustling markets, and then moved beyond into the alleys of St Giles which was know then as The Rookeries, an English slang term for 'slum'. This area was a maze of narrow streets crammed with tenement buildings, drinking dens, brothels and workhouses, and at the time was just a stone's throw from the green fields that marked the city's boundary. London's 'pea-souper' fogs, evoked for atmosphere in so many a film about that era, were particularly common here as the yellowish smog was the result of burning soft coal, and such was the density of population of The Rookeries that their collective attempts to keep warm at times reduced visibility to a few yards. Perhaps Melville may have been cheered somewhat by the familiar accents he heard as this area was also called Little Dublin, it being home to 110,000 Irish people.

In fact 6 per cent of his colleagues were also Irish and they and all Metropolitan constables were paid between sixteen and eighteen shillings a week, which was a reasonable income for the time, but was thoroughly earned considering their job – they were expected to patrol their beat at an average pace of 2.5 mph, worked thirteen nights a fortnight and received just one week's leave per annum. And of course they existed in a world of considerable peril.

Melville was determined to not to walk the beat forever and indeed he took several steps up the promotional ladder over the following years and by 1879 had risen to the rank of Detective Sergeant in the Criminal Investigation Department or CID as it is still known today. The CID had been formed just a year before, replacing the

Detective Branch and was the first attempt to properly organise and co-ordinate criminal detection in the city. This was a much-sought-after posting as not only did CID detectives earn more, but the job was viewed with some glamour due mainly to the publicity they often received in the press.

1879 was also a busy year for him in another respect. In the course of his work he'd met and fallen in love with another Irish immigrant, Katherine Reilly from Co. Mayo, and that year they were married in St George's Catholic Church in Southwark on the south bank of the Thames. They moved into a relatively comfortable home in Lambeth, where newly-built houses were just beginning to sprout up from the green fields and marshlands.

He spent his next four years as an increasingly busy and successful detective and in 1883 Katherine gave birth to their first child, named Kate for her mother. It was also the year that, with his reputation and skills as an investigator garnering him a growing reputation, he was recruited into a newly-created section known as the SIB or Special Irish Branch, formed specifically to track down teams of Irish-American Fenian bombers who had been terrorising London since 1867, but whose activities peaked between 1883 and 1885 in what became known as The Dynamite War. The unit comprised twelve detectives, several of them Irish, recruited specifically because of their understanding of the Fenian way of thinking and their knowledge of the Irish language. The SIB was the forerunner of the modern Special Branch, 'Irish' being dropped when their remit was expanded to deal with potential threats from other foreign nationals, a day that wasn't so far away.

To some Irish people at the time, this marked Melville as a traitor to the cause of Irish freedom. Yet considered in the context of the age, he simply saw himself as trying to stop terrorists from killing innocent people. He was actually a fervent supporter of Home Rule for Ireland and at the time many Irish men and women believed they could maintain their national identity within the realm of the British Empire. Added to that, even within the independence movement there was division about the methods and effectiveness of the bombing campaign in Britain.

The Dynamite War was led and financed by Clan na Gael, a sister organisation to the Irish Republican Brotherhood, and by Jeremiah O'Donovan Rossa's 'Skirmishing Fund', money raised through expatriate Irishmen in New York for the purposes of bombing England. Many of the bombers themselves were Irish-Americans recently discharged from the Union Army at the end of the American Civil War and were thus skilled in the use of weapons, explosives and survival. Repeated attempts by the British Government to have O'Donovan Rossa extradited failed.

In 1882 there was just one bombing, but over the course of the following two years this escalated greatly with nineteen separate attacks. The bombings were generally not targeted at people, but rather at the symbols of British imperialism like the Houses of Parliament, The Tower of London, Whitehall, the offices of *The Times* and Scotland Yard itself, much to the embarrassment of the force. But they didn't limit themselves to these symbolic edifices, eventually striking at targets usually crowded with civilians like Victoria, Charing Cross and Paddington train stations, killing and injuring several people. Luckily though, the casualties were relatively light considering the location of the bombs.

Melville and his colleagues in the Special Irish Branch had a very early success when they arrested five men in Birmingham and London including Tom Clarke, who was to go on to be one of the leaders of the 1916 Rising and the first of the signatories of the Proclamation of the Irish Republic. Clarke (operating under the alias 'Henry Wilson') had honed his skills as a bomber while working as an explosives and demolition operative on Staten Island in New York and was just about to put his skills to use in the demolition of London Bridge when the SIB swooped and arrested him along with four colleagues. He would be tried and sentenced to penal servitude for life in May 1883, eventually serving fifteen years.

Because the bombers were mainly based in the US, they regularly travelled back and forth between the two countries, making it extremely difficult to keep track of them or maintain any sort of surveillance. To avoid detection, republicans would often enter and leave Britain through European ports. It was decided to extend the watch on points of entry to the Channel ports in France. Katherine Melville had just given birth to their second child, William, when his father was granted the assignment of organising the surveillance of the French port of Le Havre, a mission that would last four years and ultimately prove very beneficial to the Kerryman.

Down the centuries many risings, rebellions, plots and schemes to uproot the British from Irish soil have collapsed because of paid informers. And while the SIB did occasionally manage to secretly plant the informant into the ranks of the bombers, often the secrecy was so great within CID that despite the relatively small size of the unit, most detectives had little or no idea what their colleagues were up to, or in other words the left hand didn't know what the right hand was doing, seriously diminishing the effectiveness of CID. This was compounded by the fact that many of the detectives' ambitions and the associated politicking often clouded their devotion to their ultimate goal of catching bombers, so an individual detective's career often took priority over getting results. Melville was by no means immune to this as his later career would reveal. Clearly extremely ambitious, he was now about to become involved in a mind-boggling plot that would draw groans of disbelief were it a modern-day Hollywood movie. But then, truth is so often stranger than fiction.

THE JUBILEE PLOT TO ASSASSINATE
QUEEN VICTORIA

The dynamite war subsided in 1886, by which point a hundred people had been killed – including some would-be bombers who'd accidentally blown themselves up in a London park – many more injured and ten buildings demolished. But the bombings did have the effect of terrorising the British public and of generating anti-Irish feeling, fuelled also by newspapers like the avidly pro-Tory *Times*, which regularly depicted Irish people and their leaders in a less than charitable fashion. Despite the fact that Charles Stewart Parnell's Parliamentary Party had no links to militant republicans and was devoted to achieving its aims through peaceful means, they were bitterly opposed by the Tories, who were fervently against any Home Rule Bill for Ireland.

Early in 1887, *The Times* published a series of articles entitled 'Parnellism and Crime'. These were based on a number of letters that apparently revealed that Parnell himself had personally approved of the infamous 'Phoenix Park Murders', when the Chief Secretary for Ireland, Thomas Henry Burke, and Lord Frederick Cavendish had been brutally stabbed to death in Dublin's Phoenix Park by a radical Republican group called The Invincibles. The *Times*' 'source' was a man called Richard Pigott, a Dublin journalist who himself had been an Irish nationalist, but who now opposed Parnell with something approaching hatred. Ultimately a commission of enquiry proved that Pigott had himself forged the letters. (Among the evidence was his known tendency to misspell the word 'hesitancy', an error he repeated in the letters.) The case against Parnell collapsed and *The Times* had to pay him a settlement of £5,000, a huge sum at the time. When Parnell resumed his seat in the House of Commons two years later in 1889 he would receive a standing ovation led by the then Prime Minister William Gladstone. Pigott would commit suicide in Madrid later that year.

This plot would ultimately fail, but the appetite for discrediting Irish MPs and destroying the Home Rule aspiration was clearly very real.

With the memory of the Dynamite War still fresh in the minds of the British public, in 1887 the police leaked information to the press that they had uncovered a plot to assassinate Queen Victoria on the occasion of her Golden Jubilee celebrations, which were to take place in just a few days time. 'The Jubilee Plot' had apparently been concocted by Clan na Gael and involved blowing up Westminster Abbey during Victoria's Thanksgiving Service, in one strike wiping out the monarch and the entire British Cabinet.

The main architect of the plot was General Francis Millen, a Tyrone-born republican whose funding and support was to be provided by Clan na Gael in New York. Two volunteers, Thomas Callan and Michael Harkins, would travel by steamer a few days before the Jubilee and detonate the bomb with dynamite provided by Fenians based in Britain.

What the New York Republicans didn't know about Millen was that for twenty years he'd been working as a paid informer for British Intelligence. The most extraordinary fact, however, is that it was Melville's colleagues in the British Secret Service who had in fact dreamed up the entire pantomime and had personally received the stamp of approval of the then Tory Prime Minister Lord Salisbury. At some point during the episode, Millen and his coconspirators would introduce themselves to members of Parnell's Irish Parliamentary Party in Westminster. Soon after the fake Jubilee Plot would be 'exposed' through press leaks and the Irish MPs would be linked in the minds of the entire British establishment with the terrorists, thus putting the final nail in the coffin of Parnell's Home Rule campaign.

The Special Branch were made aware of the 'Jubilee Plot' by the Secret Service, but not, of course, that it was fake. This was to ensure the plot didn't actually become a reality. But naturally the Secret Service couldn't reveal that the entire thing was an exercise in political chicanery that they'd dreamt up to discredit another politician. Neither could they tell the Special Branch that Millen was in fact working for them. As a result of this Melville and his colleagues expended an inordinate amount of time and energy in pursuit of Millen and his co-conspirators.

The only problem was that in Millen's enthusiasm for the project, it took on a life of its own and became a genuine threat. A team of republicans was organised in the US, money and explosives arranged for collection in Britain and the plan set in motion. Luckily for the British the bombers turned out to be somewhat less than adept and apparently missed the ship on which they'd planned to travel, only arriving in Liverpool on the actual day of the Jubilee celebrations, far too late to carry out the attack.

Undeterred they resolved to remain in Britain and carry out further missions for their cause. But from the moment they arrived they were watched by the SIB and in fact were allowed to move freely around the country for months, exposing many of their contacts along the way. The would-be bombers, Callan and Harkins, were eventually arrested and sentenced to fifteen years in prison and Melville in particular was singled out for praise in his surveillance of Millen – *'with the greatest tact at Boulogne and by conducting numerous inquiries in London'.*

This praise in itself seems strange as Millen 'escaped' back to New York. He was conveniently found dead in his study two years later 'in mysterious circumstances'. It is known that the SIB and Melville were made aware at some point that the 'Jubilee Plot' was a concoction of British Intelligence. The Official Secrets Act didn't exist at the time, so it might be presumed that either because of personal ambition or because of pressure from his peers, Melville was unwilling to blow the whistle on a government plan to subvert the democratic process and destroy the Home Rule Bill, something he keenly supported. At best this decision, and some of those he would make later in his career, were morally ambiguous.

The real 'Jubilee Plot', that is, the one to discredit Parnell, would ultimately fail because of its own complexity and the straitjacket of secrecy it demanded and perhaps Melville simply decided that its failure was sufficient. Revealing its true nature would certainly not benefit him in any way, the Home Rule debate would continue and after all, he was not a politician but a policeman.

But one thing was certain, the intelligence community's dark world of 'Black Ops' had begun.

MELVILLE BRIEFLY CROSSES PATHS WITH JACK THE RIPPER

By 1888, Katherine and William Melville had produced two more children, James and Celia, both born in France where he was still stationed. The preceding year, London had been horrified by the hideous murders and mutilations of at least five prostitutes in the Whitechapel area – the infamous Jack the Ripper case. One of the five principal suspects was an Irish-American quack doctor called Francis Tumblety, a man with an outspoken hatred of women who used to keep female body parts, mostly uteri, on display in jars of formaldehyde in his London apartment.

On 28 November 1888 he fled London under the alias Frank Townsend with the intention of taking a ship, *La Bretagne*, from Le Havre, where of course Melville was stationed. Various accounts, including Melville family recollections, have Melville in hot pursuit of the suspect and it has even been suggested that he all but captured Tumblety, only to be left frustrated by French bureaucrats who insisted that Melville didn't have the correct documentation to detain the man. Though much of this is speculation, and it is indeed also speculation that Tumblety was in fact the Ripper, the fact remains that the murders stopped after he had slipped through Melville's fingers and fled to New York.

'BOB'S YOUR UNCLE'

In 1887, the British Prime Minister was the aristocratic conservative Robert Gascoyne-Cecil, 3rd Marquess of Salisbury, who duly appointed his nephew Arthur James Balfour as Minister for Ireland. There was much hilarity among the press when the inexperienced Arthur referred to the Prime Minister as 'Uncle Bob', thus giving rise to the phrase 'Bob's your uncle', meaning that having the Prime Minister as one's uncle is a guarantee of success.

TRAGEDY AND PROMOTION

Before Christmas that year Melville was recalled to London and one of his first assignments was to protect the Shah of Persia during his state visit, a task that would repeatedly fall to him in the years ahead and one that would benefit his profile greatly. An illustration from that year shows the Shah in the company of members of the Royal Family enjoying a concert in the Royal Albert Hall while in the background stands a watchful figure who bears a striking resemblance to Melville.

But tragedy was just around the corner. At the age of just thirty-three, his wife Katherine contacted pneumonia and died at their home in Nursery Lane, Brixton, early in 1890. The irony of their address probably wasn't lost on Melville, who was left not just devastated, but having to nurse four children all under the age of seven.

Melville's undoubted strength of character saw him through and he carried on his police work with equal vigour, its intensity most likely serving as a welcome distraction from his grief. He was rewarded with his promotion to the rank of Inspector in 1891.

His improved position is reflected in the census of early 1891 which reveals he was in a financial position to own a house in Lambeth sufficiently large that he could take lodgers – a widowed 'tie-maker' and her five-year-old son. The other interesting thing to note from the document is that on the night the census was taken he also registered one Amelia Foy who was listed as a 'Visitor', born in Guernsey and 'Living on own means'. As it happens Amelia Foy was a widow of a former colleague of Melville's and just a couple of years younger than him. Clearly their similar predicaments drew them to each other and whether for convenience or through genuine affection, Amelia agreed to marry William and take on the responsibility of his four children.

It was an eventful couple of years and the sun hadn't yet set on 1891. In fact that year saw the seeds sown for an episode that would grow into one of the strangest conspiracies in British police history.

INSPIRING WORK

The great novelist Joseph Conrad would write a novel in 1907 called 'The Secret Agent' which featured a detective called Inspector Heat who was on the trail of anarchist bombers. There can be little doubt that Conrad's character was at least part inspired by Melville as besides various traits they shared, Inspector Heat uses a line of Melville's word for word: 'We know the whereabouts and movements of all these fellows and we can always put our hands on them when we want them'.

THE WALSALL PLOT

For a number of years many European countries had endured the terror of anarchism, which in this context was a movement of radical, often violent, left-wing individuals and groups who wished to overthrow the monarchies and governments of Europe and replace them with a new communist order. Indeed over the next decade anarchists would be responsible for the killing of the kings and queens of Portugal, Austria, Hungary and Russia. France, Spain, Germany and any other states also suffered at the hands of these violent individuals, and while their targets were often specific government figures of members of royal families, their attacks were frequently indiscriminate, causing the deaths of completely innocent bystanders – a pattern which still prevails today in acts of terrorism around the world.

At the time Britain was the only country in Europe that had no immigration restrictions, which made it a natural place of refuge for many anarchists fleeing capture from Europe. This made Britain extremely unpopular on the continent, a grievance that was aired regularly by visiting diplomats and in the European press.

Pressure grew on Melville and the Special Branch (the 'Irish' sobriquet had been dropped by now as the Branch's remit began to widen) to apprehend these fugitives, who had virtually no restrictions on their movement around the country. Miraculously it seemed, no sooner had the clampdown been demanded than a group of anarchists were identified and arrested in January 1892.

An initial arrest of a suspected anarchist, Joe Deakin, was made in Tottenham Court Road on a charge of making bombs. Under interrogation Deakin named six other 'anarchists', including a Frenchman named Auguste Coulon. Melville immediately travelled to Walsall where the ring was based and arrested four of the men. A fifth was apprehended in London. Auguste Coulon mysteriously avoided capture. At their initial court appearance it was stated that the Special Branch had uncovered information *'with reference to what he might call a widespread conspiracy throughout the country.'*

In reality, while the men may have had slight anarchist interests, there was no real evidence that they had either the skill or the equipment to manufacture a bomb. All the police recovered was a bunch of European anarchist publications, what was described as a 'plaster-cast of a bomb' and a few sketches that might be interpreted as bomb designs. Not a single ounce of explosive was uncovered.

Another man who'd been arrested and was subsequently released, claimed soon after that he'd been paid by the Special Branch to fabricate evidence against the men and during their trial several of the accused made the claim that the entire episode had been a police plot. But in the climate of fear that Britain might become another of the victims of anarchist terror, the trial was anything but fair and the men received sentences of between five and ten years each.

A year later, Melville would be appointed Commander of Scotland Yard's Special Branch and when he dismissed a veteran sergeant, Patrick McIntyre, the aggrieved detective immediately went to the press and claimed that the would-be bombers were telling the truth – that Melville had in fact staged the entire scheme in response to pressure from his superiors to demonstrate Britain's intolerance of the anarchist movement.

All of this was denied and accepted by the press and public and Melville's star rose to new heights. It would be eighty years before the mysterious Auguste Coulon would be revealed, on the official release of secret papers, as an *agent provocateur* in the employ of Melville and the Special Branch. From the off he'd been paid directly from police funds to encourage the so-called bombers to interest themselves in anarchist methods and philosophy.

Although it was partially successful in its aims, and Britain was no longer seen as a sanctuary for anarchists, it gives us a glimpse of William Melville's occasionally unsound ethics. Although personal human rights weren't afforded such a level of importance then as now, Melville was clearly of the belief that the end justified the means and was unwilling to question how far a government's rights extend over those of an individual in pursuing its own national interest.

Nevertheless his name was soon heard with trepidation by genuine anarchists throughout Europe. And though many still sought refuge in Britain, they did so in the knowledge that William Melville was on a quest to flush them from their hiding places.

ARRESTS AND FAME

The same year that the Walsall Plot was being 'uncovered', a genuine and famously violent anarchist called 'Ravachol' had been waging a war of terror in Paris. French police finally captured him outside the Café Very. In what gives us a clue to the warped mentality of these men, his associates took their revenge not on the authorities, but by bombing the Café Very while innocent Parisians were dining within. One person died and several others were injured.

The bombers, the hump-backed Theodule Meunier and Jean-Pierre Francois, fled to London to evade capture. Melville wasted no time in tracking down Francois but it would be April the following year before Meunier was located. Well aware of the value of publicity in the cause to spotlight police successes, several members of the press were present when Melville made a dramatic public arrest of Meunier in London's Victoria Station. Press reports describe how the fleeing man tried to drag Melville under the wheels of a train before finally being restrained. At this point, he yelled out (or at least it was so dramatically reported by the press),

'To fall into your hands, Melville! You, the only man I feared,

and whose description was engraved on my mind!'

Meunier was extradited to France where he was sentenced to penal servitude for life and he would die unrepentant on one of France's infamous penal colonies. Not only was Melville now becoming a household name in Britain, but he had also gained the admiration of the French authorities.

Barely a month later his attention turned to Italian anarchists Giuseppe Farnara aged forty-four and his youthful accomplice Francesco Polti, just eighteen. Melville arrested them, having uncovered their plan to blow up the Royal Exchange in London. The motivation for their crime seems laughable in today's context – it was to be in revenge for the annual invasion of Italy by British tourists! Farnara would later state that he desperately wanted to kill Melville as he had been responsible for the arrest of so many of his comrades. To anarchists throughout Europe he was now one of the most well-known and feared of policemen.

ROYAL PERFORMANCE

By the mid-1890s William Melville was almost a household name in Britain. The public appetite for crime-related stories was satiated by an ever-eager press in the way that Hollywood now tries to bring us into that shadowy world through movies. This celebrity extended

THE HONOURABLE MR MELVILLE

Honours bestowed on Melville in the course of his career included Member of the Order of the British Empire (MBE), Member of the Royal Victorian Order, Chevalier of the Order of Dannebrog, Order of Christ, Order of the Crown of Italy, Officer de la Legion d'Honneur, Commander of the Order of Isabel la Catolica, Chevalier of the Order of Francis Joseph of Austria and Knight of the Order of St Silvester of the Holy Roman Empire.

even to Europe. He had lived on the continent, spoke fluent French and was therefore a popular subject for Parisian journalists– and also because of Melville's apprehension of famed French anarchists. Upon meeting him in 1894, a French journalist no doubt expecting a hardened British copper, wrote with surprise of his demeanour that *'he did not look at all fierce or at all like a typical policeman'*.

In Britain he also became known to the public by the nickname 'The King's Detective' due to the regularity with which he was assigned the task of overseeing security for visiting royals and diplomats. There was intense diplomatic activity throughout Europe at the time and Scotland Yard was under considerable pressure to provide the manpower for these operations. This was considered a prestigious assignment, but given the number of royal assassinations in Europe during this period and the everpresent threat of indiscriminate anarchistic attacks, it was also considered highly dangerous. In fact during Queen Victoria's funeral in 1901, Melville and Gustav Steinhauer, head of the German secret police, would foil an assassination attempt on Kaiser Wilhelm II of Germany and King Leopold of Belgium.

He evidently left a lasting impression on a great number of these royals as, besides receiving an embarrassing number of state honours from a variety of European states, he was regularly presented with gifts – gold cuff links from King Alfonso of Spain, a silver cigar case from Princess Henry of Battenberg and most impressively a Fabergé Cigarette Case and watch from Czar Nicholas II of Russia – this can still be seen on display today at the Metropolitan Police Exhibition in London.

This extravagant gift was no doubt due to the close rapport that developed between the Czar and the detective. The young Nicholas (he was in his late twenties and shortly to marry) had come on a mission of education and diplomacy and having dined with all the appropriate British royals and having observed the democracy of the House of Commons in action, he secretly sought to experience the real London and personally asked Melville to essentially give him a guided tour of the city's seedier side. Melville took him and his entourage of personal bodyguards to a number of criminal haunts in east and west London, including those frequented by anarchistic anti-Czarists, but the young royal enjoyed himself immensely and came to no harm. Melville, however had to intervene on a number of occasions with his guards who apparently had itchy trigger fingers for anyone who so much as looked crooked at their ruler. Melville noted that the Russian secret servicemen *had to be taught that they could not shoot at sight and that suspects could not be carried off into the unknown without certain formalities'*.

'THE NAME'S REILLY, SIDNEY REILLY'

In 1896 Melville took his first real steps away from the relatively overt arena of the policeman and towards the covert world of international espionage. His encounters with the Czar had imbued him with a certain loyalty towards Russia and left him with no love of the many Bolshevik anarchist groups that were operating out of London. His investigations brought him into contact with a man called Shlomo Rosenblum who belonged to a Russian revolutionary group called the Society of Friends of Russian Freedom. Melville duly recruited Rosenblum who began to supply him with precise information regarding their activities. Unfortunately Rosenblum was a man of many parts, and the other role he was then playing, without Melville's knowledge, was that of a counterfeiter. When the Russian police started making enquiries about this, Melville became nervous that Rosenblum's links with his department would be blown. Using his contacts and experience, he pulled

LOCAL HERO

Although he is little known in Kerry now, his visit home in 1896 brought a flurry of interest from the local press. On 19 September, the Kerry Weekly Reporter and Commercial Advertiser reported, 'Chief Inspector Melville of Scotland Yard ... is a native of Sneem in this county, and has been there on holidays lately. He acted as one of the judges at the sports recently held in Sneem, and only left there for London on Monday week. Mr Melville was a promising athlete before he went to London many years ago, and was considered one of the best hurlers in South Dunkerron at the time. He takes a great interest in athletic sports, and is a prominent supporter of the Gaelic Athletic Society in London.' This report was taken up by all of the Kerry papers, and a week later was re-printed in the Police Review and Parade Gossip in London.

Rosenblum from cover and arranged to create a new identity for him, complete with official documents. Melville christened his recruit Sidney Reilly, and it was surely no co-incidence that 'Reilly' was his deceased wife's maiden name, though whether this indicated any sense of a brotherly relationship on Melville's part, we have no idea. It may simply have been the first name that popped into this head.

Sidney Reilly, as it turned out, was to go on to become one of the most celebrated spies in history and was believed to have been the inspiration for Ian Fleming's

James Bond character. Like Bond, he was educated, multi-lingual, debonair, a womaniser who lived the high life and was regarded as charismatic by all who fell under his spell. He lived like a gentleman, but being a master of disguise he could rapidly transform himself into a labourer, a journalist, a priest or whatever his mission demanded. Also like Bond he was a trained killer – and this is where their characters diverge somewhat – besides assassination in the course of his work, Reilly was also suspected to have killed for personal gain, though its unlikely Melville was aware of this at the time.

Over the next decade the two would maintain close links, with Reilly supplying the Special Branch with intelligence from within subversive groups both in Britain and abroad.

'M' IS FOR MELVILLE

He was fifty-three years old, respected by his colleagues and still enjoying the admiration of the public, when he suddenly announced his retirement from Scotland Yard. His friends in the force and the press were bemused. A few years after he'd stepped down the *Daily Express* continued to speculate, often wildly, as to what had become of him, even to the extent of suggesting he'd gone to work for the Russian Secret Service! Melville took the time to calmly refute this, writing to the Express: *'Like most people*

I am content to follow revolutionary movements through the medium of my daily paper and I am still in London, quietly enjoying what after thirty years of occasional excitement, I consider to be my well-earned retirement'.

Which of course was utter nonsense. In 1903 the War

HARRY HOUDINI

In 1900 a then little-known magician and escape artist called Harry Houdini embarked on a tour of Europe. Booked to appear in the Alhambra Theatre in Leicester Square, the manager eagerly agreed to Houdini's suggestion that they visit a police station where he would demonstrate his remarkable ability to escape from handcuffs, a publicity stunt he had frequently employed back in the US. With a horde of eager journalist in tow, they set off for Scotland Yard. Melville's initial scepticism was soon overcome as he watched Houdini repeatedly free himself from handcuffs with consummate ease. After the performance Melville befriended Houdini who reputedly taught him some lock-picking techniques, information he would later share when lecturing new recruits. A recent biography actually claims that Houdini was probably employed by the intelligence services on both sides of the Atlantic and that Melville recruited Houdini for espionage work in Germany. And while Houdini certainly toured Germany many times, including visiting The Krupp munitions factory, the evidence of him spying for the British or US is slim.

Office established the Directorate of Military Operations and they needed an experienced field operative to co-ordinate intelligence gathering. Melville was their man and he was given the task of general controller for British agents operating on foreign soil. He was also assigned a number of intelligence missions both at home and in Europe, reporting to a Captain Francis Davies under the alias of 'M', which would continue to be used as the alias for this department head up to the present day and is the title of the character of James Bond's superior in the series of movies, currently played by Judi Dench.

In December of that year he began his new career as a so-called 'Spymaster', working under the name 'William Morgan, General Agent' and operating out of an office in Victoria Street, which was a stone's throw from his old colleagues in Scotland Yard. Yet despite this, he managed to retain his complete anonymity and would later write: *'Few men at this time were better known in London than I was, yet during the five years I was there I never met any person going in or coming out who knew me.'*

THE D'ARCY AFFAIR

In the first decade of the twentieth century there was a sense of instability in Europe and Britain was not immune to this. The British were aware that their naval fleet was becoming outdated and in the event of a war, naval success was key to an island nation. The problem was that their entire fleet was coal-powered, which was impractical and inefficient. Oil-fuelled vessels required much less man-power and were easier to re-fuel. The only problem was, they had no oil supply.

At the time, the oil magnate William Knox D'Arcy had secured the rights to a major oil find in Turkey. The franchise for this was being sought separately by both the British and French governments. Determined to secure access to the oil, the British Government turned to Melville for help.

At the time D'Arcy was involved in negotiations with the French government's representative De Rothschild, on board his lavish private yacht in the Mediterranean.

Melville travelled to Paris where he renewed his acquaintance with the infamous Sidney Reilly. From here they journeyed south, no doubt scheming as they went as to how to usurp the French.

Quite what happened on the yacht remains a mystery, but legend has it that Reilly disguised himself as a Catholic priest, which got him past the considerable French security, and managed to separate D'Arcy from his host. Whatever offer he made or subterfuge he used worked a charm as the oil magnate granted the concession to the British. The company that would eventually emerge from this deal would be no less than BP.

SPY MANIA

Another man with deep Irish connections, nationalist Erskine Childers, was inadvertently to increase Melville's workload after 1903, with the publication of his novel *The Riddle of the Sands*. For a number of years Germany had been pursuing an aggressive policy of armament and had vastly increased its naval capabilities. Childers' novel imagined a plot whereby Britain was invaded by a German naval fleet of specially-constructed barges based in the Frisian Islands, which run the length of Germany's coast. The novel was spectacularly popular, not least with the Royal Navy who secretly sent two experts to the islands in the guise of wandering yachtsmen, to examine the feasibility of the plot. Winston Churchill actually credited the novel with the decision to establish three of Britain's principal naval bases on her east coast.

What it did for Melville and his colleagues was feed a spy mania that was running wild among the press and public. People saw spies everywhere and were happy to report them to the authorities. *The Daily Mail* stirred the paranoia when at one point it encouraged readers to take matters into their own hands: *'Refuse to be served by a German waiter. If he says he is Swiss, demand to see his passport.'* As a result Melville spent a great deal of his early years in the job chasing German ghosts. He pursued reports of mysterious figures photographing military installations, studying bays with binoculars or simply talking in a European tongue. Most of these unfortunates were simply birdwatchers or tourists.

The reality was that although Germany did have spies in Britain, the network was tiny. It was also being run by a former collaborator of his, Gustav Steinhauer, with whom he'd foiled the plot to kill the kings of Germany and Belgium.

Imaginary spies or not, the British did suspect that mobilisation for action was afoot in Germany and Melville was briefed to maintain the flow of intelligence. Over the coming years, through his long established network of agents he did manage to obtain detailed German mobilisation plans and also investigated German sympathies for the Boers, with whom Britain was currently at war, had extended to supplying military support. At one point he travelled to Germany himself in an effort to recruit more agents, these including the likes of a Courage Brewery Representative and other British businessmen who could travel freely about the country and supply information about German military and industrial capabilities.

MI5 & MI6

Frustrated at the somewhat half-hearted policy of the British Government towards espionage, Melville had been pressing for a more structured system and finally his wish was granted when in 1909 the War Office authorised the establishment of nineteen military intelligence departments MI-1 to MI-19, each to deal with a very specific aspect of national and international espionage. Only two of these survive today, MI-5, which deals with home based-terrorism and MI-6, the foreign section, in whose employ we find fictional superspy James Bond.

Given his experience in the field, Melville's section was assigned the task of unearthing German spies. Among the methods he employed was to establish a register of aliens, the first such in Britain and now common practice in almost every country on the planet. His investigations bore fruit in 1912 when Melville and his team identified what to the casual Londoner appeared to be a normal barbershop in Islington. It was run by Karl Gustav Ernst and in reality was the centre for Steinhauer's entire spy network.

Instead of pouncing, Melville had every visitor watched, identified and monitored. No doubt many an innocent Londoner who had simply popped in for a trim would have been forgiven for imagining he was being pursued by shadowy figures hiding in doorways! But the result for Melville was that over the coming months he identified twenty-one German spies. The moment war broke out the entire network was arrested, crippling German intelligence at a key moment. Melville's operation also allowed the Home Secretary, Reginald McKenna, to proclaim triumphantly in the House of Commons that '*Within the last twenty-four hours, no fewer than*

A German spy in Killarney

The first German spy to be executed in Britain during World War I was Karl Hans Lody who was eventually arrested in Killarney. Previously, while living in Edinburgh, he had sent a telegram to Germany via Sweden which read: 'Must cancel. Johnson very ill. Lost four days. Shall leave shortly. Charles', indicating that there were four ships being repaired at the dock and that there were several units about to head out to sea. The German submarine U-21 immediately received orders to attack and HMS Pathfinder became the first ship ever sunk by a torpedo fired from a submarine. Lody moved to Killarney and booked into the Great Southern Hotel. One evening while dining, several police officers approached and arrested him as a suspected German agent. Lody insisted that he was an American tourist, but the search of his room uncovered German coins, a notebook with the content of the first telegram, German addresses, drafts of his letters and a bus ticket from Edinburgh to the Firth of Forth. He was returned to London for trial, during which he refused to name any other agents, and was executed in the Tower of London, the first person to be executed there since a Jacobite rebel had been beheaded in 1747. The 'Hans Lody', a German destroyer was named after him.

twenty-one spies or suspected spies have been arrested, some of them long known to the authorities.'

Melville's efforts continued throughout World War I, when Germany desperately tried to re-build her network of agents. Some managed to get through disguised as journalists or businessmen from neutral countries, but by the end of the war thirty-five spies had been apprehended, and eleven of those were executed.

Despite being in his late sixties, Melville continued to work throughout the war, both in his position as a 'spymaster' and by putting his vast experience to use in the newly-established 'Spy School', which had been set up opposite the War Office in Whitehall. Melville lectured regularly at the school imparting his lifetime of experience including his lock-picking techniques (courtesy of Harry Houdini), breaking into houses and factories, gathering of evidence, long-term surveillance, the virtue of patience, lying convincingly and being willing to kill.

Unfortunately, the pace of his work took its toll on his health and he decided to retire at the end of 1917. His resignation letter written on New Year's Eve 1917 read: *'In leaving the Branch now, it is to me a very great personal satisfaction that I cannot remember a single enquiry or mission on which I have been engaged, which was not carried out in a satisfactory manner. Another source of satisfaction is that I have always felt I had the support and confidence of my Chiefs, and never had a wry word with any of them. I wish the Department all 'Good-Luck'.*

He never witnessed the outcome of the war, though he

would have been aware as he lay ill in his bed just two months later, his kidneys failing, that the tide was turning in favour of Britain and her Allies. He would have no doubt taken comfort from the fact that he'd played no small part in the likely victory.

He died after a surgical procedure in February 1918 at the age of sixty-eight. Unaware of his later career as a spy-master, *The Times* granted him an obituary in April 1918 entitled 'Death of a great detective'.

In many ways William Melville was an enigma, certainly from a modern Irish perspective. Some people might look back on him with disdain, an Irishman who not only worked for the British War effort, but in the early years of his career actually hunted down his own countrymen. This of course would be to adopt a terribly simplistic view.

Most Irish people now would have a firm idea of what their Irish identity means to them. Having said that, easy access to travel and the influence of foreign television, movies, books, magazines and newspapers would all tend to cloud what we would call our personal Irish identity. Most of us know or have met people with fervent nationalist leanings who are also rabid Liverpool or Arsenal supporters. Does this make them traitorous? Of course not.

In the context of the age it must be remembered that a great proportion of the population regarded themselves both as Irish and as British. Countless young Irishmen fought, and died, on the British side in World War I and when the 1916 Rising initially took place it was met with outright hostility by most Dubliners. William Melville in many respects was no different to these people. In fact, he continued to take a keen interest in all things Irish during his life in London (his house was named 'Kildare') and encouraged that interest in his children (see panel). He remained a GAA follower, was a supporter of the Home Rule campaign and his pursuit of Fenians must also be seen in context, as many Irish people, including Fenians themselves, were opposed to the bombing campaign in Britain.

SIR JAMES MELVILLE, KC

William Melville's third child, James, who was born in France, would himself go on to have a distinguished career as a leading barrister and then as a Labour MP. He became Solicitor General in Ramsay McDonald's Labour Government of 1930, the first Catholic to hold that position since the reformation. He served in WWI as an intelligence officer, reflecting his father's calling, but then ironically given his father's pursuit of anarchists, in 1911 he successfully defended two men accused of being involved in an anarchist murder and siege. Before he died at the age of forty-six he was the President of the Tyneside Irish Fellowship and closely involved in several other Irish organizations in London. His coffin was draped in the Irish tricolour.

When an exhibition about William Melville's life was held in Tralee County Museum in 2007 it brought protests from republicans, particularly because the museum is named after a nationalist volunteer who fought in the 1916 Rising – Thomas Ashe. The museum curator Helen O'Carroll expressed the alternate view that though they took very different paths in life, as a teacher Thomas Ashe would have welcomed the examination of a life as interesting as Melville's.

Whatever view one takes, there is no denying that William Melville's career as a policeman and then in the Secret Service was meteoric. He won the admiration not only of his superiors and colleagues in London, but also many of his contemporaries throughout Europe, and had he chosen to, he could have listed among his friends kings, queens, princes, diplomats and even a world-renowned escapologist.

From village baker to head of the British Secret Service – like Houdini, he'd performed quite an act of escapology himself.

John Philip Holland

Inventor of the modern submarine

SEASCAPE

Look out from pretty much anywhere in Liscannor and you'll see the same thing, the vast swell of the Atlantic Ocean. Beyond it, in the dreams of many a former resident of this tiny village in Co. Clare, lay the United States of America. And within that lay the potential fulfilment of their dreams or more simply in some cases, the potential fulfilment of their bellies, as they were often desperately poor and near to starvation.

In the mid-nineteenth century most people would have looked out at the ocean and watched as tall ships raised sails and pointed their prows at the setting sun carrying people over the waves to a new life.

But strangely, one resident of Liscannor quite likely dreamt of travelling to America not over the waves, but *under* them.

John Philip Holland was born on 24 February 1841, just four years before the beginning of the Great Famine, an event that would influence the political beliefs of a generation of Irish people far after its terrible ravages had passed over the country. His family would not be immune to the wave of post-famine nationalism that was slowly beginning to swell.

His father, John, worked for the United Kingdom Coastguard Service and was originally assigned in 1822, at the age of twenty-two, to the village of Ringabella, not far from Cork city. His first position was that of boatman and his work would have been part policeman, part intelligence officer and part lifeguard. He would have to maintain a constant lookout for smugglers, ships in distress, and later, keep an eye out for a possible French invasion force.

John Holland Senior was reassigned to Liscannor in the early 1830s and settled down happily in the small coastal community. Then in 1835, tragedy struck and his wife died. Dying young wasn't uncommon in those days and neither was the practice of staying single for very long, as it was simply considered practical for survival to exist as a family unit. So within the year he had remarried, to a local *cailín* called Mary Scanlan.

Within six years they had two children, both boys, the second of whom, John Philip, would ensure their family name lived in perpetuity well beyond the confines of Liscannor. Over the next few years, Mary would bear two more sons.

By now John's father was mostly land-bound, patrolling the shores of Clare on horseback, from the sandy beaches of Lahinch across the bay to the south, to the majestic spectacle of the Cliffs of Moher, rising seven hundred feet skyward from the churning Atlantic seas below. Surely John junior must have accompanied his father on some of his patrols, watching the tiny currachs battle with the seas to haul in nets glistening with fish, or watched during the dark days of the famine as tall ships plied their trade of transporting the starving thousands over the horizon, sometimes to America or sometimes no further than the bottom of the ocean. However he obtained it, John Philip Holland acquired a love of all things maritime during his childhood and it would drive him constantly to new horizons for the remainder of his life.

Mary Scanlan, and indeed most of the residents of Liscannor at the time, spoke only Irish as did John at home. However, he attended the local Macreehy's National School, which was state-run, so English would have been compulsory at school.

Although shielded largely from the direct effects of the famine through his father's state job, his brother Robert did succumb to the cholera epidemic which accompanied the cataclysm and died in 1847 when John was just six years old.

His parents were deeply religious and when he finished his primary education, John began the daily trek to the school run by the Christian Brothers in Ennistymon, five miles away. The rapidly expanding network of Christian Brothers' schools offered him the opportunity to pursue his education beyond childhood, something he was keen to embrace.

Then in 1853 his father retired due to ill health, and decided to uproot the family to Limerick. Sadly he died the same year leaving Mary to raise three children on her own with his father's coastguard pension their only income. John transferred to Sexton Street School in Limerick and it proved pivotal in unlocking the mechanical genius within.

BROTHERS IN SCIENCE

At Sexton Street he came across Brother Bernard O'Brien who had a deep love of the sciences; when he wasn't teaching or attending to his religious duties, he spent his time gazing at the heavens, not in search of divine blessing, but with telescopes he'd constructed himself. He also had a strong interest in the newly-emerging field of electro-magnetism and his interests captured the attention of the school's new pupil. John's letters of later years would credit this brother as having a major influence on his chosen path.

Although he was living in a large town, John's eye was always on the sea and in the 1850s he applied to join the

Merchant Marines. His application was rejected on the basis of his poor eyesight so he knew he would have to steer a different course in the search for a career that would interest him. He'd been quickly identified as a gifted student and a possible recruit to the Christian Brothers who were trawling the intellectual youth of Ireland to meet the ever-growing demand for their services. Despite the fact that he was still in his teens, John was asked to start teaching evening classes to adults who had been deprived of an education in their childhood. He accepted and stepped into the classroom, little realising that he would remain there for nearly fifteen years.

His brief spell as teacher having been a success, he was encouraged to pursue it further and in 1858 John decided to don the habit of the Christian Brothers. He moved to the novitiate in North Richmond Street in Dublin (which is still in existence, now as the Edmund Rice Centre) for his initial training as a teacher and as a member of a religious order. Before the year was out he was assigned to North Monastery School in Cork and would be known as Brother Philip. It seemed that although the Order hoped to direct Brother Philip's path through life, the irony is that here he met another Brother whose influence would ultimately make him take a sharp turn in a completely different direction.

Brother Burke is credited as the founder of vocational training in Ireland (see panel) and like the aforementioned Brother O'Brien, was a man for whom the sciences

PIONEERING A NEW SCHOOL OF THOUGHT

Brother James Dominic Burke is truly one of the unsung heroes of Irish education. Born in Limerick in 1833, he exhibited an early fascination with science, and having joined the Christian Brothers was transferred to the North Monastery School in Cork where he began a lifelong crusade to change the fundamentals of education in Ireland. Up to then, whatever education Irish children received (which was very little) was generally in the classics like Latin and English, but having witnessed the 1852 Industrial Exhibition in Cork, he resolved to change all that. He began to introduce lessons that would directly benefit the lives of poor, working-class children, introducing subjects such as subjects such as trigonometry, physics and architectural drawing. He encouraged pupils to experiment, rather than to simply sit and listen to the drone of a master reading from a book. He purchased equipment and established a laboratory, introducing methods that were unheard of in Ireland or Britain at the time. He even expanded his teachings for the benefit of adults. In 1883 his pupils were invited to compete for a Gold Medal at an industrial exhibition, which was essentially a forerunner of the Young Scientist Competition.

His new practical approach attracted widespread attention, including visits by the Duke of Edinburgh and future Prime Minister of Britain, Lord Asquith. Ultimately his ideas began to shape the future for all schools in Ireland, right to the present day.

Brother Burke died in 1904 when struck by a carriage in Patrick Street, Cork. But his influence would live on for countless years to come and for the benefit of generations of Irish schoolchildren.

held a tremendous fascination. It's said that Brothers Philip and Burke became great friends and would spend hours discussing and building models of boats and tiny submersibles and testing them in the fish pond on the monastery grounds.

Brother Philip excelled at science and mechanical drawing and also had a fascination with the mathematical qualities of music. His term in Cork was all too brief however and he was transferred to Armagh in 1860 and after a fleeting spell there he developed a form of tuberculosis and had to be sent to Dublin for treatment. His merry-go-round existence continued when he recovered as he was now moved to Portlaoise where he hoped to take his vows. Again he fell ill and it was determined that he was temporarily unfit to carry out his duties as a Brother.

TAKING TO THE WATER

He was sent to live with his aunt in Cork city; while he was there the American Civil War began. Brother Philip took a great interest in it, scrutinising the daily reports in the press. He would later record a personal memory of reading about the Battle of the Monitor and the Merrimac which was the first naval engagement between ironclad ships.

> '... it struck me very forcibly that the day of wooden walls for vessels of war had passed, and that ironclad ships had come to stay forever. I reflected that with her tremendous facilities England would apply them to the situation and become the chief naval power of the world; and I wondered how she could be retarded in her designs upon the other peoples of the world, and how they would protect themselves against those designs.'

Clearly Brother Philip was already beginning to consider ways in which England might 'be retarded'. But for the moment he was a simple teacher in a religious order and all of that was so far away it might as well have been on the moon.

When he recovered from his illness he was re-admitted to the Christian Brothers and having taken his initial vows, was assigned to Enniscorthy in Co. Wexford where he began to develop an interest not in machines of the sea, but of the sky. Mechanically-powered flight would also interest him until his final years. The fact was that all things mechanical fascinated him and he also possessed the natural bent to take his ideas from idle notions to drawings to practical working models. It was said that as a Brother in Dundalk a few years later he invented a mechanical duck which could walk, swim and – crucially – dive. It may have entertained his fellow Brothers and visitors alike, but for John Holland it was among the first of his experiments into the development of a boat that could travel underwater independently.

Despite being taken to task for allowing his love of science distract him from his religious duties, Brother Philip clearly found it compulsive. Admired by fellow Brothers and pupils alike, he spent much of his time constructing new mechanical devices, bringing order and beauty to the monastery grounds – he even constructed a wooden replica of the Rock of Cashel in front of the monastery! He built a windmill beside the monastery well so that water could be pumped directly to the building. While these inventions didn't endure, his dreams of taking his skills to a new level did and while in Dundalk he developed his first genuine submarine design, if only on paper.

TWENTY THOUSAND DREAMS UNDER THE SEA

It was 1870 and a book found its way into Brother Philip's hands by a French writer called Jules Verne. It recounted the story of Captain Nemo and his crew and their adventures in the amazing underwater ship called the *Nautilis*. Verne's book, *Twenty Thousand Leagues Under the Sea*, captured the public imagination and helped to set Brother Philip's imagination racing in a much more practical way.

Submarines of some form or another had been

THE UNKNOWN IRISH MEN
AND WOMEN OF SCIENCE PART 1

Down through the centuries Ireland has produced countless inventors and scientists whose names and work have largely gone unheralded. Among them was an officer in the British Navy, Meath-born Francis Beaufort (1774-1857), who developed what is still known in Meteorological fields worldwide as The Beaufort Scale. His scale of wind force incidentally, was first officially used on the historic voyage of the Beagle. The same year Beaufort died, John Joly (1857-1933), was born in Offaly and was among the most prolific and diverse of Irish scientists and inventors. Early in his career he developed several scientific instruments for measuring melting points, specific heats and light intensity and he also developed new techniques in the advancement of colour photography. By measuring radioactive decay in minerals he accurately estimated the age of the earth in 1913. But his most famous contribution to science and medicine is his pioneering use of radiation to treat tumours in cancer patients. Agnes Mary Clerke (1842-1907) was one of the first women to gain a reputation in the sciences. Born in Skibbereen, she studied astronomy in Florence and collated and interpreted a vast wealth of astronomical research. Her 1885 treatise 'A Popular History of Astronomy during the Nineteenth Century' brought her international renown among the scientific community. She was only the third ever female member of the Royal Astronomical Society and is probably the only Irish-born person to have a lunar crater named in her honour!

something men had dreamed about for millennia. Legend has it that in the siege of Tyre, in 332 BC, in order to attack the city walls where they ran beneath the sea level, Alexander the Great descended beneath the water in a type of submarine, which was completely sealed, yet admitted light and also air through a pipe. Whatever the truth of this, the ability to attack an enemy by stealth under the sea was something men had dreamed about for centuries.

The first recorded mention of an actual submarine was in Britain in 1578. William Bourne proposed a device constructed of wood that was water-proofed by leather hides, although he probably couldn't find a soul brave enough to take the plunge, as it was never constructed. Forty years later a Dutchman called Van Drebel takes the plaudits for building the first ever submersible craft, which he manoeuvred briefly at depths of about fifteen metres in the Thames; even King James I is said to have had a brief jaunt under the water.

There were various other attempts over the following century, many unrecorded, as the intrepid pioneer submariners never returned from the bottom of the ocean to recount their experience. By the time of the American Revolution someone had the idea of developing a submarine as a weapon. That someone was called Bushnell, a student at Yale, who created 'The Turtle'. This was an apple-shaped, one-man contrivance, driven by pedal power which would sneak under a British warship and introduce explosives through a hole drilled by a large hand-cranked screw. Luckily for the British sailors, their hull was covered in copper sheathing, which the screw couldn't penetrate. The world's first undersea attack marines returned to base alive, but thoroughly exhausted.

At first, most underwater crafts were constructed of wood. Then at the dawn of the nineteenth century, the same year John Philip Holland's father was born, American inventor Robert Fulton came up with a new idea. Fulton is most renowned as the inventor of the steamboat so was well experienced in marine matters. Hired by Napoleon, who shared a common enemy with Fulton's compatriots, he build a craft of iron ribs covered by sealed copper plates, which used a ballast tank to submerge. He called the ship *The Nautilis* and it managed to manoeuvre under a test schooner in Brest and send it to the bottom of the harbour. But Fulton soon found that under the power of just four men pedalling furiously they simply couldn't overtake a British ship in motion and their supply of compressed air quickly ran out.

With the American Civil War (1861-65) came a fresh batch of attempts to construct a working submarine. There was the *Pioneer* built by the Confederacy to try and undermine, literally, the blockade of southern ports by the Union. This was the first hand-cranked sub, but despite trials it had to be scuttled with the advance of the Union army. Later in the war the Confederates successfully launched a modified iron boiler powered by eight men with hand cranks, which towed a torpedo-like device behind it. They did enjoy a Pyrrhic victory of sorts – the torpedo sank the Union ship, the *Housatonic* in Charleston harbour, killing five men, but the explosion also sank the submarine, killing everyone on board.

On the other side of the Atlantic Wilhelm Bauer, a Bavarian officer built two submersibles, *Le Plongeur-Marin* and *Le Diable-Marin*. The first sank with Bauer and two crewmen on board, yet they managed a daring escape from sixty feet down, swimming to the surface when their air ran out after five hours. The second was built for the Russian government and was more successful in one sense, making 134 dives before being lost at sea. This time sadly, there was no dramatic escape from the sea bed. Before the tragedy, Bauer had indulged in a little theatre to demonstrate his craft. To celebrate the coronation of Tsar Alexander II, a number of musicians accompanied the crew when it was submerged in Kronshtadt harbour, where they played the Russian national anthem! It is said the patriotic strains of the music could be heard through the hulls of other moored ships.

By 1886, the electric motor and the storage battery had evolved to an extent that made them practicable in terms of power and size to be used to drive a submarine. Another *Nautilis*, this time designed by two Englishmen, made a number of successful tests in their all-electric craft, but the battery had to be recharged so often it was ultimately abandoned.

As the century drew to a close, there was intense

competition among virtually all the naval powers for the development of a practical working submarine, capable of launching repeated, successful attacks against an enemy. Strangely, only Britain, who had formerly considered herself ruler of the waves, seemed to regard the submarine as something of a flight of fancy. This would soon change.

In 1899, Maxime Laubeuf came the closest to overcoming the problems of developing an independently operating submarine that could stay submerged for extended periods. The *Narval* had two hulls, was over a hundred feet long, carried four torpedoes and was driven by a steam engine on the surface and electric motors when submerged. The ballast tanks were located between the two hulls, which was a design innovation still employed today, but at the time the design made submersion very difficult.

The world was clearly getting closer and closer to creating a practical working naval submarine. But for John Philip Holland, back in 1872, the race to build a submarine was still a far off dream.

CROSSING THE POND

It was 1872 and time for Brother Philip to take his perpetual vows. His own brother, Michael had become deeply involved in the nationalist movement and joined the Irish Republican Brotherhood, which had been formed in the great tumult of nationalist feeling that followed the famine. The IRB staged a brief rebellion in 1867 after which many were captured and imprisoned, but the twenty-year-old Michael managed to evade capture and fled to Boston in the United States.

John and Michael's mother had continued to struggle by in Limerick with their brother Alfred, but eventually, ground down by poverty, in 1872 she decided to up sticks and join her son in Boston. This had a profound effect on John Holland, who despite being deeply proud of his Irishness and having something of a nationalist leaning himself, was now torn between the love of his country and that of his family. There was also the small matter of his religious vocation.

Around that time, a new regime in the Christian Brothers decided that the order should return to basics, with emphasis on reading, writing, the Irish language and discipline. Schools were to be made more efficient and there was to be less room for so-called free-thinkers who might fill their pupils heads with all sorts of high-falutin' nonsense. His decision was effectively made for him and he declined to take his vows that year. Brother Philip reverted to plain John Philip Holland and on 26 May 1873, he took a boat for Liverpool and from there sailed for the United States, still unsure where precisely the currents would carry him.

He initially moved in with his mother and brothers in Boston and no sooner had he set foot on US soil than his feet went from under him, literally – he slipped on an icy street and broke his leg. As when he'd been confined to bed in Ireland many years earlier, John Holland put his free time to good use. He unearthed the initial submarine designs he had devised in Dundalk and began to re-work them to take account of new developments in marine technology that had transpired in the intervening years.

Once he had recovered, he took a job in an engineering firm, which afforded him the opportunity to hone his skills in an environment that had been unavailable to him within the walls of a monastery. But for reasons unknown, perhaps financial, perhaps to allow himself more time to develop his own projects, he left the firm after a year and returned to teaching, moving to Paterson in New Jersey, a town that still boasts proudly of his citizenship.

It was 1875 and he was happy that his revised plans for a submarine were workable. He submitted them to the US Navy who weren't nearly as happy and rejected them as *'the fantastic scheme of a civilian landsman.'* Despite dismissing him as a naïve landlubber, his plans nonetheless were used by a Lieutenant Barber in a lecture entitled 'Submarine Boats and Their Application to Torpedo Operations'. Clearly someone in the Navy had a notion at the back of his mind that this submarine thing had something going for it.

THE UNKNOWN IRISH MEN AND WOMEN OF SCIENCE PART 2

Having a needle plunged into your arm or backside may not be the most pleasant experience, but when the hypodermic needle was invented in 1845, it was a medical breakthrough. The invention of the hypodermic syringe is usually mistakenly credited to Scottish doctor Alexander Wood in 1853, but in actual fact it was first developed by Dublin-born Dr Francis Rynd (1801-1861) eight years earlier, and administered on a patient in the Meath Hospital. Another medical advancement originated in the mind of Arthus Leared (1822-1879). Hailing from Wexford, Leared invented probably the most familiar of all doctor's accoutrements, the binaural (or double-earpiece) stethoscope as well as contributing other important, pioneering studies on human physiology. And many may recall from their schooldays the efforts of our science teachers to drill Stokes' Law into Ireland's collective heads – describing the movement of a body through fluids of different densities. Well you can blame George Stokes (1819-1903) who was from Skreen in Sligo. George also advanced scientific study greatly with his explanation for flouresence and his contribution to advanced mathematics known as Stokes' Parameters.

THE FENIAN RAM

The US Navy and the Royal Navy may not have been fully convinced of the potential of these new-fangled submarines, but one group certainly was: The Irish Republican Brotherhood.

In 1876, John Holland's brother Michael introduced him to the famed Fenian leader and exile, Jeremiah O'Donovan Rossa, who was resident in New York at the time. O'Donovan Rossa had been orchestrating a series of guerilla-like attacks on English soil which were financed by a so-called 'Skirmishing Fund'. Ex-patriot Irishmen in New York, of which there were multitudes, were generous to a fault in helping to keep up the fight against the 'auld enemy', albeit from a distant shore.

The Fenian leader took a great interest in Holland's theories about submersibles and ultimately an audacious plan was devised to build a submarine that would have a three-man crew and would be launched through a door in the hull of an innocuous-looking cargo boat or ferry, which had casually manoeuvred to within a short distance of a British warship. It would then launch a torpedo, sink the ship and return through its secret door and none would be the wiser as to how the attack had come about.

Although he had some nationalist leanings, Holland was by no means a fanatic, a term that might have better described his brother. It's quite likely that what he saw here was not primarily an opportunity to strike a blow at

England, but to realise a lifelong ambition of actually building his submarine.

A year later the Skirmishing Fund's trustees approved the plan and voted to finance Holland's first submarine to the tune of $6,000 under the supervision of John Breslin. Holland was ecstatic and immediately set about his project with unrestrained enthusiasm. But of course it wasn't all going to be plain sailing.

Construction got under way on the *Holland I* in Todd & Raftery's yard in Paterson and the following year the fourteen-foot-long submarine was revealed to the waiting world, or rather a crowd of curious locals and journalists, as well as his Fenian backers. This was not intended to be the final design, but a kind of prototype or test dummy. The boat was transported to the Passaic River, which flows through Paterson, and lowered into its relatively calm waters from the back of a horse-drawn wagon. It was powered by a tiny four-horsepower engine and could hold only one man, in this case its designer, John Holland. He squeezed into the claustrophobic 'cockpit', which measured less than two cubic yards, and prepared to make his first dive.

Unfortunately, while the sub did submerge, it did so of its own accord as an assistant had neglected to insert a pair of screw plugs and the boat began to fill with the cold water of the Passaic River and sink in full view of the crowd and press. Holland made quick his escape and despairingly watched his first sub signal its farewell with a rush of bubbles to the surface. The local *Paterson Daily Guardian* would congratulate him the next day for getting the boat straight to the bottom without even the assistance of a captain.

Holland was nothing if not resilient and he managed to re-float the sub and repair any damage and a couple of weeks later his launch was much more successful. He dived to a depth of twelve feet and manoeuvred about under the watchful eyes of his Fenian paymasters. After Holland's initial embarrassment he was relieved to see they were suitably impressed to commit to further funding for a larger, fully functional boat.

After running a series of further tests Holland decided to remove all the useful parts and scuttle the sub. The original *Holland I* was salvaged in 1927 and is now on display in Paterson Museum.

He now launched himself fully into his new project, quitting his teaching post and devoting all his time to developing the new boat within the confines of the Delamater Iron Company in New York. The new sub would be over thirty feet long and driven by a more powerful fifteen-horsepower engine with a speed of 7 mph when submerged. It would weigh nineteen tons and would be armed with a torpedo propelled from a tube by compressed air.

As it began to take shape the press began to take an interest in rumours of the Fenians developing 'an infernal machine'. On 29 July 1881, The *New York Times* sent a reporter to the Delamater Iron Company to have a sniff around. He interviewed a director about the project that was underway in the yard below. When asked if Mr Holland was developing a 'Torpedo Boat' for the Fenians, the director informed him that anyone who inquired such from Mr Holland was given a curt answer. As far as the company was concerned they were happy to construct the boat at a cost of $18,000 as they'd received prompt weekly payments. Holland was described as *'a remarkably clever man, a perfect gentleman, well-educated, shrewd and even tempered.'* He had a *'smooth face and something of a priest-like air'*, a trait undoubtedly picked up from his many years wearing the brotherly habit of the Christian Brothers. The reporter also learned that a Consul General Archibald and Vice Consul Edwards of the British Government had visited for a snoop around the vessel. Later the reporter visited Holland's landlady who informed him that she has seen his boat but does not believe he's a Fenian, insisting *'He is a good Catholic and doesn't have anything to do with secret societies.'*

Another reporter from the *New York Sun*, equally unsuccessful at getting confirmation that the submarine was indeed a 'Fenian Torpedo Boat', decided to draw his own conclusions and christened the mysterious new invention *'The Fenian Ram'*. (Like its predecessor, the original *Fenian Ram* also eventually found its way to the Paterson Museum in New Jersey.)

In June 1881 Holland successfully launched *The Ram* in

New York harbour. The three crewmen consisted of an operator, an engineer and the armaments operator, whose job was essentially to load a six-foot explosive-crammed projectile into a tube, turn a crank which opened an outer door and turn a valve which released a 400-pound air pressure charge into the tube, propelling the torpedo towards its target.

His tests were remarkably successful and within two years he was travelling the length of New York harbour submerged to a depth of fifty feet. He also successfully fired a dummy torpedo both underwater and through the air through to distances of several hundred feet, no doubt terrifying and fascinating the burgeoning population of the fledgling city.

One description of a torpedo test read as follows: '*The projectile cleared the muzzle by eight or ten feet. Then, it leaped out of the water and rose sixty to seventy feet in the air to plunge downward and bury itself irretrievably in the mud at the bottom of the Basin.*'

As the months passed the relationship between Holland and the IRB began to deteriorate rapidly. There was considerable debate within the IRB as to the feasibility of the entire project. This in turn led to the payments to Holland being less than prompt and often shy by more than a few dollars. He continued to work on the *Ram*, but had less and less contact with the IRB. Ultimately they decided they'd had enough. In their view they'd paid for the entire project and what was theirs was theirs.

On a chilly night in November 1883, a group of Fenians led by John Breslin, steered a tug to the pier where *The Ram* was moored and using a letter of authorisation bearing Holland's forged signature, hooked up the sub and towed her up the East River, eventually mooring her at New Haven, Connecticut. Unfortunately, they soon discovered that they hadn't a clue how to operate the thing and were forced to appeal to Holland for assistance. Understandably, having devoted years of his life to it, he told them just where they could put their *Fenian Ram*.

After all, *Holland III* and *IV* were already taking shape in his mind.

THE ZALINSKI BOAT

Always with an eye on the future, in conjunction with the trial runs of the *Ram*, Holland had been developing a third design, similar in size but incorporating design changes suggested by his new-found experience. The *Holland III* was another prototype, created to explore new possibilities of manoeuvrability.

But without finance he knew the project would soon run aground. By happy co-incidence a former army lieutenant by the name of Edmond Zalinski had himself just invented a new form of pneumatic torpedo, which he wanted to incorporate into a submarine. The Polish-born engineer offered Holland a position in his Pneumatic Gun

Company with the intention of developing a submarine capable of housing his weapon.

This would ultimately lead to the formation of The Nautilus Submarine Boat Company (unashamedly borrowed from Jules Verne) and over the next couple of years the Zalinski Boat (or *Holland IV)* began to grow from a mass of wood and iron on a small island near Brooklyn. By 1885 it had blossomed into a fifty foot by eight foot, cigar-shaped submarine. Direction was determined with the use of a periscope-type device called a *camera lucida* and the pneumatic gun was fitted horizontally so that the sub would have to tilt to launch a torpedo through the air.

The prestigious *Scientific American* magazine reported the following in August 1876:

A NEW SUBMARINE TORPEDO BOAT

'*For some time past, Lieutenant Zalinski has been experimenting at Fort Hamilton, in the Narrows, with a novel submarine torpedo boat, the invention of Mr John P. Holland, of this city. The boat can be sunk to any desired depth below the surface of the water, propelled in any direction, and brought to the surface at any time. The boat has a wooden hull, is cigar shaped, and measures 50 feet in length by 8 feet in diameter at the largest part. The floating surface, under ordinary conditions, is 30 feet long.*'

His new boat benefited greatly from his previous

designs to improve manoeuvrability, but as the launch date grew nearer, he became frustrated with issues like the tilt-up requirement to fire the weapon. He began to realise that Zalinski essentially saw the submarine as little more than a vehicle to carry his weapon and had no real interest in developing a submarine that could dive to significant depths, manoeuvre stealthily, remain submerged for lengthy periods of time, attack and retreat to safety with no damage to boat or personnel. Given the technology available at the time, these were a very tall order and Holland began to feel he'd never climb to those heights in the company of Zalinski.

The Zalinski Boat did make several successful trial runs in New York in 1886, but by then the partnership had been dissolved and John Holland was once more without a job or a submarine. But by the following year he would finally embark on a voyage of a completely different nature.

TAKING HIS VOWS

Just fifteen years earlier he'd been on the brink of taking his perpetual vows as a Christian Brother. Now John Holland was on the verge of taking vows of an altogether different nature.

Having obsessed so much about his submarine research, he'd often found little time to dip his toe into the waters of romance and now, at the age of forty-six time

THE UNKNOWN IRISH MEN
AND WOMEN OF SCIENCE PART 3

Surely the earliest of Ireland's great scientists is Robert Boyle (1627-1691), who was born in Lismore Castle and was studying science while Cromwell was running rampage through Ireland. Boyle was one of the leading minds in the use of observation and experiment to advance science and is most famous for his discovery that the volume of gas varies inversely with pressure, known as 'Boyle's Law'. Other Irish inventors of renown were the so nicknamed 'mad mechanic' – Harry Ferguson (1884 - 1960), from Down, who revolutionised agriculture with his invention of the single-unit linked tractor and plough, his name forever immortalised in the Massey-Ferguson company name. He was also the first man to fly a plane in Ireland. In 1888 a Monaghan man, John Robert Gregg (1867-1948) invented the shorthand system of speed writing. Nicholas Callan (1799-1864) from Louth made a huge leap in the development of the use of electricity when he invented the induction coil, which produces a high-voltage alternating current from a low-voltage direct current supply. Lucien Bull (1876-1972) was a Dubliner who pioneered high-speed photography and made major advances in the electrocardiograph. Mary Ward (1827-1869) is uniquely distinctive for both her life and her death. Born in Offaly, she was a keen observer of the sciences and an artist and combining her skills, made thousands of drawings of life through the lens of a microscope, and was the first woman to have a book in this field published. Her studies of insects and plants life became key references for nineteenth century scientists. Her cousins had built a steam-driven automobile and tragically in 1869, she fell under its wheels and died, giving her the unfortunate distinction of being the world's first road traffic accident victim.

wasn't exactly on his side. But then in 1886 he met an Irish girl called Margaret Foley in Brooklyn and the following year they were walking down the aisle.

Keen to make up for lost ground, Margaret, who was considerably younger than her husband, was pregnant before the year was out. Their son was born in 1888, but John Philip junior tragically died while still in infancy. They would be blessed with another son, also called John Philip, two years later and ultimately Margaret would bear seven children, four boys and three girls.

The same year as his first son was born, the United States Navy began to openly show its first real interest in developing a submarine, announcing an open competition for the design of a boat with demanding specifications, including an eight-knot submerged speed, a tight-turning circle, the ability to dive to 150 feet and to be equipped with hundred-pound torpedoes.

It was the challenge he'd been waiting for. He submitted a design in competition with a famous Swedish arms manufacturer, Thorsten Nordenfelt. The Navy initially decided that Holland's design was superior, but a dispute arose as to who should carry out the testing on the boat, the designer or Navy personnel. This dragged on until eventually the project was abandoned.

The following year they held another competition. Again Nordenfelt submitted a design as well as a man called George Baker, whose previous claim to fame was the invention of a barbed wire machine. (A few years later Holland would have cause to remember Baker's name.) Once again Holland won the competition, but this time, to his extreme frustration, the Navy decided to divert the money to other, less speculative projects.

Infuriated at his lack of progress, Holland had a brief flight of fancy with his aircraft designs, but was unable to find an investor. Running low on funds and with a family to care for, he reluctantly went in search of work, accepting a position as a draughtsman in the Morris and Cummings Dredging Company. But his earlier work hadn't gone unnoticed and though he did not know it, his dreams were far from sunk.

TAKING ON THE NAVY

In 1893, a man called Elihu B. Frost, a wealthy lawyer with an eye for a good investment, read about yet another competition by the Navy to develop a submarine. This time however, Congress had appropriated $200,000 to fund the project. He realised this was an opportunity not to be sneezed at and immediately went in search of a man who could bring him a return on his investment. He found John Holland.

To Holland's delight, Frost agreed to provide a loan sufficient to finance his bid and The Holland Torpedo Boat Company was founded, with Frost as secretary and Holland as General Manager on a salary of $600 per annum.

This time the competition included the barbed wire man, George Baker and an Englishman called Simon Lake. Baker was politically connected and had already built a submarine two years earlier; it was the design for this pre-built model that he submitted. Yet because of the pace of development at the time, much of this design was already outdated.

It was reported in 1893 that Holland's submission had won yet again. A hat-trick, it seemed, yet strangely it would still be some time before he actually scored a goal. When Baker heard the news he used his political connections to insist that his boat be inspected before the contract was awarded. Holland countered that the contract was for the construction of a boat, not for the purchase of such. But Baker's influence held sway and a team was dispatched to inspect his boat in 1894. Despite Baker's best efforts, his design was still held to be inferior and as if he didn't have enough problems, he suddenly caught pneumonia and died.

His other chief competitor was Simon Lake, a brilliant young American engineer aged only twenty-seven. He heartily believed his design was superior to Holland's, but he had no investors and his youth and lack of experience probably worked against him. The contract was awarded to Holland's company, but he was further frustrated when they delayed the funding for another year.

When construction did get underway, Holland learned the hard way what it was like trying to progress his work under the 'guidance' of a committee. The submarine was to be called *The Plunger* (or *Holland V*) and the contract to assemble it was awarded to the Columbia Iron Works in Baltimore, rather than in one of his preferred locations like New York or New Jersey. Away from home for long periods of time, he soon began to come under considerable stress as disagreements over design quickly began to surface. Not one to play the prima donna, Holland was never precious about his designs and was one to gladly accept suggestions. But with the Navy he reached his breaking point. They viewed him as a landsman with no real understanding of the requirements of a naval vessel. He viewed them as amateurs with no understanding of submarine technology, it never having existed before.

Every technical plan had to be submitted to them and scrutinised in detail. They disagreed on almost every aspect of the design – steam engines versus gasoline, one propeller versus two, one torpedo tube versus two and so on. The result was that the construction of *The Plunger* proceeded at the pace of a sea snail crawling across the ocean floor.

Ultimately Holland was proven correct. He himself abandoned the project and left it to be completed by the Navy engineers. The *New York Times* reported its launch in 1897 to very little fanfare. '*The ceremonies were simple, consisting merely of the customary christening and a few impromptu speeches.*' It's hardly surprising it was a low key affair. Holland said later that the submarine was '*over-engineered*'. The Navy conducted a number of tests and slowly realised the design was never going to meet their needs. They quietly abandoned the boat a couple of years later.

A NEW CENTURY

John Philip Holland came to the decision that if he was ever going to develop his submarine the way he wanted, he'd have to do it without outside interference. He turned to the directors of his own company, the Holland Torpedo Boat Company in search of funds and they were forthcoming.

Over the following year the Lewis Nixon Shipyard in New Jersey echoed to the sounds of the *Holland VI* as it struggled to come into existence. Hammers, rivet guns, saws, welding torches, pressure valves all played in harmony under the direction of Holland's guiding hands.

By May of 1897, the *Holland VI* was ready for its initial

launch, which took place in New Jersey to a large gathering of dignitaries, reporters and members of the general public. A specially erected platform hosted the dignitaries, including the wife of the shipyard owner, Mrs Nixon, beaming as she clutched a doomed bottle of champagne. Holland arrived and joined the party, exchanging greetings with well-wishers before turning to watch as Mrs Nixon swing the champagne towards the hull of the 53-foot long craft. It shattered and amid a loud creaking of timbers and grinding of metal, the *Holland VI* began to slide down the ramp into the sea. As it settled with a tremendous whoosh, the water swelled in the dock in perfect harmony with the swelling of the applause and cheering. John Philip Holland gratefully accepted the proffered hands and back-slaps that accompanied the moment.

But hidden behind the joy and celebrations was the knowledge that the craft had not yet been acknowledged or purchased by the Navy and worse still, the project had brought their company to the brink of bankruptcy. The *Holland I* it seemed, was not the only thing that looked likely to go under.

Never having forgotten his roots, John Holland chose St Patrick's Day 1898 for the submarine's first dive. As the rigorous testing proceeded, the US Navy dispatched a Lieutenant Sergeant to inspect the *Holland VI*. He reported that '*the boat fully proved her ability to propel herself, to dive, come up, admit water to her ballast tanks, and eject it again without difficulty.*'

But Holland knew that if he didn't secure fresh funding his boat might soon be overtaken by any number of competitors in the race to secure the Navy's final blessing.

A man called Isaac Rice formed the Electric Boat Company with the specific purpose of developing and marketing the *Holland VI*. In 1899, with the trials of the

UNDERWATER FANTASIES

A New York Times reporter covering the launch of the Holland VI indulged himself in a fanciful prediction of the future use of the submarine. With the exploration of our planet and beyond still in its infancy, he gives us an insight into the imaginings of the early twentieth century public as to what lay in store. He predicted that standard naval warfare would now be rendered redundant as frigates and such would have no defence against subs. The battles would then be purely between competing submarines pursuing each other under the waves and with no means of escape, vast numbers of drownings would occur. Submarines would therefore, he speculated be used primarily for exploration, sport or entertainment. He envisaged yachting excursions to the bottom of the sea, 'cephalopod hunts', and the pursuit and shooting of whales and sharks for game, the recovering of vast hordes of treasures from sunken Spanish galleons and the great question would finally be answered: 'Is there or is there not a sea serpent?'

new submarine completed, he knew he was on to a good thing. Holland had little choice and that year he sold the Holland Torpedo Boat Company to Rice. This company would eventually be renamed as 'General Dynamics', which to this day is the primary supplier of submarines to the US Navy.

Over the coming year, Rice replaced Holland with a new Chief Engineer and also replaced the captain of the sub, appointing Frank Cable to the post. Holland had little regard for the new appointees and could see an uncertain future developing. After further inspections the then Secretary of the Navy, one Theodore Roosevelt, recommended that the Government buy the submarine. But they still weren't convinced.

Holland was dogged and continued to make alterations to meet the Navy's requirements under the watchful eye of several Navy representatives. In March 1900, the US Government agreed to buy the submarine for $150,000. With time against them, the company agreed, despite the fact that it had cost twice that to build.

On 12 October 1900, John Philip Holland's sixth submarine design was finally commissioned as the first official submarine of the United States Navy, or any navy for that matter. It would be called *The Holland*.

Financially it may not have been the outcome that he desired, but at last he'd fulfilled a dream that had begun thirty-five years earlier with a vision, a few sketches and the creation of a mechanical duck!

THE WORLD IS HIS OYSTER

Holland had won the race, but the subsequent boardroom battles would eventually defeat him. Yet over the coming years, submarines based on his design were sold to navies the world over. The Japanese had shown interest three years earlier when Holland had taken the Japanese Naval Attaché and his party for a test dive in Washington's Potomac River. With the US commissioning their first sub, they were convinced. They bought two of Holland's submarines, which helped them to a naval victory over Russia in 1905, for which the Emperor of Japan presented him with the Order of the Rising Sun.

The US now commissioned five new submarines of the Holland design, but with a supervising Naval Constructor overseeing the work and with the company imposing personnel and design constraints on him, disagreements were ongoing.

The British, who until now had demonstrated no interest in submarines, were suddenly forced to sit up and take notice. In 1900, the Royal Navy convinced their government to commission five submarines of Holland's design. Over the coming years they were built at the Vickers Sons & Maxim Shipyard in Britain. Britain's first ever submarine, like that of the US, bore the name of its creator, *The Holland I*. It was ironic really that the Royal Navy's first ever sub was named after a man whose early designs had been intended as a weapon to be used against them.

As the early years of the twentieth century passed, more and more navies began to buy into Holland's submarine. Russia commissioned five, the Japanese a further five, and one went to the Netherlands. Even Sweden built a Holland-type sub, but didn't credit its inventor!

In 1902, the now President of the United States, Theodore Roosevelt, took a dive in the Potomac in one of Holland's submarines. A little spooked at the cramped, claustrophobic conditions, he immediately ordered an increase in pay for any sailors involved in submarine duty!

Back in the boardroom, the squabbles continued. Research and development was Holland's primary objective, sales and marketing were the company's. Holland had actually designed a boat that could reach speeds of twenty-two knots underwater, unheard of at the time. But the Navy had rejected it because of the dangers such speed presented. By 1904, he'd had enough and resigned at the age of sixty-three. In his resignation note he commented: *'The success of your company can never be as great as what I ardently desired for it.'*

The company, fearing he might put his skills to use for a competitor, filed a suit against him the following year restraining him from working on submarine development in any connection. Having devoted three decades of his life to submarine design, he was now banished forever from his life's work. He quietly returned to the bosom of his family and spent the remainder of his days trying to design mechanically-propelled flying machines. The

Wright Brothers had won the race to the skies in 1903, but aviation experts studying Holland's designs in later years, believed his designs would have been successful. However, his boardroom battles and submarine obsession, meant that his aircraft designs never left the drawing board.

He retired to the small New Jersey town of Totowa and in 1914, he contracted pneumonia and died. He was survived by three children. He was buried in the town graveyard, less than one mile from the point on the Passaic River where he'd launched his first submarine.

Forty days after he died the British cruisers *Aboukir*, *Cressy* and *Hogue* were sunk by a German U-boat which bore many of John Holland's design features. It was the first major naval encounter of World War I.

REMEMBERING JOHN PHILIP HOLLAND

April 11, the day that Holland's design was finally accepted by the US Navy, is commemorated annually by the Navy as 'Submarine Day.

In 1964, the village of his birth, Liscannor, erected a plaque to commemorate the fiftieth anniversary of his death. The town also renamed Castle Street, calling it 'Holland Street' in his honour.

In 1981, the Royal Navy located the wreck of the *Holland I* and salvaged it, sixty-nine years after it had been scuttled. An extensive restoration project eventually returned the *Holland I* to near pristine condition. It can now be seen on display in the Royal Navy Museum in Portsmouth.

Holland's first ever submarine, along with the *Fenian Ram*, is on display in Paterson Museum in New Jersey, his adopted state.

In 1976, his weather-worn headstone in Totowa was replaced with a more fitting memorial.

John Philip Holland's greatest gifts were his amazing mechanical skills and great vision. He managed to combine elements like battery power, the internal combustion engine, marine engineering, ship-building skills, compressed air technology and weapons technology into one single working unit. This was done against a background of fierce competition, lack of funding and political indifference. And yet he somehow managed to emerge triumphant in the end, his submarines the first to be commissioned by four of the world's leading naval powers. His determination to succeed despite innumerable setbacks proved an inspiration for all around him, as it does for all of us today.

Monsignor Hugh O'Flaherty

Irish priest who helped to save over 4,000 people from the Nazis in World War II.

'All that is necessary for the triumph of evil is that good men do nothing.'

The words of the great eighteenth-century Irish philosopher and orator Edmund Burke could just as easily have slipped from the lips of Monsignor Hugh O'Flaherty during the dark days of the German occupation of Rome during World War II.

Yet given a snapshot of his upbringing amid the turbulence of the last years of British rule in Ireland and the brutality of the Black and Tans, it is hard to imagine that this child from a strictly Catholic background would one day be responsible for rescuing two thousand British soldiers from the hands of the Nazis along with another 2,000 Jews and people of other races.

Hugh Joseph O'Flaherty, although regarded for most of

his life as a Kerryman, was actually born in Cork in 1898, in the tiny rural community of Lisrobin, Kiskeam. He was the eldest son of James and Margaret O'Flaherty and had two younger brothers and a sister. Early in his life the family relocated to Killarney, company Kerry, about thirty kilometres to the west, and his father took up a position as the chief steward of the Killarney Golf Club, which was at that time a sport exclusively played in by the very wealthy visitors who came to view the natural beauty of the area and indulge themselves in a few gentle sporting jousts. Hugh's father's position allowed him to take up the sport himself and he would prove immensely talented, possibly skillful enough to earn a substantial living, but his calling was to come from far beyond the mountains that cast their shadows across Killarney's fairways and greens.

Hugh grew up against a background of political upheaval in Ireland. Home Rule was the issue of his early childhood, Irish proponents and opponents vied with each other in the political arenas while those who favoured complete independence sought to oust British forces from the country with more direct, violent action. By the time of his early manhood he was living amid the suppression of the notorious Black and Tans, the south west of Ireland one of the key battle grounds in which republican rebels fought a guerilla war against the ruthless mercenaries and the British Army itself. It is said that four friends of Hugh O'Flaherty were murdered in separate incidents by the Black and Tans, instilling in him a great antipathy towards the British.

As was common in Irish households of the time, the priesthood was considered among the most highly-regarded of vocations and early in his teens Hugh decided he wished to follow the path of holy orders. Having attended the Presentation Monastery and School in Killarney, he entered a Jesuit Seminary in Limerick as a teenager and in 1922, just at the outset of the Irish Civil War, he was transferred to Rome to complete his studies. Although he was unaware of its significance at the time, it also happened to be the year that the fascist dictator, Benito Mussolini, came to power in Italy.

Hugh entered the Congregation for the Propagation of the Faith (from which the word 'propaganda' derives), which was essentially responsible for overseeing missionary work and bringing Catholicism to far-flung corners of the earth. Within the beautiful walls of the Congregation's headquarters on Piazza di Spagna, which were designed by none less than Bernini, Hugh O'Flaherty found the inspiration to rapidly complete his degree in theology. He was ordained in 1925, but continued his studies for a few more years earning doctorates in philosophy, canon law and divinity.

Yet his time in Rome in those early days wasn't exclusively dedicated to his studies. Having been a keen sportsman as a boy, numbering among his skills hurling, boxing and of course, golf, he was keen not to entirely lose touch with his sporting pursuits. As boxing wasn't exactly much indulged-in around the Vatican, and hurlers were few and far between in the piazzas of Rome, he turned to his main love, golf. Even this wasn't encouraged by his superiors, but luckily a blind eye was turned. As it transpired, he was actually so proficient at golf that he would one day win the Italian Amateur Championship.

AMBASSADOR O'FLAHERTY

In 1934, the title of 'Monsignor' was bestowed upon him and he would begin to wear the scarlet-trimmed robes associated with that form of address, which was granted to clergy holding certain ecclesiastical offices such as 'Chaplain to his Holiness'. That same year he was assigned to the post of secretary to a Vatican diplomat, Monsignor Dini who was based in Egypt. Shortly after his arrival his superior died suddenly and the new Monsignor found himself appointed to take over the role and abruptly thrown in at the deep end of the diplomatic service. It turned out to be a blessing as he quickly learned to swim among the political sharks and other foreign diplomats, and actually excelled in the role so much that his superiors back in Rome soon dispatched him to foreign missions in places as far flung as Haiti, the Dominican Republic and Czechoslovakia. His diplomatic experience would serve him well in the dark days ahead.

After four years he was recalled to Rome and appointed

to The Holy Office or to give it its official title, The Congregation for the Doctrine of the Faith. The predecessor to this Vatican office had been the notorious Inquisition, but now in more enlightened days it restricted itself to holding court on challenges to the Catholic faith and examining claims of miracles, rather than burning heretics at the stake. Monsignor O'Flaherty would be soon elevated to the position of Head Notary.

In this final pre-war year, the Monsignor became a well-known face at social functions of the ruling political and business elite in Rome. Although physically he didn't seem to fit the part –a brusque, six foot-three Irishman with a heavy rural accent, wearing wire-framed glasses atop a rather generous nose – Roman high society took quickly to his intelligence and the warmth of his personality. From the time of his childhood on the Killarney golf course he'd been rubbing shoulders with his so-called 'betters' and having served as a diplomat for four years he could quickly turn his skills to charm any company. Among those with whom he is reputed to have shared a game of golf was the exiled King Alfonso of Spain and the Italian Foreign Minister, Galeazzo Ciano, who also happened to be Mussolini's son-in-law.

A SHADOW OVER EUROPE

Monsignor Hugh O'Flaherty's life was about to change. In

March 1939, Pope Pius XII was appointed to office and one of his early teachings called on the tradition of priestly heroism, to be a living example of Christ's virtue and sacrifice. This would become a central tenet of the Monsignor's life in the years ahead.

On 1 September of that year, World War II officially commenced and all over Europe men began to fall to the rattle of gunfire. Mussolini declared a 'Pact of Steel' with Hitler and in the summer of 1940, Italy declared war on Britain and France.

The tiny enclave of Vatican City, which was just over one hundred acres in size, had been granted independence as a result of the 1929 Lateran Treaty, in which Mussolini recognised it as a sovereign, independent country. This required the Vatican to remain neutral in all international affairs and conflicts. It did not however, preclude the Pope and his cardinals from making observations and criticisms of the actions of other countries. After the war the Pope would be criticised in some quarters for not having done enough to intervene in the slaughter. When in the early years of the war he stated that anti-Semitism was incompatible with Christianity and had his priests in Germany read a letter describing Hitler as an *'insane and arrogant prophet'*, persecution of the Church was instant and terrifying, with thousands of priests, nuns and monks murdered. This occasionally may have given him pause in later years, but he was regularly outspoken against fascism, ordered the opening of monasteries and churches to hide Jews and hired Jewish scholars to work in the inner enclaves of the Vatican, the very heart of Catholicism's spiritual home. After the war, many Jewish organisations would praise him for his efforts and his denunciations of racial hatred and religious prejudice, while others would denounce him as 'Hitler's Pope'.

It was in this atmosphere of legal neutrality yet open opposition to fascism that Monsignor O'Flaherty found himself in the early years of the war. Like both his home country and the country where he lived, he was officially neutral in his dealings with the opposing sides, yet like many thousands of his countrymen, he would soon find himself taking the side of the enemies of Nazism.

Initially he was assigned the task of interpreter to Monsignor Duca as they toured prisoner-of-war camps around Italy. He spent a great deal of this time talking to individual inmates, mostly British – writing down their names, listening to their needs and occasionally ministering to the Catholics among them. When he returned to the Vatican he would broadcast their names over Vatican Radio in the hope that their loved ones would know they were safe. He would also use his diplomatic experience to negotiate improved conditions for the prisoners in the camps and try to ensure that Red Cross parcels reached them.

His badgering of officials eventually brought down their wrath and after representation by the Italian government to his Vatican superiors, he was replaced and recalled to Rome.

HOLY SANCTUARY

In late 1942, in compliance with Hitler's demand for the eradication of the Jews, Mussolini's forces began a campaign of rounding up prominent members of the Jewish community – intellectuals, rabbis, leading businessmen. Among these people were many with whom Monsignor O'Flaherty had formed relationships in the days before the war.

With the tacit approval of the Pope, he initially began to smuggle these people into the Vatican itself, even accommodating some of them in his own quarters. Many others he began to house, not without a touch of irony, in the German College, so named as it had in earlier centuries been reserved for German clergy and scholars.

His initial tactics were simple. Each evening he would stand at the edge of the long portico that runs the length of St Peter's façade, clearly visible to those in the square below. A Jewish person would approach in the guise of a Catholic worshipper whereupon he would guide them into the portico out of sight of the authorities at the edge of the square. From there he would usher them to sanctuary or listen to their situation and arrange papers for their escape. There is a story, perhaps apocryphal, of a Jewish man approaching him one evening and producing a gold chain from around his waist that he offered in return for the Monsignor providing refuge for his child. He reputedly accepted the chain, took the boy and provided forged papers for the man and his wife, and when the war ended returned both the child and the chain to the eternally grateful parents.

In early 1943 the Monsignor began to have his first contacts with escaped British POWs, some of whom he'd personally met on his earlier tours of their camps. Despite his upbringing in the strictly republican, anti-British ferment of pre-independence Ireland, he had no hesitation in offering his help. He did have one major problem nonetheless; the Vatican was officially neutral and allowing a British soldier refuge on its territory would be a violation of the state's neutrality, which could bring dire consequences.

He solved the problem by approaching monasteries, friends and sympathisers around the city, slowly building up a network of secret apartments and safe houses throughout Rome, but officially outside Vatican jurisdiction. But the number of POWs soon began to escalate, their Italian guardians not as committed to security with the approach of the Allies from the south. The Monsignor realised that his informal network would not be able to cope with the demand. Funds were low to feed and clothe the new arrivals and his casual approach left the operation open to security breaches.

He arranged a meeting with the British Minister to the Vatican, Sir Francis D'Arcy Godolphin Osborne. It must have been strange for a man from such a nationalist Irish background to seek out a member of the British aristocracy and servant of the British government as an ally. Yet he reputedly made a passionate appeal for help to Sir Francis, particularly for funds, these were, after all, British soldiers he was helping. But the Minister's position was compromised as he could officially do nothing, he was on neutral foreign soil and couldn't even take a step beyond its 'borders'. His solution was to call for his butler, John May, a short Cockney man in his thirties, and inform him that the Monsignor wished to have a chat with him. He then left the room.

May began acting as the go-between for the Monsignor and the Minister, who at first provided all the funds for their enterprise from his own pocket. But John May was to become much more than that. As the year progressed he displayed an uncanny ability to source material on the black market, and to secure documentation by bribing officials in the vast Italian bureaucracy. The Monsignor would later describe him as *'the most magnificent scrounger I have ever come across.'*

Monsignor O'Flaherty and John May made contact with Count Salazar of the Swiss Legation and these men formed the Council of Three, coordinating the network of safe houses, their occupants and their supplies. The Count also proved particularly useful in providing Swiss identity papers for fleeing Jewish families.

In July 1943, the Allies began an invasion of Sicily and that same month the Allies bombed Rome itself, as much care as was possible being taken not to strike Vatican City or any of Rome's great monuments. The Italian government began to realise that the game was almost up, Mussolini's army was on the brink of collapse and his respect among the people had long since waned. The locals actually welcomed the Allied soldiers as liberators when they landed in Sicily on 9 July and in Rome, the people turned away from the propaganda broadcasts of their government and tuned to Vatican Radio to hear news of the invasion.

By September, Mussolini had been arrested and the Italian government had surrendered. But instead of improving the situation in Rome, for Monsignor O'Flaherty things had just taken a turn for the worse. Now there would be a new, ruthless and more terrifying adversary watching his every move. The Nazis.

GERMAN EFFICIENCY

On 8 September 1943, the German army occupied Rome and with the Allies still hundreds of miles to the south, prepared themselves for a long stay. Colonel Herbert Kappler was appointed the head the Gestapo in the city and immediately began stamping his authority on Rome.

Up until now, the Italians had been deliberately less than efficient in carrying out Hitler's demand for the extermination of the Jews in Italy. Kappler also knew that many Italians and members of the Catholic Church were responsible for harbouring fugitives and escaped POWs. He began to arrest and torture suspected sympathisers and activists, which soon led to a spate of arrests and executions.

One of his first actions was to demand a ransom of fifty kilogrammes of gold from the Jewish community, which would prevent the immediate deportation of two hundred Jews to concentration camps. The Chief Rabbi asked the Pope for help, but in the end it was not required as ordinary Jews across Rome surrendered their wedding rings, bracelets and pendants eventually meeting the required weight. Kappler sent the box of gold to Berlin to help the German war effort, and no doubt to impress his superiors. (It was found in the box in which it was sent, unopened, in an office in Germany, when the war ended.) But all this bought the Jews was some time, as orders came from Berlin that Kappler was to begin mass deportation of Jews soon after.

Pope Pius quickly issued orders that the doors of all monasteries and convents that came under Vatican jurisdiction were to throw open their doors to the Jewish people. Over four thousand Jews found sanctuary in hundreds of religious institutions and almost five hundred were sheltered in the Vatican itself. Yet hundreds began to be shepherded away in cattle trucks never to return.

Monsignor O'Flaherty had to up the game quickly. Using a variety of disguises, including that of a street cleaner and a policeman, he began to venture across the invisible line that divided the Vatican from Nazi-occupied Rome and make representations to more and more wealthy Italians to help fund his operation and provide shelter to the Jews. He developed a network of priests who would carry messages to the various safe-houses along with food and supplies. He continued his liaison with Sir Francis who eventually secured funding for the operation from his government – a considerable line of credit was provided, to be accessed through the Vatican Bank. With this money he rented more apartments and used his novice priests to keep them supplied, he even rented a large apartment in the street next to the Nazi HQ.

John Furman, a Jewish captain who had taken refuge in the Vatican described the Monsignor as having a *'benign, absent-minded, professorial expression'*, adding that whenever he heard of some outrage perpetrated by the Nazis the *'kindly twinkle in his eyes was displaced by a flaming passion'*.

Kappler began to grow weary of what he knew (but couldn't prove) was priestly assistance given to the Jews and POWs. To illustrate his point he had his soldiers paint a continuous white line along the Vatican 'border'. To the papal authorities its meaning was clear – don't cross the line or we'll be waiting. But the Monsignor would continue to ignore it, frequently venturing out on a recruitment mission or to seek another benefactor.

Among those he recruited to provide accommodation for his charges was a woman called Henrietta Chevalier, a middle-aged widow originally from Malta. She lived in an apartment with her six daughters and readily agreed to the Monsignor's request to conceal a couple of escaped POWs, despite the fact that the penalty for doing this was execution. She continued to provide shelter to escapees throughout the remainder of the war in Rome, sometimes harbouring as many as five POWs. She is said to have

THE BALLAD OF DELIA MURPHY

One of those who helped the Monsignor harbour prisoners from the Nazis was a woman called Delia Murphy, who at the time was much-renowned in Ireland as a ballad singer. She was the wife of Dr Thomas Kiernan, the Irish Ambassador to Rome. The Irish embassy was the only English-speaking legation remaining in the city and was often contacted by escaped POWs for assistance, but its status prevented it from becoming involved. It didn't prevent Delia from becoming involved on a personal basis, however. She frequently helped to supply or transport POWs and on one occasion drove a British Private with appendicitis to a secure hospital and then to Mrs Chevalier's home, using the Ambassador's diplomatic car. She would often find herself doing this by day and that very evening attending a function hosted by the upper echelons of the German military. When liberation did come, she remarked that she saw a soldier in the street that she thought was German until he said in an English accent: 'Say sister, come and park your arse beside me!'

mothered them somewhat, nursing them when they were ill, patching their tattered clothes, cooking them hearty meals, all the time remaining bright and cheery despite the fact that every day brought potential disaster. And she *was* suspected by the Gestapo, a fact illustrated by the raids that descended on her apartment on occasion. Yet an elaborate tip-off system among neighbours had always allowed her time to usher her guests out the back door and with the help of her daughters, hastily re-arrange the furniture to conceal their presence before the soldiers would smash down her door. There is a story that on one such occasion as soldiers milled about her home pulling open closet doors and brandishing rifles, she sat calmly in an armchair darning the escaped POW's socks in front of the SS. Mrs Chevalier was just one of the countless people who answered the Monsignor's call and daily put their lives on the line in the fight against Nazism.

The Monsignor may have been an ardent Catholic, but in offering his assistance he drew no distinctions on the grounds of race, creed or colour. He assisted the British, Italian deserters, Arabs who'd been taken prisoner in North Africa, communists, Jews, Protestants and Catholics. To the Monsignor each was precisely the same – a human being and enemy of the Nazis.

By October 1943 the Allies had advanced to a position north of Naples and hope grew among the population of Rome that the end was in sight. Unfortunately the advance stalled at the Volturno River about fifty kilometres south of Rome and would become bogged down there for the duration of the winter. Any celebrations of the Germans' departure would have to be put on hold.

But that same month, the Monsignor's organisation had a boost with the arrival of Sam Derry, a Major in the Royal Artillery who had been captured in North Africa and had escaped by dramatically jumping from a fast-moving train. Derry had been a POW before, responsible for overseeing escape committees. A local priest helped Derry to contact the Monsignor who quickly realised that the man's organisational skills could prove extremely useful to their cause.

Upon his arrival in the Vatican, the Monsignor took one look and knew he had the perfect disguise for Major Derry. He was six-three, the same height and build as himself; from then on, Derry would spend many a day out and about in Rome in the robes of a Monsignor.

The network's web had now spread out to encompass homes all over Rome and even beyond in out-lying farm houses. The numbers of fugitives it was dealing with were overwhelming. Derry brought a new level of discipline to the organization, visiting each POW and issuing strict orders, carefully regulating finance, organising relocations when necessary and always observing stringent security procedures. Commenting on the Monsignor in his 1960 memoir *The Rome Escape Line*, Sam Derry said:

'… *he is one of the finest men it has ever been my privilege to meet. Had it not been for this gallant gentleman, there simply would have been no Rome Escape Organisation.*'

A DEATH BLOW

Colonel Kappler knew that there was a network of safe-houses throughout the city and was fully aware that Monsignor O'Flaherty was behind it. Yet he had no solid evidence and he simply couldn't catch him in the act.

In early 1944 he arrested a host of suspected sympathisers and under torture forced several to reveal a number of the hideouts. Having captured the occupants it inevitably led to new information and more safe-houses being uncovered. This required the Monsignor's organisation to repeatedly relocate escapees and demanded a huge, on-going logistical operation. Yet no matter how many people were seized, the security measures put in place by Sam Derry ensured that Kappler never got the proof he required to put a stop to the organisation's activities.

In his frustration he decided to resort to more direct tactics. He approached the white line, which defined the Vatican's neutrality accompanied by two plain-clothes Gestapo agents and watched as the Monsignor took up his usual position under the arches at the front of the basilica. His plan was for the agents to slip into St Peter's and when the right moment came, seize the Monsignor and bundle him out into the city where he would then be shot as a spy. Fortunately John May had been tipped off about the plan through his underground network and when the Gestapo approached the Monsignor, they themselves were seized by the Swiss Guards who promptly delivered them to a group of Serbians taking refuge in the Vatican. Having treated the Gestapo to an exhibition of Serbian boxing, the battered and bruised men were unceremoniously delivered back across the white line to Colonel Kappler.

That same month – March 1944 – witnessed one of the most infamous massacres of the war on Italian soil and Kappler's hand was on the trigger. A group of communist partisans set off a bomb hidden in a street-cleaner's cart just as a troop of German policemen were passing. The effect of the twelve kilogrammes of TNT was devastating, leaving thirty-three dead. The German response was even more devastating. The reprisal order came directly from Hitler. Ten Italians would die for every German. Those condemned would comprise Jews and Italian POWs. When they realised they didn't have sufficient numbers, they simply seized civilians from the street.

On 24 March the three hundred and thirty prisoners were transported to the Ardeatine caves where they were executed by gunfire in groups of five, the bodies piling up on top of one another as each new group was shot in the back of the head. The German soldiers were supplied with cognac to ease their nerves, but some found the scene so horrifying they refused to carry out the execution orders. Nevertheless, the victims continued to pile up as the day wore on until the last fell that evening, after which the Germans blew up the entrance to the cave entombing the victims. This massacre became a symbol of all those carried out against Italian civilians by the Nazis and is remembered in a ceremony each year. Among the dead were five of the Monsignor's organisation.

After this outrage, the numbers of civilians willing to shelter Jews and POWs escalated and Monsignor O'Flaherty took full advantage of it.

But he himself came very close to joining Kappler's growing list of murdered civilians. In disguise, he set out on a covert mission to meet a wealthy sympathiser called Prince Filippo Pamphili unaware that Kappler was having his every move watched. When he stepped inside the Prince's palace word was immediately sent and within minutes the building was surrounded. Should he be captured the Prince and everyone present at the meeting would be arrested and probably shot. If he could escape the Germans would be unable to prove he'd been there and given the Prince's standing, Kappler would not risk taking the matter any further.

Yet the situation seemed hopeless. Soldiers stood guard at every entrance to the palace. There seemed no possible way out. In desperation he fled to the basement where he overheard the sound of coal being emptied from sacks into a coal-cellar. He reached up and grabbed one of the sacks, put his robes in the sack and smeared his face and clothes with coal-dust, then scrambled up, threw the sack over his shoulder and much to the bemusement of the coalmen, simply walked past the unsuspecting guards and climbed on board the delivery truck. It seemed almost of if God was watching his back along with the Nazis. Once again, this colourful tale may be apocryphal, or an amalgam of other close shaves he experienced, but there is no doubt that the Gestapo regularly had him under surveillance and more than once almost captured him in the act. Yet they always seemed to be one step behind.

THE END IN SIGHT

In January of 1944, the Allies had landed at Anzio just south of Rome but were unable to break out of their beachhead for months. Similarly, offensives by the Allied forces at the Volturno River had yielded no territory. But by the spring the German resistance was wearing down and in May the forces at Anzio finally advanced on the retreating enemy. A combination of US, British, French, Polish and Canadian forces also began to move northward.

On 3 June Vatican Radio reported that a British division had reached Castel Gondolfo, otherwise known as the Pope's summer palace, just thirty kilometres to the south. The Germans began to abandon their posts and flee to the north, declaring Rome an 'open city' – meaning that they had abandoned their position and the city need not be subjected to a destructive assault. This at least saved thousands of Italian lives and prevented the destruction of one of the world's most beautiful and historic cities.

With the Germans having fled, the Allied progress was rapid and at 7.15pm the very next day, 4 June 1944, Rome

THE HEROINES OF GROVE PARK HOSPITAL

Among the lesser-known Irish people to have been officially recognised for their bravery in World War II were two nurses working in Grove Park Hospital in London at the height of the blitz. Twenty-four-year-old Staff Nurse Mary Fleming from Tipperary along with fellow Irishwoman Assistant Nurse Aileen Turner were on night duty when a German bomb scored a direct hit on the building, which half collapsed and burst into flames. Realising that an entire ward was cut off, the two young nurses immediately clambered up to a first floor window and entered the burning building. In almost total darkness, the two girls were forced to crawl face down beneath burst pipes, which were spewing scalding steam above their heads, as the floor of the crumbling building swayed beneath them. They reached the ward and somehow managed to guide seventeen patients back through the corridor and help them escape through the window. A moment after the nurses clambered down the ward above collapsed. Both Irish girls were awarded the George Medal for their 'quickness, coolness and courage'. While Ireland may have been, like the Vatican, officially neutral during WWII, thousands of Irish people like Mary and Aileen played a courageous part in the battle against fascism.

was liberated. Thousands emerged from their homes to greet the victorious troops, Jews and prisoners-of-war, some of whom had spent years in hiding, finally emerged from their safe-houses to cheer their liberators. A huge throng gathered in St Peter's Square to give thanks for their survival. Waving at them from the roof were Pope Pius, his cardinals and the man who was most directly responsible for having kept so many of them alive, Monsignor Hugh O'Flaherty.

That day, 3,925 people emerged from the Monsignor's network of safe houses. Sadly the efforts of the Monsignor's organisation could not prevent all Nazi atrocity. There were ten thousand Jews in Rome at the start of the war. Five thousand of these were openly given refugee status by the Catholic Church. Thousands of others were concealed in the organisations network of apartments and houses. Yet over a thousand Jews were shipped to concentration camps. Of those, just sixteen returned.

William Simpson, a Scottish Presbyterian who worked with Monsignor O'Flaherty described his efforts as '... *the most gigantic game of hide-and-seek you've ever seen*'. As a result of his organisation's work, the sanctuary afforded by the Church and the efforts of thousands of ordinary Italian families who shielded their Jewish neighbours from the Nazis, about 80 per cent of the forty thousand Jews in Italy survived.

Colonel Herbert Kappler was arrested by the British the following year and would be extradited back to Italy in

1947 to face trial. He was found guilty and sentenced to life imprisonment in Gaeta military prison. During the 1950s Monsignor O'Flaherty began to visit Kappler on a regular basis, and in 1959 converted to Catholicism. In 1976 he became terminally ill with cancer and was transferred to a prison hospital in Rome. Calls for his release were met with outrage from Jewish organisations and from the families of those murdered in the Ardeatine Caves and the request was denied. Nevertheless he would escape from prison the following year in a most unorthodox manner. He had married a nurse while in captivity and in 1977 she entered the prison carrying a large suitcase of new clothes for her husband. As a result of the cancer, the German now weighed just 48 kg and was able to curl up inside the case. His wife then coolly walked out of the prison, at one point asking a guard to help her carry the case. She escaped to Germany and attempts to extradite him were unsuccessful. Kappler died at home the following year.

IN LIVING MEMORY

After the war Monsignor O'Flaherty continued his work in Rome. Most of the world, including his native Ireland, remained unaware of the dangerous, often heroic, work he'd undertaken during the war.

Soon after the war ended the United States Congress

awarded him the Presidential Medal of Freedom, its highest civilian award granted to individuals who have made *'an especially meritorious contribution to the security or national interests of the United States, world peace, cultural or other significant public or private endeavors.'*

In a similar gesture, the British Government made him a CBE in recognition of his work in helping to save the lives of two thousand British soldiers. He would never in his wildest dreams as a youth growing up in nationalist, pre-independence Kerry, have dreamed that he would receive such an honour and it must surely have brought a smile to his face.

In the Yad Vashem Holocaust Memorial park in Jerusalem a tree was planted in his honour and the Holocaust Martyrs and Heroes Authority conferred on him the title, 'Righteous Among Nations'.

He received no official recognition in Ireland until very recently when a grove of Italian trees was planted in Killarney National Park as a living memorial to him and a road named in his honour.

In 1960 he suffered a stroke and was forced to retire from the Holy Office. He finally returned home to Co. Kerry in 1963 and lived with relatives in Cahirciveen for the remainder of his days. He died on 30 October 1963. The following day, the *New York Times* ran an article on its front page mourning his passing.

The word 'Christian' – besides the obvious meaning referring to followers of Christ – is often used as an adjective to describe behaviour that is humane, considerate, charitable and selfless. If there was ever a man to whom that word could be ascribed, it would be Monsignor Hugh O'Flaherty. There may be no statues of him in Ireland, but in truth, the greatest memorial to his memory are the thousands of people either still living or descended from those who survived, thanks to the work of the quiet, unassuming priest from Co. Kerry.

M.J. Mc GRATH

Ireland's Unknown Olympians

Martin John Sheridan, Patrick James 'Paddy' Ryan,
Matthew John 'Matt' McGrath, Cornelius Leahy,
Peter O'Connor, Bobby Kerr, Patrick 'Babe' McDonald,
John Jesus Flanagan, Timothy 'Tim' Joseph Ahearne

Irish-born Olympians who between them won fifteen Olympic
Gold medals

THE GREEN AND GOLD

In Ireland nowadays our Olympic medallists are sadly fewer than we would wish. Gold medallists are a particularly rare breed, so much so that almost anyone you might care to stop in the street could probably rattle off most of them by heart ... Ronnie Delany, Michael Carruth, Michelle Smith, Bob Tisdall and of course, Dr Pat O'Callaghan. We rightly celebrate their magnificent achievements along with all of those other great Irish athletes who were Olympic medallists.

But for many Irish people the names of many of the greatest athletes ever born on Irish soil remain unknown, forgotten somewhere in dusty books of Olympic records, the memory of their achievements clouded by a mixture of time, politics and the one sport at which we seem to excel – emigration.

Arguably Ireland's most successful ever Olympics was in Los Angeles in 1932, when Bob Tisdall took gold in the 400-metre hurdles followed on the same day by Dr Pat O'Callaghan taking his second gold medal in the hammer. His first had come four years earlier in Amsterdam and had been the first occasion the Irish tricolour had been raised to the strains of 'Amhrán na bhFiann'.

But in reality the most extraordinary performance by Irish men and women at an Olympics came over a hundred years ago in the 1908 London Olympics, when Irish athletes took home no less than twenty-three medals. And the reason they remain mostly anonymous is that all of them were competing under another nation's flag.

For the first two decades of the twentieth century Irish athletes were considered the world force in weight-throwing events – the Irish were the guys to beat and people admired and read of the exploits of these men in the most far-flung outposts in the world. They truly did achieve legendary status. Ireland also bequeathed to other grateful nations world champion runners, jumpers and marksmen, to name but a few.

So who were these magnificent men and women who competed so heroically in the colours of other nations, but always wore their Irishness with pride?

THE WORLD'S GREATEST
ALL-ROUND ATHLETE

In 1906 the International Olympic Committee decided to hold what were called the 'Intercalated (inserted into calendar) Games' in Athens. The idea was that the Olympics would follow the four-year cycle format in different host nations, but that in between each Olympics the Greeks would host the Intercalated Games in Athens, the original home of the ancient Olympic Games. As it transpired only one Intercalated Games took place, the idea quickly losing favour with the IOC and controversially, the medals awarded were downgraded to 'honorary' as opposed to official Olympic medals. Yet at the time the world's greatest athletes competed in what they regarded as an official Olympic contest and, in fact, the Intercalated Games introduced many of the traditions that would be adopted in most subsequent competitions right to the present day. These included the separate opening and closing ceremonies with teams entering the arena behind their national flag, the raising of the winning countries' flags, the playing of the gold-medallists' national anthems

A PLACE IN THE SUN

In 1896 a Dubliner called John Pius Boland decided to take a nice little holiday in Greece where the first ever modern Olympic Games happened to be taking place. Boland was a nationalist politician who would later in life represent South Kerry as an MP in the House of Commons for eighteen years. His favourite pastime was playing tennis, which he had taken up in school and continued through his university years at Oxford where he met and befriended a Greek man called Manaos. On a holiday to Athens to visit his friend, Boland decided to attend the games as a spectator. Manaos, who was on the Olympic organising committee and was also aware of his Irish friend's prowess with a racquet, persuaded Boland to enter the competition. Boland powered through the singles and probably to the mild irritation of Manaos, defeated Dionysios Kasdaglis, a Greek, in the final, to officially become the first ever Irishman to win an Olympic gold medal. He then went on to win a second gold in the doubles partnering a German called Friedrich Traun. The Olympic Committee incorrectly recorded John Pius Boland's two golds as British wins, but they should in fact have been attributed to Ireland as he had entered as an individual and not as part of the British team. One way or the other, what a couple of souvenirs to bring back from your holliers.

and the efficient organising of all competitions within a two-week period (the London Olympics of 1908 lasted over four months!).

The most successful single athlete at the Athens games was a man called Martin J. Sheridan, who, according to the point scoring system at the time, would single-handedly amass half the points scored by the entire English team and a quarter of that scored by the Americans. Many other countries failed even to register half of Sheridan's tally under the blue skies of Athens. And although Sheridan's achievements would not be recognised officially by the IOC, he had already won gold in the discus event in 1904 and would repeat the success in the 1908 games. Including the Intercalated Athens Games, he won a stunning nine Olympic medals in a range of events, five of which were gold.

Born in the village of Bohola in Co. Mayo on 28 March 1881, Sheridan was raised in a small farmhouse on the Swinford to Castlebar road close to the Treenduff junction and attended the tiny one-roomed school in Carragowan, during which time he demonstrated an early proclivity for sports. But he was born into the time of the Land War when Irish farmers were engaged in a bitter struggle for lower rents and fixity of tenure and many found it difficult if not impossible to survive. His father, Martin senior, may have been involved directly in the politics of the time and it may have also been a factor in the family's decision to emigrate, like so many of his countrymen of that era. At the age of sixteen, Sheridan and his family took the boat to the United States and whatever fate lay in wait.

Sheridan had grown to a towering six foot three inches by the time he was in his late teens and such an obviously physical presence earmarked him almost inevitably for a career in the Metropolitan Police Force of New York. He did well in the force and earned the respect of his seniors, ultimately achieving promotion to First Grade Detective. His height and build (he was almost fifteen stone of muscle) also saw him frequently assigned to be the State Governor's personal bodyguard when visiting the city.

But it was as an athlete that Martin Sheridan truly began to rise rapidly up through the ranks. In 1901 he had his first success in the discus in New York. The following year he outdid himself by setting a new world record for the event and by 1904 he was the US title-holder in both discus and shot put. He would claim an amazing eleven American Amateur Athletic Union titles in his career. Long since a naturalised American, he was immediately selected to represent the US in the 1904 Olympic Games in St Louis.

At the Olympics, Sheridan had to call on all his mental and physical resources and probably some of his Irish fighting spirit to come back from third place in the closing rounds to force a tie with fellow American Ralph Rose. A so-called tie-off decided the winner and Sheridan emerged victorious. It was his first international gold medal, but at the tender age of twenty-three it was by no means his last.

ALL-ROUND CHAMPION,
ALL-ROUND IRISHMAN

Tom Kiely was a native of Ballyneale near Carrick-on-Suir who had an incomparable record as an athlete in the late nineteenth and early twentieth century, winning over seventy gold medals at a variety of international competitions and in a myriad of events. So respected was he that as the 1904 St Louis Games approached both the British and US teams pleaded with him to compete under their respective flags. But Kiely was a leading figure in the GAA and a committed nationalist and insisted that he would only fly Ireland's flag at the Olympics. He paid his own way to St Louis where he competed, at the age of thirty-four, in the 'All-Around Championship', known today as the Decathlon. Tom Kiely was victorious and claimed the gold medal in the name of Ireland, although the Olympic Committee again refused to recognise this and credited the victory to Britain. One of the most remarkable things about this competition and Tom Kiely's achievement is that all ten events – 100 Yards, Shot Putt, High Jump, 800 Yard Walk, Hammer, Pole Vault, 120 Yard Hurdles, 56 lb Weight Throw, Long Jump and the Mile – took place on the same day!

NEW YORK'S FINEST

Like Martin Sheridan, John Jesus Flanagan was born into a rural community in the west of Ireland, in the village of Kilbreedy about twenty kilometres to the west of Limerick city on 9 January 1873. And also like his famous fellow athlete, he would eventually join the NYPD and the hugely successful Irish American Athletic Club.

But before he ever took a step off Irish soil, John J. Flanagan had signalled to the world of athletics that he was a name to be reckoned with. At a local event in 1895, he broke the world hammer-throwing record with a throw of 47.47 metres and by the end of his career he would have broken his own record another sixteen times to 56.2 metres in 1909. Standing at a relatively short five feet ten inches and weighing fourteen stone, he would become know in the media as 'The Modern Hercules' and is widely regarded as the 'Father of modern hammer throwing.'

In 1896 he emigrated to the US and soon joined the Irish American Athletic Club which was based in the original Celtic Park, New York and whose emblem was a winged fist adorned with an American flag and shamrocks. Their motto left no doubt as to their pride in their origins – '*Láimh Láidir Abú*' meaning 'Strong Hands Forever.'

And indeed the motto almost seemed to have been written with Flanagan in mind. He quickly began to compete in local and national competitions, eventually winning seven AAU titles and was selected to represent the US at the 1900 Olympics in Paris. It was here that he first made his mark on the world stage winning the hammer with consummate ease, beating a fellow American into second by almost five metres.

Three years later he joined the police force. His initial appointment to the Bureau of Licenses seemed like a fairly tedious assignment but aware of his prowess as an athlete, this may have been a deliberate move on the part of the authorities as Flanagan soon found himself with plenty of free time to train and represent the 37th Precinct in the Police Athletic Association Games. He undoubtedly did his fellow cops a few favours with the bookies as he was so far ahead of the competition at these events it was like pitting a bear against a rabbit. A *New York Times* journalist covered one such event reporting merrily that *'Not only did he win four of weight-throwing events, but....he not only had the temerity to enter the "fat" men's race, but actually won it ... a most commendable showing, for there were many mighty policemen arrayed against him'.*

In 1904 he competed in the St Louis Olympics where he won a second gold medal, breaking the world record in the hammer. If that wasn't enough he also took part in the fifty-six-pound weight throw event and finished in the silver medal position. And despite the fact that he was now an ageing (for an athlete) thirty-one years old, he would amaze the world of athletics by throwing his hammer all the way into the next official Olympics in 1908 and beyond.

THROWING DOWN THE GAUNTLET TO
THE WORLD

Although John J. Flanagan didn't compete in the Intercalated Athens Games, his fellow policeman and countryman Martin Sheridan more than made up for his absence. In fact Irishmen would grab the world's attention not only for their sporting endeavours, but for using the Olympic stage to assert their Irish nationalism. It would be the first time the games had been used to make a political statement, a trend that would continue, not always with positive results, right to the present day.

Sheridan, competing again under the banner of the Irish American Athletic Club and the US flag, was the outstanding athlete of the games. He began by repeating his success in the freestyle discus throw at the 1904 games, taking gold with a throw of 46.46 metres – over three metres better than the nearest competitor. He then competed in the shot put, a keenly-fought contest in which Sheridan just edged out a Hungarian to take gold. He came close to a third gold in the now discontinued 'Fourteen-Pound Stone Throw', but much to the joy of the naturally partisan crowd, was edged into the silver medal position by the local Greek competitor. Not content with demonstrating his throwing skills he displayed great athletic versatility by also taking silver in the standing high jump and the standing long jump.

Besides his haul of five Olympic medals to take home,

he was presented with a ceremonial javelin by the Greek King Georgios I in recognition of his outstanding success as the games' finest athlete. The javelin is on display to this day in a pub near Bohola in Co. Mayo.

FLYING THE FLAG FOR IRELAND

Two other Irish athletes were also glory-bound, and controversy-bound, at the Athens games. Cornelius Leahy and Peter O'Connor. Leahy, born in 1876, was one of a family of seven brothers and two sisters from Cregane near Charleville in company Limerick, so right from the off, the competition was intense. All sporting enthusiasts (including the girls), their home became something of a mecca for sportsmen and sports fans of the day and would frequently be the scene of gatherings that would drift into the small hours, the crowded rooms echoing to discussions of athletic feats from around the world, all attended to by the bustling hospitality of their proud mother.

The mantel of the Leahy home became overcrowded with trophies while Con was still a child and within a few years every available space in the house was cluttered with gleaming silverware awarded for a vast range of athletic events including sprinting, hurdles, high jump, pole vault, long jump, weight throwing and of course, it being Limerick, hurling. Passionately nationalist, the family were arguably the most successful sporting family

Ireland has ever seen.

Con's elder brother Paddy had already achieved Olympic success when he won a silver medal in the high jump at the Paris games of 1900. It had rankled greatly with the family that his achievement was recorded as a British victory, Ireland then being under the direct rule of Westminster. Two other brothers Tim and Joe would later achieve international success in the high jump and long jump respectively, but it would be Con who would raise the greatest cheer among his friends and countless supporters in Ireland.

The 1906 high jump contest began in farcical circumstances with the bar set at only 1.37 metres – Con and his fellow competitors could almost have stepped over it. The organisers then proceeded to raise it just one centimetre after each jump, much to the irritation of the competitors who sat baking in the Greek sunshine for three hours before some of the weaker jumpers began to be eliminated. After two further hours of competition, the weary athletes had been reduced to just two – Leahy and a Hungarian called Gonczy. Leahy cleared his first jump and Gonczy failed on his three subsequent attempts – the Leahy family finally had the ultimate ornament for their mantelpiece – an Olympic gold medal.

Yet his Olympic endeavours were not yet finished, he still had to compete in what was then known as the 'hop, skip and jump', now called the 'triple jump', and this time one of his main rivals would be another

Irishman, Peter O'Connor.

Competitors on the field of sports they may have been, but in another respect they were very much allies in the same cause – that of Irish independence. Three Irish athletes had been entered in the games by the GAA and the Irish Amateur Athletics Association (IAAA): O'Connor, Leahy and John Daly. To stress their nationality each had been presented with green blazers and caps adorned with gold shamrocks. They'd also been given a large green flag bearing the slogan '*Erin go brágh*'. But as Ireland was not an independent nation and had no Olympic Committee of its own, the Greek authorities simply registered the athletes as British. This outraged the men, particularly as the British had contributed nothing to their attendance in Athens, their expenses were being paid by the GAA and IAAA. Yet despite a letter of protest submitted to the Greek King's son, Prince George, a member of the Olympic Committee at the games, their protests were in vain and their appeal to have their national identity recognised fell on deaf ears. This was much to the delight of the British delegation who recognised that the athletes presented them with an excellent chance of topping the overall standings. Naturally O'Connor, Leahy and Daly weren't going to let the matter drop so easily.

Peter O'Connor was born in 1872 and although raised in Wicklow he would eventually make Waterford his home where he would develop a thriving career as a solicitor. Yet in his early days the only law that occupied his thoughts was that of gravity – and how to defy it. Having joined the GAA at an early age, O'Connor was soon mesmerising crowds at athletics meetings all over Ireland, particularly at the length and height of his jumps. By the age of twenty-seven he had won All Ireland medals in the long jump, high jump and triple jump and as he moved through his thirties he consistently emerged victorious at international competitions. In 1900, the British Athletic Association recognised in him their best hope of a gold medal in the Paris games, but O'Connor turned them down as he would only compete for his own nation.

The world long jump record was held at the time by an American named Myer Prinstein. It stood at 7.5 metres, although official records had not yet begun. In May 1901, O'Connor, competing in an event in Dublin under the gaze of Olympic officials, jumped 7.54 metres and became the first official holder of the world long jump record. Three months later, this time before a huge, devoted crowd in Dublin's RDS, he stunned the athletics world by jumping 7.6 metres – or twenty-four feet, 11 and three quarter inches – an agonising quarter of an inch short of the holy grail of jumping, 25 feet. To put this achievement in context, the record stood for over twenty years and remained an Irish record until 1990!

By 1906 O'Connor and Prinstein were regarded as the world's two greatest jumpers and sure enough, they ended up head-to-head in the Athens games. The event was marked by controversy as two of the judges who were

British, and resentful of the Irish athletes' protest, failed to turn up. This left only one judge, Matthew Halpin, who happened to be the manager of the American team. Despite protests that the competition would be biased in favour of Prinstein, the Greek authorities wouldn't back down. To make matters worse Halpin controversially refused to declare the length of each jump as it occurred, declaring that he would only reveal the lengths achieved at the end of the contest. O'Connor was outraged yet had little choice but to compete. When the results were announced, Prinstein was declared the winner by a preposterous six inches, with O'Connor second. He would always believe he had been cheated of the gold medal and said in an interview for the *Limerick Leader* many years later that *'If my wife had not been present looking at the contest, which restrained me, I would have been beaten Halpin to a pulp.'*

Things went from bad to worse during the medal presentation ceremony. As the flags were hoisted representing the winners' nationalities, the Stars and Stripes for gold and bronze, O'Connor saw that his silver medal was to be awarded under the Union Jack. After their earlier protest and the refusal of the British judges to adjudicate, this was the final insult. Con Leahy, who was equally outraged, quickly conferred with O'Connor and a number of other Irish officials and one of them hastily produced one of their 'Erin go Brágh' flags. O'Connor, who among his many talents could count that of gymnast, ran to the flagpole followed by the Irish entourage and began to clamber up the pole, much to the surprise and excitement of the crowd. At a height of about twenty feet he unfurled his green flag and waved it vigorously to cheers from the mainly Greek audience. As officials hastened to stop the protest, Leahy and the other Irishmen formed a circle around the base of the flagpole and refused to allow any interruption of the protest. The incident received coverage around the world and was certainly one of the most overtly political acts to occur at an Olympic games.

Yet Peter O'Connor and Con Leahy still had unfinished business and two days later they would put on a demonstration of a completely different nature. Leahy already had his gold medal, but O'Connor had, up to this point, to settle for silver. The political allies became sporting opponents as they competed for the hop, skip and jump honours. As the contest reached its final stages three men were in the running, an American called Thomas Cronan and the two Irishmen. Leahy eclipsed Cronan's jump by 28 centimetres only to see his own leap bettered by O'Connor, who soared another 9.5 centimetres beyond his teammate's mark to claim his first and only gold medal. O'Connor, at thirty-four became the oldest winner of the triple jump, a record that would not be equalled until Jonathan Edwards won for Britain in the 2000 Olympics, also at the age of thirty-four.

With a gold and silver medal apiece alongside Martin Sheridan's haul of two golds and three silvers, the 1906 Athens Intercalated games had truly announced the arrival of Irish athletes, if not the Ireland team, on the world sporting stage. And yet there was even greater glory to come.

LONDON CALLING

If the 1906 games had got Olympic political controversy off the starting blocks, the 1908 games in London saw it burst into an unstoppable sprint, earning it the nickname of 'The Battle of Shepherd's Bush'. It was one of the most memorable Olympics in history for events both on and off the field and Irish men and women played a significant role in the battles that were played out in the political and sporting arena.

Originally the event had been scheduled to take place in Rome, but when Vesuvius erupted in April 1906, devastating Naples, the funds earmarked for the Olympics were diverted into relief efforts, leaving the games temporarily homeless. Eventually London was selected as the new venue and displaying an Edwardian efficiency that would put present day developers to shame, the British built the White City Stadium in just ten months. It could hold 68,000 spectators and cost a mere £60,000, cheap even in those days. (The stadium was demolished in 1985 and is now the site of BBC White City).

As in 1906, flags were fluttering at the centre of several

political storms. During the opening ceremony the Finns (then part of the Russian empire) refused to march under the Russian flag and marched as a group separate from the Russians. The flag of their fellow Scandinavians, Sweden, had been omitted from the display above the stadium, so the Swedes boycotted the ceremony altogether. But it was the similar omission of the American flag that caused the greatest rumpus.

At the time the British government and aristocracy tended to have a view of the Americans as 'upstart colonials', so the atmosphere was rife with tension before the first starter gun had even been fired. The majority of the US team were also from the Irish American Athletics Club and either Irish-born or of Irish descent and most of these men had been raised with a nationalist Irish tradition, adding even more fuel to the fire.

It was a tradition in the Olympics that each country's flagbearer would respectfully dip the flag when passing the head of state. Incensed by the British attitude to their team, the American flagbearer Ralph Rose strode past King Edward VII with the Stars and Stripes held high. This act has often been mistakenly attributed to the Irish athlete, Martin Sheridan and assigned some Irish nationalist motivation. There is also a story, likely an apocryphal one, that Irish weight thrower Matt McGrath, also a member of the US team, slipped up behind Ralph Rose and whispered that if he dipped the flag to a British king, he'd spend the night in hospital!

The upshot was that the British were outraged at this slight on their royal family. At a press conference, Martin Sheridan, who was the US team captain, was asked by the British press why the flag had not been lowered for King Edward to which Sheridan is famously reported to have replied, *'This flag dips for no earthly king.'*

If the political pot hadn't been stirred enough, relations between the Irish and British were by now bubbling over into what threatened to be an unseemly mess. A large proportion of the Irish competitors were protesting once more about having to compete in the name of Britain. As the row escalated the British began to fear an Irish boycott, which would rob their team of several precious medals (the games being in London, they dearly wanted to claim top spot). At the last minute, a compromise was agreed in that the team name would be changed to Great Britain / Ireland, with Ireland competing as an individual nation in team sports like hockey and polo. Despite this, official Olympic records to this day list the Irish medals only under 'Great Britain'.

In the arena meanwhile, to paraphrase another Briton, Shakespeare's Henry IV, 'The games were afoot', and Irish-born athletes were already involved in the heat of the battle.

The hammer event was whittled down to a handful of contestants and every one of the men in medal position was born in Ireland. Con Walsh from Cork, competing for Canada (whose points were awarded to Britain, as were those of all the athletes from the Commonwealth) was eventually nudged into the bronze medal position leaving a titanic struggle between two-time Olympic gold medallist John J. Flanagan and Matt McGrath, another New York cop who would achieve legendary status himself in future years. But his time had not yet come and Flanagan claimed an astounding third gold medal in successive Olympics, out-throwing McGrath into second place by seventy centimetres.

He would soon be joined on that esteemed triple-gold medallist platform by the brilliant Martin Sheridan, who was to enjoy his most successful 'official' games. Two days after Flanagan's triumph, he out-performed two fellow members of the Irish American Club to take gold in the discus. Soon after he beat another American and a Finn to take gold in the Discus Greek Style and, as a little bonus, he also added a bronze in the Standing Long Jump. He didn't compete in the Shot Put although he was the reigning champion, the gold going to US flag-bearer Rose, with Irishman Denis Horgan taking silver.

The running track was offering the spectators a rich mix of competition and controversy. In the 100-metre sprint, Enniskillen-born Bobby Kerr, competing for Canada, was initially disappointed to finish in the bronze medal position, but pointed his anger in the right direction and used it to hurtle himself to victory the following day in the 200-metre race.

The 400-metre race brought the British-American

rivalry to a head. The final was contested by three Americans and a Briton and in the closing stages one of the Americans, J.C. Carpenter, was adjudged to have cut across the Briton, Halswelle, blocking his run. Whether he had deliberately interfered with the Briton was down to the differing interpretations of the rules between the British and US athletics committees. Yet without authorization a British official took it upon himself to run on to the track and signal for the tape to be broken, thus rendering the race void before any judgment could be pronounced. After a hotly-disputed inquiry it was determined that the race should be re-run, but the Americans, already outraged, refused to take part. The following day Halswelle ran 400 metres around the track alone, taking the gold medal in the only ever Olympic race to feature just one runner.

The level of nationalism and patriotic zeal seems almost fanatical in the context of today's games. The notion of the Olympian spirit transcending nationality was some way away at this point, one of the earliest Olympic Games. This combined with the fact that many of the competing nations were also political enemies, and once-great empires were in their death throes with emerging nations trying to assert their new-found national pride. The Olympics contestants symbolised for the onlookers the political struggles and ambitions of their respective countries. In effect the Olympic arena represented something of a battlefield.

Back in the in-field, the Irish athletes' gold fever was continuing apace. Timothy Joseph Ahearne was born in the village of Athea in Limerick. Whatever they put in the water in Limerick in those days, it remains an astonishing fact that three Irish gold medallists (Ahearne, Con Leahy and John J. Flanagan) all hailed from within a ten mile radius of one another in the county. Like the Leahys, the Ahearne family, were all outstanding sportsmen with a 'never-say-die' attitude. And it served him well as throughout the triple jump contest he repeatedly fell short of Canadian Garfield McDonald's jumps. Going into the final jump, the Canadian was the clear favourite, yet summoning all his reserves, Ahearne launched himself into the leap of his life out-distancing his competitor by 16 centimetres, breaking the world record. His brother Dan, although never successful as an Olympian, would break this record the following year, his leap remaining unsurpassed for eleven years.

THE 'RACE OF THE CENTURY'

One of the most famous events in Olympic history would also occur in London in the marathon race. The curious length of the modern race – twenty-six miles and 385 yards or 42.195km – is often erroneously ascribed to a demand in 1908 by King Edward that the race be lengthened to facilitate it finishing in front of the royal box. In

BULL'S-EYE BEATIE FROM LOUTH

Wearing gut-throttling corsets, cumbersome head-to-toe dresses designed for utmost modesty and decidedly florid bonnets, the women of the early Olympics lined out to compete in one of the few events open to their sex, archery. One of the competitors in the 1908 London Games was Miss Beatrice Geraldine Hill-Lowe from Co. Louth, although she was officially competing for Britain. If ever it was certain that a nation was going to win gold in an event it was in this one, as every single competitor was British (if you include all the nationalities that fell under the GB banner). But to her credit, Beatrice performed heroically, scoring an impressive 618 points, which placed her in the bronze medal position. This gained her the unique place in Irish sporting history as the first ever Irish woman to win a medal at an Olympic Games.

fact the length of the race varied considerably during the first seven Olympics before being settled upon in 1924 at the 1908 distance. The length did change in 1908, but due to several factors (avoiding cobbled streets and so on) and one of those did involve the race finishing before the royals, though not at their behest. However it transpired, ultimately the King and the 68,000 spectators were treated to what was regarded as the 'race of the century'.

With a couple of miles to go there were only three competitors still in contention. An Irishman, Charles Hefferon, running for South Africa (whose points also tallied for

Britain) was in healthy lead. In second place was an Italian pastry chef called Dorando Pietri, who judging by his skeletal hundred-pound frame had never indulged himself in a single one of his own pastries. In third place came John J. Hayes, the son of Irish immigrants from Nenagh, running for the Irish American Athletic Club.

The streets of London, under oppressive summer heat and humidity, were crammed six-deep with cheering crowds passionately encouraging Hefferon forward. At some point a supporter ran out and gave him a glass of water, which he unwisely accepted (in the more colourful versions the water has been miraculously transformed into champagne); within two hundred yards Hefferon began to experience violent stomach cramps and his pace floundered. Before he knew it Pietri had overtaken him, followed by Hayes about three hundred yards behind. The stage was set for a dramatic finish.

By the time Pietri entered the stadium he was so dehydrated and exhausted he became disorientated and turned in the wrong direction, his legs almost giving way beneath him. He was 385 yards from the finishing line, but he still had a 250-yard advantage. A number of officials ran onto the track and supported him, turning him in the right direction. He collapsed twice and was helped up by an entourage, which now numbered about twenty officials and London bobbies. Pietri staggered around the track yard by yard on legs that seemed to be made of soft linguini, yet was repeatedly assisted. To huge cheers he finally lurched through the tape and collapsed on the side of the track, just as Hayes approached around the final bend.

The unfortunate Pietri was disqualified, although he had no hand in the officials' assistance, and the Irish-American, John Hayes was awarded the gold with the Irishman Hefferon, taking silver. In recognition of his run, Pietri was presented with a specially commissioned gold cup by the Queen a few days later. It was a remarkable climax to one of the most discussed Olympics in history.

Over the course of the 1908 games Irish athletes had continued to notch up success after success. George 'Con' Kelly from Dunmanway in Cork won a gold medal in the freestyle heavyweight wrestling event. Edmond Barrett from Ballyduff in Kerry, who had been renowned locally as a field athlete and hurler and who had emigrated to London as a young man, won a gold medal as a member of the London Metropolitan Police Tug-of-war team. Colonel Joshua Kearney Millner won another gold for shooting and set quite a unique Olympic milestone. The Colonel, from Carlow, famously shot while lying on his back with his feet pointed at the target, using his feet to support the barrel of his rifle. When he scored ninety-eight points out of a possible 100 to take gold in the free rifle event, he became at the age of sixty-one, the oldest winner of an individual Olympic event in any sport.

It is both wonderful and sad to reflect that the Irish-born competitors' twenty-three medals in the 1908 Olympics,

SPORT IS ELEMENTARY, MY DEAR WATSON

One of the most famous images of 'The Race of the Century' is that of Pietri just feet from the finishing tapes being assisted by officials. For decades after, one of the men helping the Italian was mistakenly identified as Sir Arthur Conan Doyle, creator of Sherlock Holmes. Conan Doyle was indeed present at the race, but was actually in the stand, having accepted out of interest the offer to cover the race for the Daily Mail. He, like so many others that day, was enthralled, using his undoubted literary talent to convey the drama to the readers – 'It is horrible, and yet fascinating, this struggle between a set purpose and an utterly exhausted frame'. He said of Daniel Pietri that '... the Italian's great performance can never be effaced from our records of sport, be the decision of the judges what it may.' When Pietri was disqualified, it was Conan Doyle who organised a fund to purchase the gold cup awarded to Pietri, contributing £5 of his own. On that hot afternoon in London, Arthur Conan Doyle came to recognise the importance of the Olympic movement as a means of fostering international goodwill through competition and he would subsequently become an influential supporter of Britain's still fledgling Olympic Committee.

would have ranked Ireland fourth in the world had the athletes being competing under an Irish flag. For a country of Ireland's population it was an astonishing achievement and is arguably the greatest ever collective Irish sporting success.

TOWARDS SPORTING INDEPENDENCE

As the early years of the twentieth century progressed, Ireland began to see great political upheavals, but another sixteen years would pass after the London games before Ireland as a nation, would have official representation at an Olympic games.

Yet Irish athletes would continue to shine in those years and even achieve legendary status. One such was Matt McGrath, born into a farming family near Nenagh in 1878. At some point, while a young man, he decided to swap the muddy fields of Tipperary for the cobbled streets of New York and like some of his illustrious fellow-sportsmen, swap his plough for a policeman's baton.

McGrath was a huge man, almost six feet tall, weighing a colossal 17.5 stone, square-jawed and broad-shouldered, with muscles straining against his skin, he surely presented a terrifying sight for the unfortunate wrong-doers who crossed his New York beat.

As an athlete, success did not arrive at his doorstep until relatively late. Enjoying the benefit of the blind-eye frequently turned towards the time-keeping of aspiring NYPD athletes, McGrath slowly improved his hammer-throwing skills until they began to match the proportions of his physique. He was in his mid-twenties before he began to achieve any measure of success, first in New York police events, then slowly building a national reputation. By the relatively old age of twenty-seven, he was ranked seventh in the world but the suspicion was that he surely had left his athletic career too late. But in Matt McGrath's mind, he was in the prime of his youth. He was just beginning.

Like so many other Irish-born athletes, he joined the Irish American Athletics Club and by the time the 1908 Olympics came along he had already claimed a number of AAU Hammer-throwing championships. When he took the silver medal behind Flanagan in London, McGrath was already thirty and surely this would represent the pinnacle of his career? Not a bit of it.

He continued to notch up AAU wins in the following years as well as securing the world record, including his lifetime best throw of 57.10 metres in New York's Celtic Park in 1911. By the time the Stockholm Olympics of 1912 came along, McGrath was at the peak of his powers. Amazingly the shortest of his six throws was more than six metres longer than the two runners-up and he claimed the gold medal that had been denied him in London by his compatriot Flanagan.

Another giant, in every respect, who won international

acclaim at the Stockholm games was Patrick 'Babe' McDonald. He was born just six months before McGrath in 1878 in the tiny village of Killard, near Doonbeg in Co. Clare. Toiling for long hours on his family's tiny tenant farm, Patrick soon began to develop into a muscular, bulky youth. Emigration was forced upon him and he departed for America at the age of twenty-seven. His surname was actually McDonnell, but his Clare brogue was misinterpreted in Ellis Island where the official registered him as Patrick McDonald.

Like Sheridan, Flanagan and McGrath, he soon joined the New York police force who welcomed him with open arms – they probably found it hard to believe that they'd found a recruit who was even bigger than Matt McGrath. McDonald was a towering six feet five inches and weighed in at a colossal twenty-one stone! Good looking, fair haired and sporting a fashionable moustache, he quickly came to be a familiar sight on the streets of the city, as he had been assigned to the traffic department. A reporter once described him as a *'living Statue of Liberty'* and commented that no chauffeur would dare disobey his directions as they negotiated their automobiles around McDonald's bulk in Times Square.

His chosen athletic discipline was the shot put and also like McGrath, he was a relatively late starter. Having competed with great success on the national stage, he arrived in Stockholm at the age of thirty and found himself in the final shakedown of his event, with his primary contender, fellow teammate and veteran Ralph Rose. These pair traded places at the top of the leaderboard (the next nearest was over a metre short) until Rose threw an impressive 15.25 metres. McDonald readied himself inside the wooden marker ring, raised his left hand skyward and nestled the shot put high on his shoulder behind his right ear. He then swirled and let fly, the metal sphere thumping down a full nine centimetres beyond that of Rose. The crowd leapt to its collective feet at the sight of what was a new world record!

His other event, the two-handed shot put, was only ever held at the Stockholm games. It involved throwing the sphere first with the right and then the left hand, the aggregate score then being taken. Rose and McDonald again were the outstanding competitors, but on this occasion they traded places with Rose taking gold and McDonald silver. It was a fitting conclusion for the long time teammates.

World War I intervened to deny the athletes the opportunity to compete at what would have been the Berlin 1916 games and it seemed that both McGrath and McDonald, now in their mid-thirties, had reached the end of their careers. This certainly seemed to be the case for McGrath when he attended the 1920 Games in Antwerp in Belgium. After an initially impressive two throws he twisted his knee and was forced to drop out. Despite this he still managed to finish fifth!

The victor in the hammer contest that day was, sure

enough, yet another Irishman, Paddy Ryan. Born in Pallasgreen in Limerick (where else?), he emigrated to New York in 1910 and after initially working as a labourer, joined the seemingly ever-growing band of Irish athletes among the ranks of the police force. He rapidly established himself among the elite of the weight throwing Irish, who collectively would earn the nickname the 'Irish Whales'.

Ryan had failed to establish his citizenship in time to compete for the US at the 1912 games so would have to wait eight long years to avail of his opportunity to challenge the best hammer-throwers in the world. Yet he continued to take part in local and national events with great success and in 1913, at the oddly named Eccentric Fireman's Games, (which included novelty sports like trying to hit a suspended ball with a jet of water from a fireman's hose!), he set the first official world record for the hammer with a throw of almost sixty metres, a record which would stand until 1938.

He won his first AAU hammer title in 1912 and repeated the feat every single year with the exception of 1918, when he was serving with the US armed forces in Europe during the war. When he next returned to Europe it was to do battle of a different kind – at the hammer event in the Antwerp games.

Another colossus of a man at six feet three inches and weighing almost nineteen stone, perversely he was said to be nimble on his feet, which considerably aided his throwing skills. Unfortunately, he was also renowned for his drinking skills, which almost called time on his bid for Olympic glory. He is said to have spent the evening before the contest 'sampling' the local wines only to awake the next day with a dreadful hangover, greeting the US coach with his hand to his forehead and the words *'I'm dyin'...'*. Insisting on a 'cure', the coach deposited him, rather unwisely, at the nearest bar where Paddy Ryan and an American teammate shared enough 'cures' to heal the dead. Eventually Lawson hauled him from the bar whereupon there ensued a headlong dash to the stadium, aided by a lift on the back of a passing truck, arriving somewhat the worse for wear just in time to see the last of the other entrants hurl the hammer.

Flags marked the throws of the previous contestants and with his vision slightly impeded by the Irish whiskey floating across his eyes, he asked a young official if he would do him the favour of standing just beyond the furthest flag to serve as a target. Somewhat nervously the young man agreed and his apprehension was justified as a few moments later he had to dive for cover as Ryan's hammer sailed overhead, out-distancing the next best throw by a stunning 4.5 metres, the widest winning margin ever recorded.

He competed in one other event, this time against 'Babe' McDonald, in the fifty-six-pound weight throw. McDonald had been granted the honour of carrying the US flag at the opening ceremonies and also appointed the

US team captain and he certainly led his team by example. He broke the world record in the event and took the second gold of his career. Ryan rounded off another hugely successful Olympics for Irish athletes by taking the silver medal. At the age of forty-two this made Peter 'Babe' McDonald the oldest track and field gold medallist, a record that stands to this day.

By the time the 1924 Paris Olympics came around, Irish athletes would compete for the first time under the Irish tricolour and the golden era of the great ex-patriot Irish Olympians was drawing to a close. But Matt McGrath would bring the curtain down in some style, taking a silver medal in the hammer at the age of forty-six, making him the oldest member of an American track and field team to win an Olympic medal. He would remain in the top ten throwers in the world until he was fifty years of age.

CLOSING CEREMONIES

Matt McGrath returned to New York where he attained the rank of Inspector in the police force. To add to his medal haul of one Olympic gold and two silvers, he was also awarded the NYPD's Medal of Valor on two occasions. A statue depicting him in action stands in Nenagh, alongside two others of the sprinter, Bob Tisdall and the 1908 Marathon winner, Johnny Hayes, all of who had close ties to the area. In a *London Times* Poll to celebrate the Beijing

Olympics in 2008, he was ranked in 66th position of the top 100 athletes of all time. He died in 1941 at the age of sixty-three.

John J. Flanagan retired from the NYPD in 1911 and returned to his native Limerick in 1924 after his father died. He there resumed the life of a farmer but continued his involvement in athletics, coaching Dr Patrick O'Callaghan, Ireland's first ever official gold medallist. When O'Callaghan won the hammer event in 1928, Ireland became the first country besides America to win the event. Flanagan's medals total included three golds and one silver. He is one of an elite group of people to have won gold in the same event at three consecutive Olympics, 1900, 1904 and 1908. He was ranked 19th in the *Times* Top 100 Athletes list. He died on the family farm in Limerick in 1938 at the age of sixty-five and is buried in Ballingaddy graveyard.

Con Leahy emigrated from Limerick in 1909 to join his brother Patrick. Con was the winner of an Olympic gold and two silvers, Pat the holder of a silver and a bronze medal. The achievements of the Leahy family are still a source of great pride in their native county and particularly in the Cregane area. In 1906 a memorial plaque to Con was unveiled in Bedford Row in Limerick city. He was listed in joint 94th place in the *Times* Top 100 athletes. Con died in Manhattan in 1921 at the young age of forty-five.

Peter O'Connor reached the peak of his powers in 1906 with his gold and silver medals and his passionate and dramatic defence of what he believed was his right to participate under his own nation's flag. He was invited to later Olympics to participate as a judge. He enjoyed a long an successful career as a solicitor in Waterford and his achievements were celebrated in a book entitled *The King of Spring* by Mark Quinn. He died in Waterford in 1957 aged eighty-five.

Timothy J. Ahearne remained in Athea in Limerick all his life, his 1908 gold medal the pride and joy of the entire community. His brother Dan, who broke Tim's world triple jump record, emigrated to Boston in 1909. Tim lived to be eighty-three years of age and died in 1968.

Pat 'Babe' McDonald lived the remainder of his life in the US. He was the winner of an Olympic gold and a silver medal and his achievement is remembered with a monument near the White Strand beach at Killard in Co. Clare. He died aged seventy-six in 1954.

Bobby Kerr became a successful athletics and football coach in Canada and was an official at subsequent Olympics. He was the winner of a gold and a silver Olympic medal and a park in his home town of Hamilton was named in his honour. He died in 1963 aged eighty and is buried in Hamilton.

Paddy Ryan eventually returned to Ireland, throwing his considerable bulk behind the running of the family farm. His athletics career had brought him the treasured reward of a gold and a silver Olympics medal. In 2004, an impressive life-size bronze statue of Paddy in action, flanked by the Stars and Stripes and the Tricolour, was unveiled in Pallasgreen in Limerick.

Martin J. Sheridan was described in a *New York Times* article of 1906 as 'The World's Greatest All-Round Athlete'. After the 1908 London Games he returned to his native Bohola in Mayo where he was rightly feted as an all-conquering hero of the athletics world. While there he took part in exhibitions for the people of Mayo, one of which included breaking the then British record for the pole-vault, which wasn't even his particular discipline. In 1966 a permanent memorial featuring a bronze bust of the great athlete mounted on a pedestal was unveiled in Bohola. The NYPD instituted the 'Martin J. Sheridan Award for Valor' to honour his name, an award which would endure until the late 1960s. In total he was the winner of five Olympic gold medals and three silvers along with countless other awards, prizes and accolades. The *Times* Top 100 Athletes of All Time placed him at number four. Tragically, Martin J. Sheridan's life ended prematurely when he, like millions of others, fell victim to the 1918 flu epidemic. He died in St Vincent's Hospital in Manhattan on 26 March 1918, the day before his thirty-seventh birthday and was buried in Calvary Cemetery, Queens. The inscription on the cross above his grave reads:

An intrepid American; an ardent lover of his motherland;
A peerless athlete; devoted to the institutions of his country

And to the ideals and aspirations of his race.

On his visit to Bohola, the local priest presented Martin J. Sheridan with a scroll bearing an inscription which seems particularly appropriate not just for the athlete, but for all those Irish men and women who travelled to distant lands and there scaled the greatest of all mountains – to make of themselves the very finest they could be. The opening lines of the message from the people of Bohola are a fitting epitaph for all of those sportsmen, artists, engineers, scientists, politicians, soldiers, architects and countless other Irish who did their native land proud in those far-flung corners of the globe:

Breathe there a man with a soul so dead
Who never to himself hath said
This is my own, my native land
The Irish exile may climb the ladder of fame.
Irish prowess may win a name that will evoke the admiration of all nations,
but the Celtic heart ever fondly clings to the dear old land of the harp.

References

In this section, I list the books, websites, periodicals and other resources I made use of when researching this book. They are listed, approximately, in the order in which their information appears in each chapter.

Chapter 1 Paddy Hannan & Charles Yelverton O'Connor

Le Page, J.S.H., (1986) *Building a State: the story of the Public Works Department of Western Australia 1829-1985*, (Water Authority of Western Australia)

Goldfields and Agricultural Areas Water Supply, (Water Authority of Western Australia)

'A Glimpse of one of the giants who built our nation', *The University of W.A. Press*

Constructing Australia – Pipe Dreams, Australian Broadcasting Corporation. A FilmAustralia Making History Production

Australian Dictionary of Biography Online Edition, O'Connor, Charles Yelverton (1843-1902), Hannan, Patrick (1840 - 1925)

A.G. Evans, A.G., (2001) *C.Y. O'Connor: His Life and Legacy* (Nedlands: UWA Press)

en.wikipedia.org/wiki/Charles_Yelverton_O'Connor

'Poverty Before the Famine, County Clare 1835' (www.clarelibrary.ie)

McMahon, John T. (1936) *Ramblers from Clare and Other Sketches* (Dublin: Talbot Press)

www.clarelibrary.ie/eolas/coclare/people/paddyhannan.htm

Coolgardie – 'Mother of the Western Australian Goldfields'

(www.coolgardie.wa.gov.au/history)

Encyclopedia Britannica – Kalgoorlie, Western Australia, Australia (www.britannica.com)

'Australian Prospectors and Miners Hall of Fame Historical Profile' – Patrick (Paddy) Hannan (www.republicofmining.com)

'The town full of miners *en route* to Hannan's find', *The West Australian*, 1 August 1893

'Hannan's Croesus Gold Mining Company', *The West Australian* 16 May 1896

Parliamentary Gazetteer of Ireland 1845

Lewis, Samuel (1837), *County Clare: A History and Topography 1837* (www.clarelibrary.ie)

www.nullarbornet.com.au/towns/kalgoorlie.html

'History of gold in Australia – The Aussie Gold Prospector' (users.tpg.com.au/dtdan/index.htm)

'Australian Gold Prospecting – History & Methods' (www.goldfeverprospecting.com)

Gordon Clarke, Francis (2002) *The History of Australia* (Greenwood Press)

TheAustralianGoldRush (www.cultureandrecreation.gov.au/articles/goldrush)

en.wikipedia.org/wiki/Paddy_Hannan

en.wikipedia.org/wiki/Eureka_Stockade

www.cultureandrecreation.gov.au/articles/eurekastockade

Chapter 2 Alejandro O'Reilly:

Encyclopedia Louisiana (http://enlou.com/elindex.htm)

Encyclopedia Britannica, 'Treaty of Aix-la-Chapelle' (www.britannica.com/EBchecked/topic/11186/Treaty-of-Aix-la-Chapelle)

'Irish Migration Studies in Latin America' – Society for Irish Latin Studies & 'The Irish Presence in the History and Place Names of Cuba' – Rafael Fernández Moya (www.irlandeses.org)

en.wikipedia.org/wiki/Alejandro_O'Reilly

'The Works of Lord Byron, Volume 6 / Byron, George Gordon
  Byron, Baron, 1788-1824'
  (infomotions.com/etexts/gutenberg/dirs/1/8/7/6/18762/18762.ht
  m or tinyurl.com/nhdbtx)
www.rte.ie/travel/2007/0605/cuba
www.iadb.org/exr/cultural/catalogues/orleans/spanish_period
'Military history of Puerto Rico'
  (en.wikipedia.org/wiki/Military_history_of_Puerto_Rico)
www.travelnet.cu/en/hotel-o-farrill
'Irish Migration Studies in Latin America – Ricardo O'Farrill'
  (www.irlandeses.org/0707.pdf)

CHAPTER 3 ALBERT D.J. CASHIER AKA JENNIE HODGERS:

'The Civil War Archive – 95th Infantry'
  (www.civilwararchive.com/Unreghst/unilinf8.htm#95th)
'Civil War Women – Jennie Hodgers'
  (civilwarwomen.blogspot.com/2007/08/jennie-hodgers.html)
'87 years ago: Jennie Hodgers: Army Vet' , *The Irish Echo*, October
  2002
www.albertcashier.com
'An Irish Cailín Goes to War: Jennie Hodgers, Private, Co. G,
  95th Illinois Infantry' (civil-war-irish-l@rootsweb.com)
Eggleston, Larry G. *Women in the Civil War*
Ruckman, Leigh, 'Jennie Hodgers: A True Survivor', Illinois
  Historic Preservation Agency, Good Shepherd Lutheran
  School, Collinsville
Irish identity – population
  (www.irishidentity.com/extras/people/stories/population.htm)
The Flax Growers of County Louth – 1796
'Reflections on Irish Linen' by Leslie Calvert, *Journal of the
  Craigavon Historical Society Vol. 5 No. 1*
Irish Medal of Honor Winners (www.thewildgeese.com)
en.wikipedia.org/wiki/Albert_Cashier

en.wikipedia.org/wiki/Chevalier_d'Eon

en.wikipedia.org/wiki/Siege_of_Vicksburg

en.wikipedia.org/wiki/Irish_Brigade_(U.S.)

'The Irish Brigade'
  (www.historynet.com/the-irish-brigade-fought-in-americas-civil-war.htm or tinyurl.com/nsekrd)

Karmakar, R. N., *Forensic Medicine And Toxicology – (Eonism)*

'Who was Jennie Hodgers?', Jennie Hodgers' Memorial Society

'Women Soldiers of the Civil War' – DeAnne Blanton
  (www.archives.gov/publications/prologue/1993/spring/women-in-the-civil-war-2.html)

'Female Warrior's Death', *The Irish Times* 6 November 1915

CHAPTER 4 MARY 'MOTHER JONES' HARRIS:

Jones, Mary Harris (1925)*The Autobiography of Mother Jones* (Chicago: Charles H. Kerr & Company)

1821 Census Inchigeela Parish, Co. Cork. Ireland.

Ballingeary History Society – Sean O'Sullivan

1827 Tithe Applotment for the Parish of Inchigeelagh (Iveleary) Co. Cork

Griffith's Valuation 1852

Debs, Eugene V. (1907) 'A Tribute to Mother Jones' (originally published in the *Appeal to Reason* 23 November 1907)

'Civilization in Southern Mills & The Rope Factory' (from *International Socialist Review*, Vol. 1, No. 9, March 1901)

Hawse, Mara Lou 'Mother Jones: The Miners' Angel' (www.kentlaw.edu/ilhs/majones.htm)

'Yellow Fever', *New York Times* 19 October 1867

'Mother Jones speaks to Coney Island Crowd' – *New York Times* 27 July 1903

'Mother Jones at Oyster Bay' – *New York Times* 30 July 1903

'Mother Jones, Free, Defies Governor' – *New York Times* 17 March 1914

'Two women depict Battle of Ludlow' –

New York Times 4 February 1915

Chicago Historical Society – 'The Chicago Fire'
(www.chicagohistory.org/fire)

en.wikipedia.org/wiki/Catherine_O'Leary

Did the cow do it? (www.thechicagofire.com)

Musil, Emily, 'Mary Harris "Mother" Jones (1830-1930)' Drew
University, New Jersey
(depts.drew.edu/wmst/corecourses/wmst111/timeline_bios/MoJo
nes.htm or tinyurl.com/lyymlr)

Encyclopedia Britannica – 'Mother Jones American labour leader',
'Gatling gun', 'John D. Rockefeller, Jr' (www.britannica.com)

Dictionary of Canadian Biography – 'Harris, William Richard'
(www.biographi.ca)

Alhadef, Tammy (2007) 'Last Survivor of Ludlow Massacre dies at
94', *The Pueblo Chieftain*, July 2007

Sandburg, Carl, 'She'll be coming round the mountain', *The
American Songbag*

'Barnes & Noble Sparknotes: Mother Jones'
(www.sparknotes.com/biography/motherjones)

Labour Heritage Foundation – Hall of Fame, Power of the Arts
and Creative Expression: Mother Jones
(www.laborheritage.org/?p=249)

en.wikipedia.org/wiki/Mary_Harris_Jones

en.wikipedia.org/wiki/Ludlow_Massacre

Chapter 5 James Hoban:

Bogart Bryan, Wilhelmus (1916) *A History of the National Capital
from its Foundation through the period of the Adoption of the Organic
Act* (The Macmillan Company)

Ecker, Grace Dunlop (1951) *A Portrait of Old George Town*

The White House Historical Association
(www.whitehousehistory.org/podcasts/whha_hoban.html)

Warner, William W. (1994) *At Peace With All Their Neighbors:
Catholics and Catholicism in the National Capital*

Encyclopedia Britannica – 'James Hoban, Irish Architect'
(www.britannica.com)

National Inventory of Architectural Heritage – 'Desart Court,
Kilkenny' (www.buildingsofireland.ie)

Friday, Mike Livingston (2001) 'Georgetown Tavern serving
history since John Adams' *Washington Business Journal* 31 July
2001

Bushong, William B. *Imagining James Hoban: Portraits of a Master
Builder*

Bob Arnebeck, 'The Use of Slaves to Build and Capitol and White
House' (www.geocities.com/bobarnebeck/slaves.html)

'History of the R.D.S.' (www.rds.ie)

Houses of the Oireachtas – A guide to Leinster House
(www.oireachtas.ie)

Encyclopedia Britannica – 'Andrea Palladio – Italian architect',
'Leinster House – Palace, Dublin, Ireland'
(www.britannica.com)

Ashurts, John & Dimes, Francis G. (1998) *Conservation of building
and decorative stone* (Butterworth-Heinemann)

'James Hoban Family' (trees.ancestry.co.uk)

'Architects of Ireland – Thomas Ivory (1732-1786)', 'Architects of
Ireland – Richard Cassels (1690-1751)', 'Architects of Ireland –
James Hoban (1762-1831)', 'Architects of Ireland – Sir Edward
Lovett Pearce (1699-1733)' (www.irish-architecture.com)

'Social Life In 18th-Century Dublin' (www.chaptersofdublin.com)

'Otway Cuffe, 1st Earl of Desart' (http://thepeerage.com)

'Charleston's Historic, Religious & Community Buildings'
(www.nps.gov/history/nr/travel/charleston/ccc.htm)

South Carolina Department of Archives and History – 'William
Seabrook House'
(www.nationalregister.sc.gov/charleston/S10817710031/index.htm)

'George Town Taverns, Shops, and Schools'
(www.accessgenealogy.com)

'The National Register of Historic Places,

The L'Enfant & McMillan Plans' (www.nps.gov)

en.wikipedia.org/wiki/James_Hoban

en.wikipedia.org/wiki/Pierre_Charles_L'Enfant

en.wikipedia.org/wiki/Richard_Cassels

'James Hoban memorial now set in stone', *The Kilkenny People* 6
    August 2008

Phoenix Masonry Masonic Museum
    (www.phoenixmasonry.org/masonicmuseum/white_house.htm)

Barolini, Helen (2007) *Their Other Side* (Fordham University Press)

Bunbury, Turtle 'The Cuffe Family'
    (en.wikipedia.org/wiki/Pierce_Butler)

Biographical Directory of the United States Congress – 'Pierce
    Butler' (http://bioguide.congress.gov)

Colonial Hall – Butler (http://colonialhall.com/butler/butler.php)

'Carlow man to "blame" for protracted American election' – *The
    Carlow Nationalist*, 17 November 2000

The Historical Marker Database – 'Rhodes Tavern'
    (www.hmdb.org/marker.asp?marker=9651)

Watkins, T.H. 'A Heritage Preserved', *American Heritage Magazine*

CHAPTER 6 LOLA MONTEZ:

Lola Record of filing of case of James v. Lennox – *Morning Herald*
    (London)

7 December 1842

Baptismal certificate for Elizabeth Rosanna Gilbert

Morning Post 1-5 June 1843

Evening Mail (London) 2-5 June 1843

The Observer (London) 4 June 1843

The Era (London) 20 August 1843

Morning Herald (London) 10 July 1843

Journal des Debats (Paris) 7 October 1843

Letter to the *Sunderland Herald* 31 August 1849

File of James v James, an action in the Consistory Court, *The Times*
    (London) 16 Dec 1842

Chronology of the life of Lola Montez
(By kind permission of Bruce Seymour, author of *Lola Montez : A Life* (1998) Yale University Press)

'Lectures of Lola Montez (Countess of Landsfeld) : Including her autobiography' (1858: Rudd & Carleton, New York)

Wyndham, Horace (1935), *The Magnificent Montez – From Courtesan to Convert* (Ayer Co. Pub)

Letter from Lola Montez, *New York Times* 1 April 1852

Obituary – Death of Lola Montez, *New York Times* 21 January 21 1861

Lecture by Lola Montez on 'Gallantry' – *New York Times* 11 February 1858

Art Gallery of Ballarat – 'Lola Montez – The art of the erotic dance' (www.balgal.com/)

Lola Montes: The Tragic Story of a Liberated Woman (1973: Heritage Publications)

Death Notices, *The Cork Examiner* 2 July 1856

www.victorianweb.org

Walker, Alan (1983) *Franz Liszt* by Alan Walker (Cornell University Press)

A History Of Castle Oliver (www.castleoliverireland.com)

Johnson-Woods, Toni 'Lola Montez: The Reluctant Victorian' (www.uq.edu.au)

Encyclopedia Britannica – 'Fanny Elssler, Austrian ballerina' (www.britannica.com)

Australian Dictionary of Biography – 'Montez, Lola (1818-1861)' (adbonline.anu.edu.au)

'Montez, Lola (1818 - 1861) – Australia Dancing' (www.australiadancing.org)

'Her name was Lola', *Hidden History*, RTE Television

Encyclopedia Britannica – 'Lola Montez Irish dancer', 'George Sand French novelist' (www.britannica.com)

Major, Fanny 'Mariners and ships in Australian Waters' (mariners.records.nsw.gov.au)

Find a Grave – 'Lola Montez' (www.findagrave.com)

Lola Montez Trail, Northern Sierra Nevada, Nevada County
(www.trailsgalore.com)

'Lotta Crabtree and Lola Montez' (www.standingstones.com)

The National Library of Australia – 'The Lola Montez Polka' by
Henrion, Paul, 1819-1901 (http://nla.gov.au)

Sierra Nevada Virtual Museum – 'Lola Montez'
(www.sierranevadavirtualmuseum.com)

'Racy life of our Lola', *Sunderland Echo* 27 March 2006

'Sex, porn and a discreet taste for the bizarre', *The Times* June 5
2007 (http://women.timesonline.co.uk)

en.wikipedia.org/wiki/Lola_Montez

en.wikipedia.org/wiki/George_Sand

en.wikipedia.org/wiki/Marie_d'Agoult

en.wikipedia.org/wiki/Alexandre_Dumas

en.wikipedia.org/wiki/Daily_Express_(Dublin)

en.wikipedia.org/wiki/Monto

en.wikipedia.org/wiki/Lotta_Crabtree

Nevada County Gold – 'Lotta Crabtree'
(www.ncgold.com/History/LottaCrabtree/lotta.html)

Chapter 7 Guillermo Brown:

Institutio Nacional Browniano – El Almirante Brown
(www.inb.gov.ar)

Society for Irish Latin American Studies, 'Was Admiral William
Brown Admiral Someone Else?' (www.irlandeses.org)

'Boston honors Bill Brown, now that it knows who he was', *The
Miami Herald*, 22 July 1998

Mulhall, (1878)*The English in South America* (Buenos Aires)

Society for Irish Latin American Studies, *Dictionary of Irish Latin
American Biography*, William Brown (ww.irlandeses.org)

'Admiral William Brown' (www.triskelle.eu)

'The ten greatest Britons of all time' (www.bbc.co.uk)

en.wikipedia.org/wiki/William_Brown_(admiral)

en.wikipedia.org/wiki/Battle_of_Monte_Santiago

The Admiral Brown Society
(local.mobhaile.ie/admiralbrownp/Home/tabid/9716/Default.aspx)

'Admiral William Brown (1777-1857)' (towns.mayo-ireland.ie)

'Biografia de Guillermo Brown'
(www.portalplanetasedna.com.ar/brown.htm)

Scheina, Robert L. (2003), 'The fall of Montevideo' , *Latin
America's Wars: The age of the caudillo, 1791-1899* (Potomac books)

Dictionary of Irish Latin American Biography – 'O'Brien, John
Thomond'
(www.irishgenealogy.com.ar/genealogia/B/OBrien/john_thomond
.htm)

Murray, Thomas (2008), *The Story of the Irish in
Argentina*(BiblioBazaar LLC)

MacLoughlin, Guillermo (William) (1998), 'The forgotten people:
the Irish in Argentina and other South American countries',
Celtic News (Buenos Aires: March, April, May/June, 1998).

'British built sub, first Chilean nautical museum' *Merco Press*,
South Atlantic News Agency, 3 December 2008

O'Leary, Daniel Florence (www.irlandeses.org/dilab_olearydf.htm)

en.wikipedia.org/wiki/Daniel_Florencio_O'Leary

O'Leary, Peter, 'General Daniel Florence O'Leary', Ballingeary &
Inchigeela Historical Society

Wright, Thomas Charles James
(www.irlandeses.org/dilab_wrightt.htm)

en.wikipedia.org/wiki/William_Bulfin

Bulfin, William (1902), *Rambles in Eirinn*

Kiely, Benedict, 'William Bulfin – Man from the Pampas' *The
Capuchin Annual 1948*

'Irish Migration Studies in Latin America' – Juan MacKenna
(en.wikipedia.org/wiki/Juan_Mackenna)

en.wikipedia.org/wiki/Benjam%C3%ADn_Vicu%C3%B1a_Macke
nna

en.wikipedia.org/wiki/Ambrosio_O%27Higgins,_Marquis_of_Osorno

Encyclopedia Britannica – Ambrosio O'Higgins
  (www.britannica.com)

Chapter 8 George McElroy:

Census of Ireland 1911
Bowyer, Chaz & Lewis, Gwilym Hugh (1976) *Wings over the Somme, 1916-1918* (Kimber)
Addington, Scott (2006), *For Conspicuous Gallantry* ... (Matador)
National Archives of Ireland – 'Dublin in 1911/The Suburbs'
The Supplement to *The London Gazette* 26 March 1918
The Supplement to *The London Gazette* 26 July 1918
en.wikipedia.org/wiki/George_McElroy
en.wikipedia.org/wiki/No._40_Squadron_RAF
en.wikipedia.org/wiki/Battle_of_Ypres
The Aerodrome – 'George McElroy'
  (www.theaerodrome.com/aces/ireland/mcelroy.php)
'An Illustrated History of World War One – George McElroy'
  (www.wwiaviation.com/aces/ace_McElroy.shtml)
'Battle of Ypres', 'Who's who of WWI', 'Weapons of War: Poison Gas' (www.firstworldwar.com)
Century of Flight – Aces of World War One
  (www.century-of-flight.net)
'The Aerodrome Forum – Who was McScotch?'
  (www.theaerodrome.com)
'Inflatable Aircraft of the Great War' (www.diggerhistory.info)
'Wings of Valour' (http://wings-of-valor.net)
Bradbeer, Thomas B., '"Always above": Major Edward "Mick" Mannock in World War I', in *Air Power History*
O'Shea, Walter S. (1998) 'A Short History Of Tipperary Military Barracks' (www.freewebs.com/tipperarybarracks/index.htm)
'Fokker and His Aircraft' (www.centennialofflight.gov)
'Les Chevaliers du Ciel – George "McIrish" McElroy' – 'Deadeye Mac' (http://membres.lycos.fr/asduciel/index.htm)
'Capt George Edward 'McIrish' Henry

McElroy'(www.findagrave.com)

en.wikipedia.org/wiki/Horatio_Kitchener,_1st_Earl_Kitchener

BBC Historic Figures – 'Lord Kitchener of Khartoum (1850–1916)' (www.bbc.co.uk)

The Western Front Association: Major 'Mick' Mannock, VC (www.westernfrontassociation.com)

en.wikipedia.org/wiki/Edward_Mannock

CHAPTER 9 WILLIAM MELVILLE:

O'Carroll, Helen, 'William Melville – Spymaster' (Curator, Kerry County Museum)

The Metropolitan Police Service Historical Archives (www.met.police.uk/history)

1891 Census of England

1901 Census of England

England & Wales Death Index, 1837-1983

'The Irish Dynamite War' – *New York Times*, 11 March 1884

'The Walsall Anarchists' – *New York Times* 22 January 1892

'Anarchist Meunier guilty' – *New York Times*, 27 July 1894

Campbell, Christy, *Fenian Fire: The British Government plot to assassinate Queen Victoria*

en.wikipedia.org/wiki/Jubilee_Plot

www.rte.ie/tv/hiddenhistory/jubilee.html

www.casebook.org/suspects/tumblety.html

en.wikipedia.org/wiki/Walsall_Anarchists

Barrell, Tony, 'And now for my last trick' – Did Houdini lead a life as a secret agent? *The Sunday Times*, 30 July 2006

Roberts, Andrew, 'When the prime minister plotted to kill the queen' *The Telegraph* (www.telegraph.co.uk)

Conrad, Joseph *The Secret Agent*

http://www.sneem.net/

Fleming, Diarmuid, 'Irish spymaster "M" sparks debate' (/news.bbc.co.uk/2/hi/uk_news/northern_ireland)

en.wikipedia.org/wiki/William_Melville

en.wikipedia.org/wiki/Sidney_Reilly

Encyclopedia Britannica – 'Sidney Reilly, Russian spy'
(www.britannica.com)

London Metropolitan Archives – 'The Theatres of the Strand'
(musicaltheatreguide.com)

Urbinato, David 'London's Historic "Pea-Soupers"' (US
Environmental Protection Agency)

'MI5 History: The German Spy Ring' (www.mi5.gov.uk)

Le Queux, William (1915) *German Spies in Britain. An Exposure*

CHAPTER 10 JOHN PHILIP HOLLAND:

John P. Holland – The Liscannor Man who invented the Sub – *The
Phoenix, Clare Champion*, 9 August 1996 (www.clarelibrary.ie)

Knowles Morris, Richard (1966) *John P. Holland 1841 – 1914
Inventor of the Modern Submarine*

Beard, Annie E.S. (1922)*Our Foreign-Born Citizens and what they
have done for America* (Thomas Y. Crowell Company, New York)

Frost, James *The History and Topography of the County of Clare*

'How John P. Holland Solved the Problem of Submarine
Navigation', *The Evening Star,* 6 January 1900.

'A Fenian Torpedo Boat' *The New York Times* 29 July 1881

'The Submarine Vessel' *The New York Times* 24 May 1897

'"The Plunger" Launched' *The New York Times* 8 August 1897

Ahern, Richard (1987), *A History of the Christian Brothers in Limerick*

Fitzpatrick, Jim *Br. James Dominic Burke (1833-1904) Forgotten Hero
of Cork's Working Class*

New Advent – 'The Christian Brothers of Ireland'
(www.newadvent.org)

'Civil War Battles – The Monitor and The Merrimac'
(www.sonofthesouth.net)

Development of the Submarine (www.maritime.org)

UK National Archives – 'The Origins of the Coastguard'
(http://yourarchives.nationalarchives.gov.uk)

Office of the Chief of Naval Operations: The Saga of the

Submarine – 'Early Years to the Beginning of Nuclear Power' (www.navy.mil)

McCue, Gary 'John Philip Holland And His Submarines (1841-1914)' (www.geocities.com/gwmccue)

John Philip Holland (http://everything2.com)

'Liscannor – Kilnamona Cemetery' (www.ancestry.com/~nymets/liscannor.html)

en.wikipedia.org/wiki/John_Philip_Holland

en.wikipedia.org/wiki/Agnes_Mary_Clerke

en.wikipedia.org/wiki/John_Robert_Gregg

Encyclopedia Britannica – 'John Joly, Irish geologist' (www.britannica.com)

Irish Midlands Ancestry – John Joly 1857-1933 (www.irishmidlandsancestry.com)

en.wikipedia.org/wiki/Mary_Ward_(scientist)

Mary Ward, 1827-1869 (www.irishmidlandsancestry.com)

'Beaufort, Sir Francis (1774-1857)*World of Earth Science*' (www.enotes.com/earth-science/beaufort-sir-francis)

'Lucien Bull 1876-1972 Pioneer Of High-speed Photography' (http://our-ireland.com)

National Science Museum, Maynooth – 'Reverend Professor Nicholas Callan (1799-1864)' (www.nuim.ie)

'The Human Face of the Chemical Sciences – Robert Boyle' (www.chemheritage.org)

Dr Francis Rynd – Inventor of the Hypodermic Needle and Syringe (http://our-ireland.com)

Irish Patents Office – 'Irish Scientists and Inventors – Harry Ferguson – Arthur Leared – George Stokes' (www.patentsoffice.ie)

CHAPTER 11 MONSIGNOR HUGH O'FLAHERTY:

'Monsignor Hugh O'Flaherty, the Scarlet Pimpernel of the Vatican', The Holocaust Educational Trust of Ireland

Hugh O'Flaherty Memorial Society (www.hughoflaherty.com)

Simpson, William C. (1995) *A Vatican Lifeline* (Leo Cooper)

Derry, Sam (1960) *The Rome escape line* (Norton)

Gaffney, Mary, 'The Vatican Pimpernel' *Catholic Ireland*
  (www.catholicireland.net)

Hugh O'Flaherty (www.findagrave.com)

Congregation for the Doctrine of the Faith (www.vatican.va)

Encyclopedia Britannica – 'Pact of Steel Italy', 'Germany (1939)',
  'Lateran Treaty – Italy (1929)', 'The Allies' invasion of Italy
  (1943)', 'Ardeatine cave massacre' (www.britannica.com)

County Kerry Genealogy 'Hugh O'Flaherty: The Scarlet
  Pimpernel of the Vatican'
  (www.rootsweb.ancestry.com/~irlker/index.html)

'A Brief History of WWII – Sicily and Italy'
  (www.worldwar2history.info)

McIntyre, Ben (2008) 'Was Pope Pius a moral coward or a saint?'
  The Times, 23 October 2008 (www.timesonline.co.uk)

Dalin, Rabbi David G.(2005) *The myth of Hitler's Pope* (Regnerey)

Rebecca Weiner, 'Rome', The Jewish Virtual Library – Rome
  (www.jewishvirtuallibrary.org)

Zimmerman, Joshua D. (2005) *Jews in Italy under Fascist and Nazi
  rule, 1922-1945* (Yeshiva University, New York)

Lucey, Anne '"Scarlet Pimpernel" of the Vatican honoured in his
  native Killarney', *Irish Times* (www.irishtimes.com)

The History Guide – 'Edmund Burke, 1729-1797'
  (www.historyguide.org)

en.wikipedia.org/wiki/Hugh_O'Flaherty

en.wikipedia.org/wiki/Congregation_for_the_Evangelization_of_Peoples

en.wikipedia.org/wiki/Monsignor

en.wikipedia.org/wiki/Pope_Pius_XII

en.wikipedia.org/wiki/Ardeatine_massacre

en.wikipedia.org/wiki/Delia_Murphy

Fleming, Mary G.M. and Turner, Aileen G.M., 'The War Room'
  (www.csn.ul.ie/~dan/war/people.htm)

'WW2 Talk – Mary Fleming' (www.ww2talk.com)

Chapter 12 Ireland's Unknown Olympians:

'The History of the Olympic Games 1896-2008'
  (www.guy-sports.com)
'The 1908 Olympic Games', *The Irish Times* 4 August 2008
McGrath, Roger D. 'These Colors Run' – Article by Roger D.
  McGrath (www.amconmag.com)
en.wikipedia.org/wiki/Irish_American_Athletic_Club
Ireland in the Olympics (www.eurolympic.org)
Ware, Seamus, 'Irish-born medal winners in the early Olympic
  Games' *Journal of Olympic History* (www.la84foundation.org)
The Intercalated (Olympic) Games of 1906 in Athens Greece
  (www.letstalkgymnastics.com)
'Top 100 Olympic athletes of all time' *The Times* 30 July 2008
  (www.timesonline.co.uk)
Belam, Martin, '1906 Athens "Intercalated" Olympic Games
  anniversary' 22 April 2008 (http://www.currybet.net)
Guiney, David 'The Olympic Council of Ireland'
  (www.la84foundation.org)
'Martin J. Sheridan, World's Greatest All-Round Athlete', *The New
  York Times* 6 May 1906
'New York Athletes take Everything', *The New York Times* 20 June
  1909
'Martin Sheridan is Dead', *The New York Times*, 28 March 1918
1901 Census, Bohola, Co. Mayo (www.ancestry.com)
en.wikipedia.org/wiki/Martin_Sheridan
'Martin Sheridan – Early Discus Star' (www.olympic.org)
Carragowan National School (www.castlebar.ie)
Bohola Civil Parish – County Mayo (www.irelandgenweb.com)
'Martin Sheridan 1881-1918' (http://towns.mayo-ireland.ie)
'Athletic Policemen in Celtic park Games', *The New York Times* 22
  October 1905

Encyclopedia Britannica – 'The hammer throw', 'John Flanagan' (www.britannica.com)

John Jesus Flanagan (www.sports-reference.com)

John Jesus Flanagan – Modern Hercules (www.wingedfist.org)

en.wikipedia.org/wiki/John_Jesus_Flanagan

'John Jesus Flanagan – Triple hammer Champion' (www.olympic.org)

'Olympic Game Trials in America (Con Leahy)' – *New York Times* 16 December 1907

O'Ceallaigh, Seamus, 'Great Limerick Athletes – Con Leahy of Cregane' *The Limerick Leader* (Publication date unknown)

O'Ceallaigh, Seamus, 'The Leahys of Cregane', *The Limerick Leader* (Publication date unknown)

en.wikipedia.org/wiki/Cornelius_Leahy

Cornelius 'Con' Leahy (www.sports-reference.com)

Irish Family History Foundation Online Genealogy Database – 'Cornelius Leahy' (https://brsgenealogy.com)

O'Ceallaigh, Seamus, 'Great Limerick Athletes – Paddy Ryan of Pallasgreen', *Limerick Leader* 20 December 1952

en.wikipedia.org/wiki/Patrick_Ryan_(athlete)

Paddy Ryan, Olympic Gold Medal Winner Antwerp 1920 (croom.wordpress.com)

Dooley, Bill & Guiney, David, 'Paddy Ryan – Olympic Hammer Throw Champion' (www.la84foundation.org)

'Athea's Ahearne Athletes' – *Éagsúil* (Arts and Culture Show) West Limerick 102 FM

Timothy Joseph 'Tim' Ahearne (www.sports-reference.com)

en.wikipedia.org/wiki/Timothy_Ahearne

'Matthew J. McGrath – Overwhelming Hammer Winner' (www.olympic.org)

USA Track & Field Hall of Fame – Matt McGrath (www.usatf.org/halloffame)

'Doctor Pat – The Boy from Duhallow', Castlemagner Historical Society

REFERENCES

'M.J.McGrath' – Mecca Cigarettes Trading Card

en.wikipedia.org/wiki/Matt_McGrath

Matt McGrath Promoted, *The New York Times* 30 May 1918

en.wikipedia.org/wiki/Patrick_McDonald

Lucas, John A. 'Pat 'Babe' McDonald Olympic Champion and Paragon of the Irish-American Whales' (www.la84foundation.org)

en.wikipedia.org/wiki/Doonbeg

Quinn, Mark *The King of Spring: The Life and Times of Peter O'Connor* (The Liffey Press)

en.wikipedia.org/wiki/Peter_O'Connor

'Olympic Champion Wins – Bobby Kerr', *New York Times* 25 June 1911

Robert 'Bobby' Kerr (www.sports-reference.com)

en.wikipedia.org/wiki/Bobby_Kerr

'John Boland – The Spectator Who Won an Olympic Championship' (www.olympic.org)

en.wikipedia.org/wiki/John_Pius_Boland

The Rambling Man – 'Unsung Irish: John Pius Boland' (cp1302ger.wordpress.com)

Olympic History – Ireland – J.P. Boland (www.eurolympic.org)

en.wikipedia.org/wiki/Tom_Kiely

Guiney, David 'Olympic Council of Ireland – Tom Kiely' (www.la84foundation.org)

Scott, Sir Walter 'The Lay of the Last Minstrel'

Picture Credits
(cover & internal images)

C.Y. O'Connor: portrait courtesy of Battye Library, Australia (JA Clarke Collection Of Glass Lantern Slides Of Western Australia), sculpture photograph courtesy of Tony James; portrait, standing, courtesy of the State Library of Western Australia. Paddy Hannan: photograph (1920) by John Joseph Dwyer, 1869-1928, sculpture photograph courtesy of Pauline Murphy. Alejandro O'Reilly: street sign photograph courtesy of Brian O'Donovan. Albert Cashier: courtesy of Tony and Marylin Thorsen, Dwight Historical Society, Illinois, thanks also to Ruth Morehart. Guillermo Brown: Argentine stamp photographed by Facundo A. Fernandez. Mother Jones: photograph (1902) by Bertha Howell (United States Library of Congress), newspaper © Mount Olive Library; march photograph from *The Autobiography of Mother Jones* (Charles Kerr). James Hoban: stamp provided by Stephen Carr, used by permission of An Post. Lola Montez: portrait by Joseph Karl Stieler, Schönheitengalerie, Munich. William Melville: © The Metropolitan Police. Mgr O'Flaherty: golfing photograph courtesy of Brian Fleming (author of *The Vatican Pimpernel*), other images courtesy of Hugh O'Flaherty Memorial Society. J.P. Holland: courtesy of The Paterson Museum, Edward M. Graf Collection of John P. Holland, thanks also to Gary McCue.

From Colin Murphy & Donal O'Dea

The Book of Feckin' Irish Trivia

More trivia about Ireland than you ever needed to know!
Distract yourself from doom-and-gloom with useless
information: guaranteed to make you a hit at parties or
gatherings of more than one person!

This book contains jewels like the following:
- During the first half of the nineteenth century, the average
number of CHILDREN per household in Ireland was 10.
- An ancient Irish marriage ritual called 'handfasting', involved
tying a rope between the newlyweds' wrists for 366 days. It is said
that this is where the expression 'TYING THE KNOT' originated.

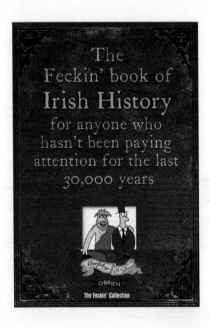

THE FECKIN' BOOK OF IRISH HISTORY FOR ANYONE WHO HASN'T BEEN PAYING ATTENTION FOR THE LAST 30,000 YEARS

Forget the boring stuff you learned in school. Here's the REAL skinny on Irish history.

Invasions, Emergencies, one Big Rising, all sorts of Troubles; the Siege of Limerick (continuing), Paddy of the Snakes, Niall of the Nine Hostages, The Big Fella, The Long Fella, Aer Lingus and the Flight of the Earls, Daniel O'Connell, Wolfe Tone and other singers, Gun-running at Howth, Wind-surfing at Lahinch; the IRB, the IRA, the EEC, the GAA, the Celtic Tiger, RIP.

With illustrations that put the Book of Kells in the ha'penny place.

www.obrien.ie